Citizenship, democracy and justice in the new Europe

What does political theory have to say about citizenship, social justice and political legitimacy in the new Europe? Can normative political theory adequately assimilate what is happening in Europe?

This book demonstrates the important role political theorists must play in shaping the new Europe. The contributors lead us to reflect in novel ways about the conditions that might make a European union possible. They engage with cultural questions of citizenship, democracy and justice thrown up by integration. What is clear from their dialogue is that there are no easy solutions; indeed, European integration represents a formidable challenge to existing normative theories.

Percy Lehning is Professor of Political Theory and Public Policy at Erasmus University, Rotterdam. **Albert Weale** is Professor of Government at Department of Government, University of Essex.

European Political Science Series
Edited by Hans Keman
Vrije Universiteit, Amsterdam, on behalf of the European Consortium for Political Research

The European Political Science Series is published in association with the European Consortium for Political Research – the leading organisation concerned with the growth and development of political science in Europe. The series will present high-quality edited volumes on topics at the leading edge of current interest in political science and related fields, with contributions from European scholars and others who have presented work at ECPR workshops or research groups.

Sex Equality Policy in Western Europe
Edited by Frances Gardiner

Democracy and Green Political Thought
Sustainability, rights and citizenship
Edited by Brian Doherty and Marius de Geus

The New Politics of Unemployment:
Radical Policy Initiatives in Western Europe
Edited by Hugh Compston

Citizenship, democracy and justice in the new Europe

Edited by Percy B. Lehning and
Albert Weale

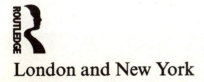

London and New York

First published 1997
by Routledge
11 New Fetter Lane, London EC4P 4EE

Simultaneously published in the USA and Canada
by Routledge
29 West 35th Street, New York, NY 10001

Typeset in Times by RefineCatch Limited, Bungay, Suffolk

Printed and bound in Great Britain by
Mackays of Chatham PLC, Chatham, Kent

Brtitish Library Cataloguing in Publication Data
A catalogue record for this book is available from the British Library

Library of Congress Cataloging in Publication Data
Citizenship, democracy, and justice in the new Europe/edited by
  Percy B. Lehning & Albert Weale.
     p.   cm.
1. Citizenship – European Union countries.   2. Democracy – European
  Union countries.   3. Legitimacy of governments – European Union
  countries.   4. Social justice – European Union countries.
  5. European Union.   I. Lehning, Percy B. (Percy Blanchemains)
  II. Weale, Albert.
  JN40.C57   1997
  323.6′094′09049 – dc21   97–8963

ISBN 0–415–15819–2 (hb)
      0–415–15820–6 (pb)

Contents

List of contributors

Deborah Fitzmaurice. Late Department of Philosophy, University of Essex.

Ryszard Legutko. Associate Professor at the Institute of Philosophy, Jagellonian University, Kraków, Poland.

Percy B. Lehning. Professor of Political Theory and Public Policy at the Erasmus University, Rotterdam, and at the University of Leiden.

Elizabeth Meehan. Professor of Politics and Jean Monnet Professor of European Social Policy, Queen's University, Belfast.

Julian Nida-Rümelin. Professor of Philosophy, Georg-August Universität, Göttingen.

Philippe Van Parijs. Professor, Chaire Hoover d'éthique économique et sociale, Université Catholique de Louvain.

Angelo M. Petroni. Professor of Philosophy of Social Sciences, University of Bologna.

Ursula Vogel. Senior Lecturer, Department of Government, University of Manchester.

Albert Weale. Professor of Government, University of Essex.

Acknowledgements

This book has its origins in a conversation between the editors when we were trying to work out how we might respond to the challenge of the European Consortium of Political Research which had advertised that it wanted to convene a series of research workshops on 'The New Europe'. As we talked we tried to think what normative political theory might have to say about the subject. It became apparent to us that the political theory of the new Europe promised much for our understanding of central topics in political theory, as well as offering an opportunity to contribute to reflection on the processes of European integration. Since that original conversation this project has been through many modulations, and we should like to take this opportunity to thank all of those who have helped us refine our thoughts and who have contributed to the making of this volume.

Our first thanks must be to the Research Committee of the European Consortium of Political Research whose original invitation sparked our enthusiasm and whose subsequent support enabled the preparatory workshop to take place in Rimini on 26–29 September 1990. The three participants, apart from ourselves, in that workshop (Brian Barry, Peter Graf Kielmannsegg and Jean Leca) gave freely of their time and knowledge to help us in the development of our first tentative ideas. They will recognise not only some of their ideas, but even some of their words, in the pages that follow.

The preparatory meeting was followed a year later by a conference at the Department of Public Administration of the Erasmus University, Rotterdam. As well as hosting the event, the department also provided funds for travel for the participants. We should like to take this opportunity to thank it for this support. Versions of most of the papers that appear in this volume were presented at that conference and we are grateful to the participants for their involvement in the enterprise and for their constructive contributions to the discussion. We are also grateful to Ryszard Legutko and Angelo Petroni for agreeing to allow their papers to be included in this collection, even though they were not able to be present at the Rotterdam conference.

We are also grateful to Hans Keman, the academic editor of the ECPR series, for his help and patience, and to Patrick Proctor and Sarah Brown at Routledge for managing to a successful conclusion what must have seemed an extraordinarily complicated project.

We must, however, end on a sad note. It is with the deepest regret that we record that Deborah Fitzmaurice, one of whose papers appears in this volume, died in tragic circumstances in August 1992. She was at the beginning of her professional career, and yet she was able to combine deep moral commitment with luminous philosophical clarity. Her contribution to this volume will evidence what a great loss to European political theory occurred with her death.

Percy B. Lehning
Albert Weale

Preface

Since the European Community was enlarged and became a Union the term the 'New Europe' is used more and more to indicate the changes that have taken place within geographic Europe as a whole. This idea of a changed Europe gained even more momentum when Central and Eastern Europe moved into the camp of democracies in the late eighties.

Both developments, the European integration through the European Union, and the walls that separated East and Western Europe tumbling down, have had and will have great consequences for the political configuration of the 'New Europe' as such, as well as for the shaping and functioning of national democratic policies.

These developments raise questions that seemed to have been settled some time ago, but which have now come to the top of the political agenda again. And rightly so: what is the nature of 'citizenship' in the 'New Europe', be it in the European Union, or in the new democracies in Central and Eastern Europe? How should one cope with the tensions arising from regional identities in the EU, or from the minorities in the East? What rights and obligations can link citizens to one another in the 'New Europe'? Under these changing circumstances what role can ideas about justice and equality play in both the civic community and the political systems that are *in statu nascendi* or in transition?

In summary: the 'New Europe' faces not only challenges in terms of economic development and the reshaping political institutions, but transformation of the value systems that exist and are in need of reflection, reformulation, and – if necessary – of new foundations. This is precisely what this volume aims at: asking these questions in view of the drastic changes that have occurred globally and in Europe. The volume is a collection of essays written by political theorists and philosophers who do not try to come up with an ultimate or universally correct answer. Rather, they attempt to ask these questions in such a way that any suggestions and answers may guide us through the changed circumstances of the 'New Europe'. This is not an easy assignment. Breaking new ground and doing away with hackneyed insights never is. Yet, every contributor delivers a thought-provoking chapter which revolves around two basic themes.

These themes are both essential and daunting. Broadly speaking the contributions cluster around ideas about 'liberalism, community and culture', on the one hand, and the creation of 'substantive legitimacy and social justice', on the other.

The first theme involves, for example, the notion of the nation-state and the issue of national boundaries from the perspective of social justice (for whom?) and the feasibility of political autonomy (of whom?). Other contributions focus on the issue of democratic citizenship as well as the extent to which this enables people to share common cultural values instead of creating divisions within a community.

The second theme is treated in the volume by rethinking the idea of European Constitutionalism. For example by contemplating on the relation between size and democratic procedures, like majority rule *vis-à-vis* (large) minorities and within quite different political cultures and identities. Issues such as European Federalism compared to existing types of national federalism are questioned in the light of legitimate decision-making for all involved at the European level. This is particularly important with respect to socio-economic and political developments which are, and have been, cross-*nationally* different across Europe and over time. Hence, what are the implications across Europe for solidarity with the less well-off in societies? What about the emancipation of minorities in the context of European citizenship? And, finally, how does one develop a justified basic income for the 'New Europeans' that is politically and economically right?

These are just a few of the questions raised in this volume and which make the volume as a whole not only an important one within this European Political Science Book Series, but also a valuable and timely contribution to the debate about the future of the 'New Europe'.

Canberra, February 1997
Hans Keman
Book Series Editor

1 Citizenship, democracy and justice in the new Europe

Percy B. Lehning and Albert Weale

INTRODUCTION

The new Europe raises hopes and fears, aspirations and resentments, passions and indifference. For some it is the promise of continental unity born out of local diversity, the ultimate experiment in political pluralism. For others it is the site of atavistic nationalism. For some it is the prospect of an economic giant that will be capable of taking on the global dominance of Japan and the United States. For others it raises the spectre of transnational capital breaking up and overturning the social and political gains of national welfare states. For some it is the free movement of people and ideas across boundaries that, in the lifetime of the vast majority of adults now alive, have been maintained only by violence, fear and persecution. For others it is the erosion of the little local particularities that have given to the peoples of Europe their history, traditions and identity. For some Europe is a grand ideal. For others it is merely a geographical expression.

Amid these conflicting feelings and attitudes, however, one thing is clear: the current pace and scale of European integration and the crumbling of the old order in eastern Europe pose major questions of social choice and political principle. Suppose that all were to go as well as possible with the major political issues of Europe. Suppose that aggressive nationalism could be tamed, full employment recreated, economic growth made compatible with environmental protection, and education rendered a European experience. Even under these highly optimistic assumptions there would still be major questions to answer. What might be the nature of citizenship in a politically unified Europe? What framework of rights and obligations would link the members of culturally, linguistically and socially diverse European states to one another? What role should ideas of social justice play in the shaping of institutions and policies, and what are the relevant theories of justice anyway? How would difference be made compatible with civic and political equality? What should be the role of constitutional courts? How much power should be given to majorities? On what principles can a European constitution be established?

Despite the obvious centrality of these questions to the construction of the new Europe, they have received little discussion in public and professional debate about the future of Europe, which has tended to be dominated by techno-bureaucratic considerations. This is most clearly evident in the political and institutional development of the European Community. During the 1980s the renewed impetus for European integration came from the programme to complete the single European market, the '1992' project. The creation of the single European market was of course a long-standing ambition of the European Community, going back to the Treaty of Rome, but the manner of its eventual implementation reflected the closed and elitist character of EU political practice as it has developed over the years. Thus, the social dimension of 1992 came as an afterthought to legitimate the *fait accompli* of market liberalisation. Environmental considerations were side-lined or ignored in the planning of the single market. The negotiations surrounding the Maastricht Treaty were conducted behind closed doors. And the 1996 post-Maastricht Inter-Governmental Conference on political institutions has not been a constituent assembly for a democratic European constitution, but a continuation of the bargaining, log-rolling and pork-barrel politics that are the usual fare on these occasions.

Within this context, the purpose of this collection of essays is to discuss the questions of political principle raised by the creation of the new Europe and the processes of European integration. The distinctive features of these essays is that they employ, or engage with, the techniques of contemporary analytic political theory to discuss the issues involved. Their aim is to provide novel and insightful ways of looking at fundamental problems, as well as using discussion of the problems associated with the new Europe to recast familiar themes of political theory. All the authors argue in their various ways that the emergence of the new Europe poses fundamental questions of value and principle, as well as providing an intellectual challenge to hitherto unquestioned assumptions of political theory.

Why should political theorists have anything of interest to say about the new Europe? One answer to this question is that many of the large questions of political principle raised by the new Europe have been at the forefront of the revival of political theory in the wake of John Rawls's *A Theory of Justice* (Rawls, 1972). In the last few years, political theorists have fashioned and refined techniques of argument that have helped clarify questions about social justice and political legitimacy as well as delineate the logical structure of answers that different theories give to these questions. Thus, Rawls laid out what many have taken to be a left liberal or social democratic conception of justice, whilst Nozick (1974) articulated a libertarian conception. More recently, Barry (1995) has argued for a conception of justice based upon notions of impartiality and equality. Parallel explorations have been taking place in democratic theory in such writers as Barber (1984) and Held (1995). It would be surprising if the collective efforts of those who have tried to think about the fundamental principles of political life were irrelevant to the construction of the new Europe. Thus, in seeking answers to the questions of principle that Europe faces, we can reasonably expect that the tools, techniques and concerns of political theory will be relevant.

Why, however, should political theorists be interested in the new Europe? Is the new Europe simply another source of examples for competing conceptions of political life? Can we assume that the conditions of the new Europe can be easily assimilated to the predominant working principles of contemporary political theory? Our answer is 'no'. The new Europe poses novel questions that political theorists need to consider. Moreover, reflection upon the circumstances of the new Europe can, in our view, help political theorists in their task of delineating conceptual structures and investigating the character of political argument. The new Europe is not simply an example; it is a form of political life which should have its own corresponding distinctive political theory.

In what follows we should like to suggest that the new Europe requires political theorists to address three sets of issues: liberalism, community and culture; reasoning about the structure of political authority; and the place of economic and social rights within the emerging European political order. These are by no means the only issues to consider, but they do help set the scene for other, equally fundamental, questions.

LIBERALISM, COMMUNITY AND CULTURE

The currently dominant theories of justice all presuppose the institutions and politics of the nation-state. Within these theories political institutions are seen as providing a network of rights and obligations in terms of which social goals are to be pursued. The principal theories of social justice differ in the ways that they characterise this network. For example, according to the one conception, the network is to be seen as a series of constraints upon actions preventing the violation of antecedently specified rights, whereas, according to another conception, the network is seen as a context within which civil and political liberties are protected and the welfare of members of society patterned according to a principle of social justice. Both approaches, and others, are united, however, in the tacit assumption that the nation-state with its associated conception of citizenship is the appropriate political community for the implementation of the ideals of social justice.

However, the Europe of the 1990s has entered a state of political development in which the central role of the nation-state can no longer be assumed. In the wake of the Maastricht Treaty on European Union and its review in the Inter-Governmental Conference, the European Union (EU) is wrestling with the problem of how to create structures leading to closer political union, even if fully fledged federation is some way off. Western and central European countries outside the EU are looking for ways to establish new political and economic relationships with those within. And the new democracies of eastern Europe are seeking not only to define their relationship with western Europe but also determining their social and welfare provision. In other words, the circumstances that are normally taken for granted in theories of social justice will no longer apply. Just as important is the fact that recent work that has looked at questions of justice beyond borders will also not be directly relevant. The question therefore will be: what does social justice demand in this new institutional and historical context?

One way of examining these questions is to begin with the observation that social justice is sometimes seen as one of the conditions essential to securing the achievement of democratic citizenship. The circumstances of the new Europe suggest that the notions of justice and citizenship, and the relation between them, will have to be redefined. The questions to be raised include the following. How far should there be common standards of welfare provision across Europe, and how should the costs of achieving the standards be shared? Would it be just to offer workers and their families from the east less favourable political and economic rights than western workers? If the rights that are accorded to those living in the new Europe are not the rights of citizenship, does this imply that social provision is based upon a notion of 'human rights'? If there is a notion of human rights at work, what does this imply for the pressing obligations that Europeans might have to those beyond their boundaries?

Such questioning in turn leads to issues concerned with the foundations within practical reason of principles of justice. Within recent political theory there has been a significant dispute between liberal and communitarian conceptions of justice and political life (Mulhall and Swift, 1992). As theorists have considered rival conceptions of justice, it has seemed that these varying conceptions themselves embodied various understandings about the way in which individuals related to the community of which they were members and presupposed competing accounts of the way in which the human good related to notions like rights, duties and obligations. These questions in turn raise fundamental issues about practical reasoning and political principles.

Consider as an example the communitarian critique of liberal theories of justice. As Mulhall and Swift (1992) have shown, these have a number of logically distinct components, not all of which are espoused by every communitarian critic, but one central theme has none the less been the constitutive role that a political community is supposed to have for its members. As Sandel puts it, in an oft quoted passage:

> But we cannot regard ourselves as independent in this [deontological] way without great cost to those loyalties and convictions whose moral force consists partly in the fact that living by them is inseparable from understanding ourselves as the particular persons we are – as members of this family or community or nation or people, as bearers of this history, as sons and daughters of that revolution, as citizens of this republic.
>
> (Sandel, 1982: 179)

It is of course a contested question whether this criticism in fact damages Rawls's political theory, which is its intended target (Mulhall and Swift, 1992: 167–205), or whether, even if Rawls is vulnerable on this point, the general point is one that liberals have to concede (Kymlicka, 1989: 53–6). It should be clear, however, in the present context, that the circumstances of the new Europe raise fundamental questions about the approach to political theory that Sandel advocates. For the project of European integration rests upon the premisses that the particular identities that make up the present states of Europe need to be transcended if Europeans are to create an identity that matches their needs and aspirations.

Here we should be careful about the theoretical relevance of the processes of European integration. The question is not one of the substantive merits or demerits of pursuing a European union, though political theory should be able to contribute to an understanding of the issues that are involved in the project, but rather one of whether it is a coherent conception of practical reason and political identity to suppose that political cooperation and union can take place across the boundaries of existing European nation-states. Can we reason ourselves out of the bounded identities that we have inherited from the past, and, if so, what sort of relationship is thereby presupposed about the relation between individuals and the political communities of which they are a part?

In the first chapter in this volume, Deborah Fitzmaurice argues that any adequate theory of international justice must both have a coherent theory of practical reasoning and provide an account of how the moral significance of boundaries can be transformed in the direction of increasing the scope of justice. Adopting a constructivist viewpoint, in which principles of action are reasons for anyone given minimal assumptions about her starting-point, the chapter argues that an acceptable account of the moral significance of boundaries should: provide a vindication of the good of autonomy; suggest an account of the institutional conditions of the good and the grounds upon which rational individuals should support such institutions; and show the extension of the scope of such institutions across state boundaries. The chapter, in particular, explores the notion of inherently collective goods in this context.

The significance of this chapter is that it makes the scope of political institutions and community organisation dependent upon a judgement about the circumstances under which the good of human autonomy can best be promoted. In essence, this is to say that the citizens of Europe are not simply the interpreters of traditions that they inherit, but that they are also the potential authors of their collective fate in the light of some shared understandings about the human good.

Nida-Rümelin complements this approach by developing the idea of structural rationality. This chapter argues that it is possible to construct an account of democratic citizenship that transcends the ideas of a cultural melting pot, on the one hand, and divisive nationalism, on the other. Structural rationality is a particular conception of practical rationality, involving the idea of 'we-attitudes'. We-attitudes involve a consensus on secondary rules – the rules for changing rules – and they give rise to we-intentions. Such intentions provide us with the logical foundations for a concept of democratic citizenship in which it is possible for persons to participate in a variety of communal associations.

It can be argued, however, that there are cultural conditions necessary for the development of a sense of collective identity. In his chapter, Ryszard Legutko distinguishes between two ways in which we might conceive the political processes of European integration. In the first way, emphasis is placed upon the existence of a common culture underpinned by a shared metaphysical conception of the social order. In the second, an effort is made to abstract individuals from their cultural context, and the assumption is made that universal metaphysics and cultural absolutism are politically divisive and therefore harmful in the rational choice of a just order. Arguing that if we accept the second approach we are then culturally agnostic, the chapter also argues that the converse does not hold: to be aware of the importance of cultural rootedness prevents our accepting too easily the prescriptions of analytic political philosophy. The problem is therefore whether we can talk about European integration whilst ignoring fundamental cultural processes that bestow identity upon individuals.

There is, then, no simple consensus among the contributors to this volume about the conditions of practical reason and cultural commitment that make European integration possible. But we hope that we have shown that the questions posed by European integration have theoretical as well as political significance. They lead us to reflect in novel ways about the conditions of practical reason that might make a European union possible. Implicitly, they pose the further question of the sources of political authority and legitimacy for such a union. And this is the topic of the second set of essays.

DEMOCRATIC LEGITIMACY

One of the central features of the new Europe is the strengthening or development of new institutions at the cross-national level with responsibility for important aspects of public policy. But, as much of the motive force for integration has emerged from economic and techno-bureaucratic imperatives, problems of democratic legitimation have received little attention. Yet, reflection upon the question of whether it is possible to create a European constitutional system suggests that there are a number of issues that need discussion. We should not simply assume, for example, that decision-rules can be transferred to higher levels of social aggregation without a change in their significance and operation.

This problem of the basis of the legitimacy for cross-national political institutions is related to familiar debates in political theory about size and democracy. No nation-state embodies the Athenian notion of citizenship in which active participation in public affairs was a central value, and yet it may be argued that pan-European institutions, covering over 400 million people, raise problems that do not occur in nation-states of even 50 to 80 million people. These problems do not spring from size in the sense of physical scale, but from the diversity of languages, cultures and historical experience that is a feature of European populations. There are, of course, examples of political systems that have successfully confronted diversity of language and culture, for example, Switzerland, but no doubt it is easier to sustain consociational solutions in small countries where social elites from different social groups meet regularly. Such conditions do not prevail at the pan-European level.

The problem of size also raises the issue of the role of participation in maintaining democratic legitimacy. The efficacy of personal political action tends to zero as much in a population of 40 million as in a population of 400 million, and in that sense pan-European political institutions face no greater difficulties than existing nation-states. However, if we see democracy not simply as a system of political coalitions operating within voting rules, but also as a system of public debate through mechanisms of political accountability, then the problem of European citizenship and the putative identity on which it rests becomes more serious. The lack of a common culture and language makes the creation of a public discourse within which political accountability is discharged an inherently precarious exercise.

The problems are well illustrated in the workings of the European Union, and the political presumptions of its development hitherto. The present process of political integration has been predominantly driven by bargaining between representatives of national governments. The representation of populations has therefore been indirect, with implications both for democratic accountability and for democratic legitimacy. Taking a broad theoretical perspective, it is possible to question the assumptions that are built into this approach. The nature of the present processes of bargaining leads to confederal, or inter-governmental, solutions exemplified in the role and standard operating procedures of the EU Council of Ministers. But it is possible to see individual citizens within the European Union sharing common conditions of citizenship and relating directly to EU institutions. The institutional embodiment of this approach would be the Court of Justice, which has federal rather than confederal operating procedures. The difference of emphasis between a collectivist and an individual approach is therefore reflected in the institutional mechanisms of the EU.

Elizabeth Meehan argues that a meaningful conception of citizenship is emerging at the level of the European Union. The currently dominant conception of citizenship was rooted in the idea of the nation-state. Yet, this is only one conception of citizenship, and others, involving the idea of participation in a common moral order, are not only logically possible but have been historically held. Moreover, the practice of coordinating different national social policies by the European Union and their implementation by the European Court of

Justice creates a regime of common legal rights that can form the basis
for a form of European citizenship. Changing values and psychological
orientations among members of European nation-state populations
reinforce these developments.

In his contribution Angelo Petroni also sees the European legal system as playing a crucial role in the construction of a European constitution. He begins by noting that the jurisprudence of the European Court
of Justice has insisted upon the pre-eminence of Community/Union
law over the national systems of members of the European Union. The
centrality of the legal system in the development of European integration has significant long-term implications. Whereas constitutional
devices, like the right of secession, are unlikely to protect the liberal
freedoms, according to Petroni, a strong role for the judiciary tends to
block the growth of centralized political power. Going beyond the ideas
both of a confederal Europe and of a European super-state therefore
depends upon the ability of the European legal system and its associated jurisprudence to develop principles that limit the constitutional
scope of government.

Percy Lehning considers what the philosophical basis of this citizenship might be. He argues that the pluralism that has led theorists to
offer a conception of citizenship based upon principles of right, rather
than the common good, applies even more strongly at the level of
the European political order. Developing a contractarian theory of
federation, he offers an account of the basis of a European citizenship
in which federalism emerges out of an overlapping consensus of
European citizens on the terms of their political association.

Federal institutions differ in the way that constitutional powers and
legal consequences are allocated to elements of the political system.
European institutions are currently interventionist in economic and
social affairs, whereas, by contrast, control over military power and
foreign policy-making remains, and is likely to remain, a national
responsibility. Classical notions of citizenship would suggest that it is
difficult to create a common citizenship with different national armies.
Moreover, the usual pattern of federal systems is to allocate foreign
and defence policy to the federal level and domestic policy substantially to the provincial/state level. A European federation would appear
to invert this pattern, with possible implications for political
legitimacy.

Albert Weale questions whether European federalism should differ in
the character of its powers from other federalisms. He argues for the
application of a constrained principle of majority rule as the basis for
the legitimate exercise of political power within the European Union.

The grounds for majority rule are to be found within the requirement that political authority take the form of constitutional democracy, if it is to be legitimate. However, the scope of majority rule may be properly limited by considerations of distinctions of political identity and the variations in collective choice that can accompany such distinctions. An account of political identity is advanced in which individuals may possess a complementary variety of identities depending upon their participation in a range of cooperative political practices.

SUBSTANTIVE LEGITIMACY AND SOCIAL JUSTICE

The character of modern political systems is such that governments cannot secure legitimacy unless they can demonstrate some connection between their policies and social justice. Yet, the meaning and implications of social justice at the European level are by no means obvious.

In all countries in the EU there is some framework of public provision for the common social and economic insecurities of ill health, disability and old age, but the extent and quality of provision are highly variable, reflecting both the level of economic development that different countries have reached and their distinctive political traditions. Moreover, the existence of these differences means that members of the EU may have more in common with countries outside than they do with other member states, for example Denmark and Sweden will have more in common with Norway than they do with, say, Portugal or Greece. How powerful are the arguments for seeking to eliminate differences in the quality and extent of welfare differences of EU member states? How should an EU system treat workers who were not EU members, but who might be extensively involved in economic activity within the EU?

If we assume that social justice requires some reallocation of resources from the outcomes markets produce, then the problems of policy strategy and legitimacy loom large. Social justice would require various forms of transfer or rectificatory action depending on whether the focus was primary income distributions, vertical transfers from rich to poor, horizontal transfers over the life cycle, non-contributory 'demo-grant' type benefits or benefits in kind. Orthodox economic theory would suggest that the liberalization of capital and labour markets would tend to equalize marginal returns, but also make it more difficult for national governments to pursue policies of compression for primary economic returns in so far as this compression involved a departure from competitively determined returns to labour factor inputs. Moreover, in so far as other forms of redistribution involve possible transfers between distant geographical regions (Copenhagen to Calabria) there are important questions about the extent to which this scale of redistribution can be sustained.

There is a general problem of method raised here. If we suppose that the sense of social solidarity is bounded by the existing borders of the nation-state, how should this enter our reasoning about social justice? Should we simply take it as an empirically given boundary condition limiting the application of a general principle, or should we seek to incorporate the notion of limited responsibility in our theory of justice? The latter approach might, for example, be based on the claim that the limitation of solidarity was essential to the idea of responsibility. We cannot feel responsible for undifferentiated others, but only for those with whom we have ties of culture, language and identity. There is a difference of perspective here about the moral importance of existing feelings of social solidarity: some theorists regard them as having only pragmatic implications, relevant to the implementation of moral principles in practice, but not themselves carrying any ethical significance, whereas others think of them as intrinsically related to our sense of obligation to others.

Ursula Vogel raises the question of what contribution feminist political theory on the politics of difference can make to present debates about social solidarity and ethical relations within a theory of European citizenship. This chapter considers two divergent tendencies. First, from its historical origins in the European Enlightenment, on the one hand, and from the experiences of an international political movement, on the other, feminism is less constrained by the paradigm of the nation-state than other political ideologies. Feminist scholarship has established the common pattern of patriarchal institutions in otherwise different political systems. It has, equally, been able to accommodate the significance of cultural differences in the expression of gender. In this regard, however, recent developments have emphasised a conception of emancipatory politics which calls for the demolition of the universalist principles of the Enlightenment heritage. This 'politics of difference' – premissed upon the assumption of an irreducibly heterogeneous civic public – challenges the very goals of integration and communal identity because they imply hierarchical oppositions between groups and a dualism of inclusion and exclusion.

Social justice within an integrating Europe sharply raises the theoretical problem of how we are to distinguish the grounds of public policy, and in particular what we count as issues of social justice and what we count as matters of collective preference. Clearly such problems arise within all political systems, but the cultural and historic diversity of Europe makes the need to draw a distinction between these domains unusually pressing. On the one hand, the claims of social justice within an integrated Europe would indicate common standards of service provision and social protection; on the other hand, the existence of cultural and historic diversity indicates the need for a domain of collective choice in which diverse preferences can be developed. The logic of these two demands indicates the need for a principled basis to the distinction between collective preference and social justice, as well as the need to ensure that the common standards of the latter do not simply become low standards.

Philippe Van Parijs proposes one way in which a feasible European solidarity can be developed. Noting that the European Union has been interested in the idea of a basic minimum income since the early 1980s, he argues the case for assuring a basic income to all citizens in Europe unconditionally. The merits of such an arrangement are in part general, connected with the anti-poverty advantages of such a strategy in any society, but they also have specific appeal to the new Europe. In particular, in the wake of the collapse of socialism in eastern Europe, the provision of an unconditional basic minimum meets the aspirations of the emancipatory ideal of the 'realm of freedom' contained in communism. Moreover, such a Eurogrant would avoid many of the problems that can be expected to be associated with piecemeal reforms of national social security programmes in the aftermath of the completion of the single European market.

But how far in practice is this likely to go? In the concluding chapter, Percy Lehning sets the ambitions for a European theory of citizenship against the reality of developments to date. Asking the question of whether the European Union can become the basis of a citizens' Europe, he reviews the empirical evidence available in the light of the demands of citizenship theories. He argues that the reality falls far short of the aspirations. Neither in its welfare provisions, nor in its treatment of migrants, nor in the development of institutions for citizens' control do the achievements of the European Union to date provide much ground for hope. In the mid-1990s a Europe of the citizens seems further off than it was at the beginning of the decade.

CONCLUSION

The reader will have noted, even from the brief summaries that have been given here, that these chapters do not all speak with one voice. Nor should we expect them to. For many of its inhabitants, it is the diversity of Europe that makes it such an exhilarating place to live and work. Whatever theoretical account we offer of European politics and society, the plurality of the European experience is one of its abiding features. Rather than dwell upon the conditions of its existence, we should like to conclude by suggesting three problems that a political theory of Europe might address, which are not treated directly in the present volume but to which we feel the present volume naturally gives rise.

The first of these questions concerns the theory of practical reason that is most appropriate when constructing an account of political developments in the new Europe. Are we to think of European political identity as something to be made or found? Earlier in this introduction we suggested that reflection on the circumstances of the new Europe should prevent theorists from slipping into easy assumptions about the sources of the self provided by the political community within which persons lived. As the chapters included in this volume have often made clear, in their different ways, Europeans are citizens of something yet-to-be. Their identity is not something that can simply be found. Yet, it is equally clear that the European is not something totally alien to previous European experience. If it is not something to be found, neither can it be something simply made. Perhaps the idea of Europe is neither made nor found but intimated within some traditions of European nation-states. Like all intimations it has to be worked upon and developed before its meaning can be discovered. But much more needs to be said than we can say in this volume about the conditions under which the understanding of such intimations, if that is what they are, can take place.

The second set of questions follows on from the first. What theoretical account are we to give of the relationship between the justifiable principles of public action that have been discussed in this volume and the processes of European integration and political bargaining that are taking place all the time within the new Europe? The United States of America could only become the first new nation by ignoring and suppressing the political traditions of indigenous peoples. That option is clearly not available within Europe. We are not discussing the creation of a constitution *de novo*, but the principles that apply to legitimate political entities who themselves have to agree to the changes that will be necessary to create political legitimacy and social justice within the new Europe. We could simply retreat at this point to a form of procedural agnosticism, and say that whatever comes out of the programme of bargaining between legitimate governments is itself to be regarded as just and legitimate. For reasons that we have already given, we think this an inadequate response. But the question remains of how we are to conceive of the relation between theoretical activity, on the one hand, and political bargaining, on the other.

The final question is the most pressing in practical terms and one that also requires a clear theoretical formulation. What obligations does Europe have to the rest of the world? We do not want to parrot the currently fashionable idea that a sense of identity is only given by contrast to the other, but there is clearly a danger that a new European community would be created at the expense, or at least in disregard of, non-Europeans. We would hope that the breaking down of boundaries within Europe would provide a convincing demonstration that political barriers could be broken down elsewhere. But if this is to be more than a pious hope, it will need more argument and analysis than we have been able to give in this volume. We would simply conclude by saying that we would not want to see great European unity purchased at the expense of a weakening of Europe's obligations to the rest of the world.

BIBLIOGRAPHY

Barber, B. (1984) *Strong Democracy*, Berkeley and Los Angeles: University of California Press.

Barry, B. (1995) *Justice As Impartiality*, Oxford: Clarendon Press.

Held, D. (1995) *Democracy and Global Order: From the Modern State to Cosmopolitan Governance*, Stanford, CA: Stanford University Press.

Kymlicka, W. (1989) *Liberalism, Community and Culture*, Oxford: Clarendon Press.

Mulhall, S. and Swift, A. (1992) *Liberals and Communitarians*, Oxford: Blackwell.

Nozick, R. (1974) *Anarchy, State and Utopia*, Oxford: Basil Blackwell.

Rawls, J. (1972) *A Theory of Justice*, Oxford: Oxford University Press.

Sandel, M. (1982) *Liberalism and the Limits of Justice*, Cambridge: Cambridge University Press.

2   Justice, practical reason and boundaries

Deborah Fitzmaurice

INTRODUCTION

There is a model for the explanation of international relations, pessimistically named 'realism', which takes it that states are necessarily engaged in a competitive struggle for power. The model, in both its explanatory and normative aspects is, of course, Hobbesian. The power of Hobbes's original theory derives from the integrity of his theory of political obligation and his theory of practical reason. A reasonstatement of the form 'A ought to Φ' means 'A has instrumental reason to Φ' which means 'A has some interest which is best served by Φ-ing'. The universal interest in security is the basis for the universal rational obligation to contract into a state, governed by an absolute sovereign. Thereafter, the authority of the sovereign derives from his effectiveness in sustaining peace, and his effectiveness derives from his monopoly of coercive power within the state. Since, however, we lack a global sovereign, states continue in the state of nature with respect to one another. It is quite unclear how this model can account even for limited cooperative behaviour between states, since the absence of a Leviathan means that the conditions for trust, and hence for contract, are absent. However, in so far as it tries to do so, such cooperation is explained in terms of the perceived national self-interest of the cooperating parties. If it makes sense at all within a realist framework to speak of the obligations of one state to another, these are limited to positive obligations derived from specific treaties made with some mutual benefit in view, and honoured for just as long as it is expedient to do so.

There have been a number of recent attempts to utilise Hobbes on behalf of a normative theory of political obligation, or even justice, in the modern state. But all such attempts suffer from at least this flaw: no set of laws and institutions which could conceivably be derived from a Hobbesian contract bear the smallest resemblance to those embodied in

Western constitutional democracies.[1] We seem to live our domestic political life according to a conception of justice that cannot plausibly be given Hobbesian foundations. In the international arena, however, the Hobbesian model still holds considerable sway. Part of the reason for this must surely be that it reconstructs the past and present state of international relations, and the actual practice of international cooperation, hitherto quite narrowly military and economic, with tolerable verisimilitude. But the arena is changing. International cooperation is no longer limited to the creation of minimal treaty obligations, but increasingly consists in the construction of transnational institutions. And as our common institutions come to bind us to other states as well as to fellow citizens, questions of justice, as the first virtue of social institutions, will increasingly be raised in the international context.

Any theory of international justice which is to prove adequate to our practical and theoretical needs in a new era of global cooperation must have in larger measure the virtues which sustained Hobbesianism. First, the theory of justice must incorporate a theory of practical reason and motivation which demonstrates both that acting justly can be rational and that persons can be motivated to do so. Second, if the normative theory is to illuminate the actual historical transformations through which we are living, it needs to give an account of how the moral significance of boundaries can be transformed in the direction of increasing the scope of justice. Since I shall contend that the dominant political philosophical theories lack one or both of these virtues, this chapter will be in the main critical rather than constructive.

The models for political theorising which I shall discuss are as follows: neo-Hobbesian, Kantian, 'Kantian' with an empirical motivational base and neo-Aristotelian or communitarian.[2] All assume, in one way or another, that principles of justice are principles for the organization of social life to which rational persons can, or in appropriate circumstances would, assent. Hence, the content and scope of the principles commended by these theories are deeply bound up with their underlying theories of reason and motivation. For the purposes of mapping theories of justice onto theories of practical reason, the latter can be usefully divided into two categories: those which take all reasons for action as internal and those which take it that there are external reasons. This distinction corresponds roughly to that between hypothetical and categorical imperatives. I borrow in what follows from Bernard Williams.

Briefly, Williams argues that an individual A has an internal reason to Φ if Φ-ing is appropriately related to some antecedently existing member of her motivational set, or S. A person's S is her motivational set, her desires in the widest sense: that is, her ends or goals. One very obvious relation to S in which Φ-ing might stand in order for A to have a reason to Φ is that of being causally efficacious means to the fulfilment of a member of S, but it is not the only one. For Williams argues that a large part of practical reasoning is constitutive, not instrumental. Constitutive reasoning occurs when an agent entertains some goal at too high a level of abstraction for instrumental practical reasoning to begin, as when one wants 'a satisfying career' and must locate an adequate determination of that goal, for example, being a doctor, before one can start actively to pursue it by applying for courses and so on (Williams, 1981: 101–13).

Putting this together with what Williams says elsewhere, it seems clear that he takes ethical reasoning to be the location of constitutive solution to the problem of how best to embody one's ethical ideals in one's conduct. A moral agent is one who already has standing goals of, say, kindness, fairness and courage, and whose moral thinking consists in trying to tailor her actions in some given context to the initially vague and possibly competing goals which these ideals present. What *political* reasoning is like is therefore crucially dependent on the politico-moral culture of the negotiating bodies. When interaction takes place between parties, each of whom regards the other as a mere instrument of its own purposes, but the conditions are such as to make contractual arrangements tolerably stable, political negotiation approximates to the *modus vivendi* model. If, however, the parties share an ideal of justice or the common good, however abstractly, and understand it to be applicable in the given context, then the negotiations will be an attempt to arrive at an agreed determination of its requirements.

Williams's aim in the piece from which this discussion is drawn is to refute the external reason theorist. The external reasons theorist is one who claims that certain reason statements (of the form: A has a reason to Φ) may be true of a person quite independently of her actual motivations – of her existing ends and values. That is, the theorist takes it that at least some reasons have an unconditional ground and therefore universal scope. Another way of putting this is to say that there are *agent-neutral* reasons for action. A useful way to understand the difference between internal and external reasons theories is to see how and when they construe as true or possibly true the claim that A has reason to Φ, when A acknowledges no such reason. For an internal reasons theorist, this claim is true if it is the case that if A were to reason deliberatively, on the basis of her existing ends and goals, she would come to acknowledge her reason to Φ. For the external reasons theorist, there is a special sub-class of reasons of which it is true that if A were to reason adequately she would come to acknowledge them *whatever* her starting-point. The external reasons theorist therefore incorporates a conception of practical rationality which goes beyond deliberation in the ordinary sense. On this conception, fully adequate practical reasoning necessarily leads to the conclusion that certain principles of action are reasons for action for any agent. But a non-deliberative practical argument is a philosophical argument, that is, a transcendental or quasi-transcendental argument along Kantian or Habermasian lines, so the demonstration that there are external reasons depends on the success of such an argument.

JUSTICE AND PRACTICAL REASON

The two classical models for reasoning about justice, those of Hobbes and Kant, represent opposite poles of the spectrum of theories of practical reasoning. Hobbesians are internal reasons theorists of a pure and paradigmatic sort. The principle that A has a reason to Φ if Φ-ing is a likely effective means to one of A's ends extends into the principle that A has a reason to obey laws, or support, or accept, legally constituted institutions just in so far as such institutions further A's private ends. Laws and institutions are rationally vindicable to those whose private ends they serve: universally rationally vindicable if the end which they serve is universally desired.

Kantians argue that some principles for public institutions can be shown to conform to the requirements of non-instrumental reason. Just institutions are those which would be acceptable to agents thinking in conformity with the principles of pure practical reason, hence their legitimacy is quite independent of the contingent and varied desires of the actual agents who live under them. However, some theorists who offer apparently formal or procedural vindications of principles of justice are not Kantian in any deep sense. For their superficially procedural vindications are properly understood as articulations of some fundamental value of fairness, or equal respect, or a fundamental ideal of the person. The resulting principles of justice are then justifiable to only those who desire to realise the ideal. Rawls, who was once (at least arguably) strongly Kantian and conceived of choice in the original position as a procedural equivalent of the categorical imperative, now acknowledges that his principles presuppose a contingently shared ideal of the person as rational, equal and free. His theory is superstructurally 'Kantian', but has an empirical motivational base.

When we come to the theorists who may be called communitarian or neo-Aristotelian, a clear-cut theory of justice is harder to discern. This is partly because these theories lack the sharp discontinuity between reason and value, and therefore between principles of justice grounded in reason and merely contingent value-commitments, which marks both Hobbesian and Kantian theory proper and, in the form of a sharp discontinuity between political and private values, their modern inheritors. Neo-Aristotelians regard rational action as necessarily conforming to an order of value. Rational action is intelligible action, and intelligibility demands that the end to which action is oriented falls under a value-concept, or desirability description. Whereas Aristotle bound values together in a conception of human flourishing ultimately grounded in a conception of human nature, most neo-Aristotelians are tacitly or explicitly historicist. What provides the order of value to which action, in order to be intelligible, must be appropriately oriented, is a given tradition or culture. Justice is conceived as one value amongst others, with no unique power to generate compelling reasons for action.

Of the four kinds of theory just outlined, only Kantians presuppose external reasons. Hobbesians rest on the claim that, roughly, we are all desiring beings and therefore have internal instrumental reason to pursue the means of desire fulfilment. Theorists like the later Rawls, who rest on the fact that some value-commitment is generally prevalent in the relevant audience, are internalists. The neo-Aristotelians, I suggest, should also be placed in the internal reasons camp, since they eschew transcendental moral argument and treat the demands of morality, including political morality, as historically and culturally specific. Since there are no unconditional requirements of rationality, whether or not I ought to do such-and-such depends on the moral ideals I actually have, which in its turn depends on the culture I inhabit. The difference between Hobbesian internalism, on the one hand, and late Rawlsian and neo-Aristotelian internalism, on the other, is that the two latter positions assume standing desires for justice or dispositions to virtue, and then focus on constitutive rather than instrumental practical deliberation.

We might ask just what the distinction is between a communitarian theory of justice like Walzer's and that of the later Rawls, which is plausibly thought of as a sort of communitarian liberalism, since the principles of justice rest ultimately not on a-historical principles of reason, but on a shared cultural ideal, for the realisation of which there is a very widespread 'highest-order desire'. The differences are not all easy to discern or to articulate, but one of them lies in different conceptions of how far political philosophy or theory can underwrite radical criticism of actually existing institutions.

LATE RAWLS VS. COMMUNITARIANISM

The theory of the early Rawls embeds two incommensurable models of justification in moral and political philosophy. One is the Kantian: the provision of a purely rational ground for principles of justice (Rawls, 1972: 254–7). It is this that has been decisively dropped by the time of 'Justice as fairness: political not metaphysical'. The other is the method of reflective equilibrium. High-level, abstract ideals are played off against more concrete moral intuitions. The idea is to show that abstract and concrete intuitions can be exhibited as having a structure whereby the more concrete can be derived from the more abstract. Abstract and concrete intuitions are initially put forward on the basis of mere intuitive plausibility, but in due course a relationship of mutual support develops. High-level principles or ideals are confirmed if they have the capacity to subsume and organise a body of concrete moral intuitions: once confirmed, the abstract principles provide grounds for the dismissal of initially plausible concrete intuitions with which they are incompatible (Rawls, 1972: 48–51). This is to say that the non-Kantian aspects of Rawls's methodology in *A Theory of Justice* are coherentist.

However, Rawls's methodological position changes. In 'Kantian constructivism in moral theory', he acknowledges that his principles of justice are only justifiable to those who have a highest order desire to realise an ideal of the person as rational, equal and free (Rawls, 1980). Principles of justice are then 'constructed', that is, derived from this ideal of the person via the device of the ideal hypothetical contract. So the ideal of the person here bears a weight independent of its capacity to organise our concrete moral intuitions. Now, the Rawls of the middle period acknowledges that the conception of the person as rational, equal and free is an ideal contingently shared by the members of Western constitutional democracies. It is not rationally inescapable and not compulsive for members of other epochs and cultures. Nevertheless, one might think that despite this admission, Rawls may still aspire to the reformative and critical power of a Kantian theory. For if the relevant 'we' share an ideal of the person, and reflection reveals that such an ideal has implications for the good practice that many of our institutions do not live up to, then presumably 'we' have grounds for radical reform of those institutions.

In 'Justice as fairness: political not metaphysical', however, Rawls characterises the ideal of the person as one we must conceive of ourselves as having in virtue of our actual constitutional democratic institutions and practices (Rawls, 1985: 228). What our ethico-political commitments are, are those which our institutions embody. It now becomes quite unclear how far the theory of the later Rawls is meant to be able to provide a basis for a radical critique of actual social and political arrangements. If the theory has gone fully communitarian, the attempt to derive radically reformatory concrete requirements from ideals and principles shared in the abstract must be given up. For the communitarian, what high-level ideals mean is fixed by their concrete instantiation in the actual social institutions and practices of the relevant culture or society. For a culture to share an abstract value concept is for its members to share paradigmatic applications of the concept. To put it crudely, we do not share the principle that cruelty is wrong unless we share the concept of cruelty, and we do not share the concept of cruelty unless we agree that, say, torturing a cat to death *is* cruel.

If the meaning of the concept of justice, like that of any other abstract value term, is given by its paradigmatic applications, by its forms of embodiment, then it is surely not possible to show by means of philosophical argument that a culture's actual social institutions are unjust in terms of some abstract principle of justice. There can be no such thing as a rationally compelling determination of what justice requires, arrived at by theoretical reflection on the implications of some high-level principle or ideal, but hitherto not instantiated in the actual institutions and practices of the society. For the only compelling – rationally inescapable – determinations of the concept of justice are those which provide the paradigmatic applications of the concept of justice. Slavery, for example, is emphatically unjust, and anyone who argues for its justice would be semantically out of court. This is not to say that all moral criticism is impossible on this model, but that it is necessarily piecemeal, and proceeds largely on the basis of analogy. If, for example, we have well-established principles of compensation for industrial accidents, there are good grounds for arguing that the victims of the Bhopal disaster were entitled to such compensation. But to argue that, say, our failure to give aid to the Third World until we are reduced to the level of penury at which further transfers would begin to reduce aggregate utility, is unjust, or an infringement of rights, is to attempt to substitute a philosopher's ethic, divorced from social practice, for real ethical language embedded in practice (compare Singer, 1977). So even supposing that 'we', as members of Western liberal democracies, all share an ideal of the person as free, equal and rational, it does not follow that we can all be rationally compelled to accept, say, radical and concrete principles of transnational distributive justice that will massively transform our way of life.

A useful illustration of this point is provided by Charles Beitz's criticism of the early Rawls's treatment of international distributive justice. Briefly, Beitz argues that Rawls is inconsistent with his own premisses when he treats the difference principle as applying only within the boundaries of the individual nation-state. The argument falls into two parts. The first focuses on one of the arguments Rawls offers on behalf of the difference principle, namely, that an individual's natural and social advantages are morally irrelevant in deciding what goods she should receive, since they are purely a matter of luck. Beitz points out that this is even more clearly applicable to natural resources. It is irrelevant to one's moral desert that one is a member of a country which is rich or poor in natural resources. Therefore, Rawls's argument against the system of natural liberty within states applies equally well to relations between states. If the naturally and socially disadvantaged within a state should be given sufficient aid to compensate for their disadvantage in a competitive social system, then surely countries disadvantaged before they even begin on productive cooperative activity by scarcity of natural resources, e.g. minerals or quality arable land, should be regularly compensated from a global resource fund (Beitz, 1975: 366–70).

Beitz argues that the claim to be compensated for scarcity of natural resources owes nothing to the fact of cooperation. Claims to goods based on membership of a cooperative system must be directed towards the additional value created by cooperative productive activity. Therefore, fully self-sufficient countries have obligations and entitlements derived from the requirement that the initial distribution of resources be just. Notice that this is markedly weaker than the requirements of a global difference principle. A country which receives compensation for the paucity of its natural resources, but fails to produce because its internal organization fails, has no further call on international assistance.

Beitz's second criticism is that Rawls takes it that what count as the boundaries of a cooperative scheme are given by the notion of a self-contained national community. This, he says, is false to twentieth-century economic reality. And it will not do to suggest that national boundaries mark a sharp discontinuity between levels of intensity of cooperation. Sub-national regions generally have more intense levels of cooperation than those which obtain in the nation as a whole, and Rawls has not suggested that these should be treated as autonomous units, beyond which the difference principle does not apply. Therefore, on the basis of Rawls's own arguments, the difference principle should apply globally (Beitz, 1975: 373–83).

Given early Rawlsian parameters, Beitz's arguments are strong. But we should now ask what the implications of Rawls's communitarian turn are for the idea of a global difference principle. The burden of the criticism which forced Rawls's communitarian turn was that Rawlsian principles are justifiable only to those who share an antecedent moral community. An antecedent moral community is one which shares an account of the scope and limits of moral responsibilities and entitlements, including obligations and entitlements of justice, which are embodied in social practices and grounded in history and tradition, rather than in a-historical principles of reason, either instrumental or Kantian.

Even Rawls's assumption that 'our' shared ideals compel acceptance of the difference principle as a structuring principle for national institutions is contentious enough. When, however, we come to reflect on our own institutionally embodied commitments to transnational distribution, they do indeed bespeak a certain unity: namely, that whatever positive obligations of justice, as opposed to charity, there may be, these stop at the boundaries of the nation-state. Beitz, who is working within a strongly Kantian framework, recognises that nationhood may be the basis of political identity, but treats this as a purely contingent motivational problem (Beitz, 1975: 378). But no broadly communitarian model can do so. Although the theory of motivation and reason embedded in communitarianism is not empiricist in the traditional desire–fulfilment sense, the theory cannot treat concrete moral motivations as contingencies which enter a theory of justice only as natural obstructions presenting merely strategic problems for the noumenally rational and just agent. And if we glance at the other internalist theory, neo-Hobbesian contractualism, what becomes quite obscure is not why the boundaries of obligations and rights are drawn so narrowly as the boundaries of the nation-state, but why they are drawn so as to include the less advantaged at all. If the basis of each individual's political obligation is the advantages to herself of the cooperative scheme, then surely sub-national formations between the most powerful and productive members of society fix the limits of justice and of rights.

Let me, then, briefly summarize how each theory must construe the significance of boundaries in relation to the obligations and entitlements of justice.

1 For the Kantian, there exist universal obligations of justice, grounded on non-instrumental reason, and corresponding rights. There are some obligations and reciprocal rights which bind or are held by all rational agents. Boundaries, national or cultural, are morally irrelevant.

2 For the Hobbesian, all obligations and rights are the product of a

hypothetical contract, made by instrumentally rational agents who take no interest in one another's interests. Such a contract is rational for, and therefore can be deemed to bind, only those who have a common interest in cooperation. Since there is no reason for anyone to respect another's rights unless she benefits from the other's reciprocal willingness to treat her as a right holder, we have rights only against those to whom we bear obligations, and vice versa. On this model, all obligations and rights, since they derive from a hypothetical contract, are special. That is, they attach to human beings not merely *qua* human, but in virtue of some prior commitment or relationship. The significant boundaries are those which surround the group of individuals for whom mutual cooperation, on appropriate terms, is self-interestedly rational.

3 For those who espouse a Kantian superstructure with an empiricist motivational basis – 'liberal communitarians' – obligations and rights are grounded in some fundamental moral principle, such as equal respect, or fundamental moral ideal, such as the conception of the person as free, equal and rational. Principles of justice bind only those who share an ideal, but they apply universally. That is, we, the inhabitants of late liberal culture, conceive of ourselves as bound by principles which confer the same basic rights on all, but since these principles are ultimately based on an ideal of the person as free, rational and equal, they are rational principles of action – obligations – only for we who share the ideal. Obligations of justice turn out to be special on this account, since not all are subject to them. But since they are the concomitants, not of a contract, but of shared moral ideals, and the ideal specifies that all should be treated equally in certain respects, the corresponding rights are universal.

4 For the communitarian, all rights and obligations presuppose an antecedent moral community. The scope of such rights and obligations depends on the conception of their scope which is concretely embodied in the dispositions of persons and in the political and social institutions of the community. In all actual societies, nested and interlocking social, cultural and national boundaries mark highly differentiated levels of both moral responsibility and moral entitlement.

All four theories are marked by deep difficulties, some of which I have already indicated. But they all conspicuously fail to provide a construal of the significance of boundaries which can provide a basis for a theory of the development of international justice which does not track merely contingent shifts in interests or in moral sentiments. Kantianism proper treats boundaries as morally insignificant. But actual boundaries mark very different levels of acknowledged moral responsibility and moral entitlement; acknowledgement, that is, in the sense of being embodied in concrete social practices, including political institutions, and in the dispositions of persons. Therefore, the *onus probandi* is on the Kantian to show that they should not. This requires the success of some transcendental moral argument, demonstrating that certain principles of action are incumbent upon rational beings as such. Kant offered such an argument, his less metaphysically inclined inheritors, on the whole, do not. Both neo-Hobbesians and communitarians treat boundaries, merely by their existence, as having moral significance. Hobbesian boundaries mark the limits of coincidence of non-moral interests, communitarian boundaries mark the limits of moral interests. Late Rawlsianism, as an uneasy compromise between Kantianism and communitarianism, aspires to a disregard of the moral significance of boundaries which its theoretical foundations do not permit.

SKETCH OF A THEORY OF JUSTICE

What follows is the merest sketch of a theory that may be able to provide an adequate account of both intra- and international justice. I shall take it as a minimal requirement of just institutions that they do not obstruct human flourishing and that they provide at least some of the necessary conditions of its realisation. That is, I shall present a theory which unashamedly makes the good prior to the right. The traditional liberal requirement that, in order to be just, institutions must command the assent of those who are to live under them, in so far as they are rational, is then interpreted in the light of this substantive requirement. In order to justify social institutions to a rational individual, one needs to show that (a) she herself, and anyone else relevantly similar, requires certain institutional conditions in order to flourish or enjoy a good life and (b) that there are reasons for her to support social institutions which provide (some of) those conditions for others beside herself. The scope of justice is then the scope of the institutions which the representative individual, appropriately characterised, has reason to support.

Thus stated, there is nothing at all unusual about the structure and methodology of the theory. Apart from Kant's own theory, which dispenses altogether with the notion of flourishing, any of the models of political philosophy discussed above can be conceived as different ways of fulfilling conditions (a) and (b). One standard way of doing so, common to the early Rawls and others, is to interpret (a) in a broadly empiricist or Hobbesian and (b) in a broadly rationalist, Kantian manner. The conditions of the good life are taken to be the necessary means of want-satisfaction. Hence, there is instrumental reason for any purposive agent to want them, which is to regard them as good. Then the agent-neutrality of reasons is invoked to show that if there is reason for anyone to regard these objects as good for herself, there is reason for anyone to regard them as equally good for all, and hence reason for each to act in ways which contribute to an equitable distribution of such goods to all, where such action includes supporting social institutions which secure such a distribution.

A theory which combines a want-satisfaction theory of the good and an account of justice based on the agent-neutrality of reasons embeds inconsistent assumptions about the nature of practical reason. In what follows, I shall defend a theory of the good and of justice which, I believe, makes coherent assumptions about practical reason. Since there is no scope here to articulate the theory in full, let me merely state its basic tenets. There are reasons to be just which are reasons for an individual with a correct conception of the good, and the correct conception of the good is rationally vindicable to all, given the cultural conditions of modernity. It may appear, then, that what I am offering is a philosophical argument which claims for itself the status of a transcendental derivation of principles of justice, and which offers external reasons to pursue the good life and support just institutions.

There is, however, a form of reasoning, mid-way between practical deliberation and 'pure' philosophical argument, which may tend to blur the distinction between internal and external reasons theory. This is the kind of argument which aims to show that certain principles of action are reasons for anyone given fairly minimal assumptions about her starting-point, assumptions which in certain historical and cultural contexts may be indisputable. Constructivist arguments, for example, those of Rawls's middle period, are of this kind.[3]

Williams's scepticism about external reasons, and by implication about the legitimacy of constructivist and transcendental argument in political philosophy, is based on scepticism about the power of such arguments to motivate those to whom they are addressed. I consider that a deeper understanding of the nature of practical reasoning will allow that constructivist arguments can have the power to motivate. Williams's account of reasoning is a correct account of ordinary practical deliberation, but ordinary practical deliberation is not the only form of reasoning about practical matters. Constructivist arguments in moral and political philosophy are also forms of practical argumentation. What follows, then, is a sketch of a construction of principles of justice on the basis of a conception of the good, namely the good of autonomy.[4]

The full version of the theory has three parts: (a) a vindication of the good autonomy; (b) an account of the institutional conditions of the good and the grounds on which rational individuals should support such institutions; and (c) an account of the extension of the scope of such institutions across state boundaries and the grounds on which rational individuals should support that extension. For the purposes of this chapter, I shall merely presuppose that autonomy is valuable, with the excuse that its status as the regulative ideal of liberalism is widely acknowledged in contemporary political philosophy, and I shall utilise Raz's definition. The ideal of autonomy is 'the vision of people controlling to some degree their own destiny, fashioning it through their own decisions throughout their lives', and the conditions of autonomy are 'appropriate mental abilities, an adequate range of options, and independence' (Raz, 1986: 369–70). 'Appropriate mental abilities' are the capacities to determine what one has most reason to do through rational reflection, rather than remaining subject to appetites, habits or conventional norms, and the strength of will to act on the conclusion of one's reasoning. To have an adequate range of options is to be confronted by a range of different modes of good life. And independence is material independence, without which there is no choice but only subjection to the imperatives of survival.

How, now, to argue from the good to justice? Raz sometimes appears to take the route sketched above and to rely on the supposed agent-neutrality of reasons. From the objective goodness of autonomy, there follows the principle that we should respect and support the development of others' autonomy (Raz, 1986: 408). From this principle it follows that we should establish and support social institutions which secure the conditions of autonomy for all those who live under them. This is the short route to the justice of institutions which supply the Rawlsian primary goods: civil and political liberties, equal opportunity, income and wealth. The civil liberties secure freedom from coercion and allow for the exercise of the critical capacities. The political liberties extend the scope of reflective choice to the institutions which structure the agenda of options. The requirement that positions and offices be open to all under conditions of equal opportunity secures to each an adequate range of professional and vocational options. Income guaranteed under the difference principle occludes 'choice' forced by material necessity.

It is, however, quite unobvious that, because there is an objective reason for any agent to pursue a certain mode of life, there is a reason for all agents to be devoted to the provision of the conditions of such a mode of life for any or all others. Since the objectivity of the good does not automatically give rise to the agent-neutrality of reasons, the provision of convincing arguments for the former does not absolve the theorist from the requirement to produce further arguments on behalf of a conception of justice. Elsewhere in *The Morality of Freedom*, however, Raz suggests that other-regarding principles may be founded on the good of autonomy if we recognize that at least some of the constitutive conditions of autonomy are 'inherently collective goods'.

A good is a collective good if it cannot be enjoyed by a single individual, but only by a collectivity within which it is provided on a non-excludable basis. It is contingently collective if it is merely contingently impossible, or contingently very difficult, to provide the good for some individuals and not for nearby others. Clean air and water are examples of such goods, as are public utilities like street lighting and sewage. However, a collective good is inherently collective if it cannot be enjoyed by a lone individual, because it is constituted by or logically dependent on conditions which are states of collectivities, not individuals. Such goods can be enjoyed by the individual only in virtue of her membership of the relevant collectivity. These goods include not only those produced by participation in specific practices, such as that of medicine, and those constituted legally and institutionally, such as marriage, but the overarching good of living in a society which makes possible the specific collective goods (Raz, 1986: 198–203).

I now propose the following axiom of practical reasoning. If a good is inherently collective (that is, if there is a logical relationship between that good and the characteristics of a collectivity), then anyone who intrinsically values the good has a *non-instrumental* reason to value the flourishing of the said collectivity (see also Raz, 1986: 206). This axiom simply depends on the requirement that instrumental reasons recapitulate only causal relationships: if there is a non-causal relationship between a good, x, and its collective conditions, X, then if A values x she has a non-instrumental reason to value X. And to have a non-instrumental reason to value X is to have a reason intrinsically to value X. Non-instrumentally to value a collectivity is necessarily to have non-instrumental relations with some other *persons*. For the flourishing (*qua* participants) of the other members of the collectivity is a constitutive condition of one's own.

If, now, I value autonomy, which encompasses both the capacity reflectively to choose one's mode of life and the actual availability of a range of modes of worthwhile life from this to choose, then I have non-instrumental reason to value the existence of many more modes of life than that in which I presently engage, and to value the autonomy capacity and its exercise in a large and indeterminate number of others. To see this more clearly, consider the three components of autonomy: appropriate mental capacities, an adequate range of options, and (material) independence. Both appropriate mental capacities and an adequate range of options are clearly inherently collective goods. The capacity for reflective criticism and evaluation of different modes of life depends on membership of a language community with the conceptual repertoire and discursive openness to allow discussion about complex issues of value. The conditions under which free debate can be sustained and 'experiments in living' pursued, demand at minimum the institutional protection of freedom of expression, association and information and a private sphere of protected negative liberty. If a multiplicity of different modes of life, too many and various to be realised in the span of a single human life, but compossible in a wider community, are valuable, then there is reason intrinsically to value the protection of the opportunity to pursue any one of these forms of the good life. If autonomy is valuable, each has reason to value the existence of the civil liberties *for* a community sufficiently large to sustain both discursive flexibility and diverse modes of life.[5]

If autonomy is the reflective determination of how one shall live, then the autonomy-valuing agent clearly has reasons to value not only the conditions of *individual* reflective choice between *existing* practices, but also the existence of and access to mechanisms of collective decision-making which make it possible for a community actively to structure the larger institutional context which determines what practices and combinations of practices are concretely available. This is to say that the autonomy-valuing agent has reason to value membership of a democratic political community, the scope of whose powers extends to control of the highest-level institutions which determine the shape of the social world she inhabits. This political community must embed the principle that decision-making is to be based on rational dialogue, since this is the only method of determining common legal and social institutions compatible with autonomy. Finally, the members of a political community concerned for the excellence of their common social institutions have reason to want all their co-members to share in the capacity for reflective reasoning about how best to realise the institutional conditions of autonomy. Since rational and reflective powers develop only in those who have received appropriate upbringing and education, all members of a dialogical political collectivity have reason to support the provision of such conditions for all co-members.

The proper instrumentalist response to the above argument is to claim that at least some of the 'reasons' cited above are instrumental, hence the reach of my reasons for intrinsically valuing others' autonomy is more limited than the argument suggests. The only difference between this position and pure instrumentalism about political institutions is that it places more emphasis on the inherently social nature of some valuable ends, and hence on the intrinsically valuable nature of some collectivities. The autonomy-valuer logically must intrinsically value the conditions of autonomy for some moderately large social group, because leading an autonomous life is constituted by participation in a certain sort of social world. But it does not follow that she must non-instrumentally value the conditions of autonomy for larger groups. The question for the instrumentalist, it should be stressed, is not merely 'What reason does the autonomy-valuer have to value the personal and political autonomy of others outside the boundaries of her own nation-state?', for it is unclear that she has over-riding reason to value the political autonomy of all co-nationals. The Greek *polis* and Swiss cantons were famously good at sustaining the political autonomy of citizens whilst excluding from political participation the non-citizens within their own boundaries. But the question of the scope of rational concern for others' autonomy arises most sharply in considering those who lie beyond one's own national boundaries. Why should the autonomy-valuer value the conditions of autonomy for distant others with whom her own collectivity either has minimal interaction or is able successfully to dominate? The instrumentalist's objection can be summarised as follows: the individual's intrinsic valuation of some inherently collective goods need not reach 'all the way up' through the nested institutions which constitute the world she inhabits. Even if the argument for the inherently collective nature of autonomy holds, it merely shows that there is reason for each intrinsically to value the existence of an autonomy-supporting community containing an indefinite number of others, and does not provide a rationally conclusive argument against the instrumentalization of some norms and of some other persons in all contexts of human interaction.

It is appropriate, however, to emphasize again that personal autonomy is the direction of one's life through the use of reason, and political autonomy the determination by a collectivity of its own social and legal institutions through rational debate. The equation of autonomy and rationality demands that autonomous persons mark the boundary of the intrinsically valuable autonomy-supporting community in a rationally defensible way. A collectivity which values both personal and political autonomy cannot consistently act on the basis of purely arbitrary distinctions between persons. If some are to be excluded, it has to be on the basis of reasons. If some are included but on merely instrumental grounds, there has to be some reason for having a profoundly different moral stance towards these others than towards the primary co-members whose autonomy is a constitutive condition of one's own. Such reasons cannot be merely preferential reasons, based on the interests or prejudices of some powerful group. For the defining characteristic of the social institutions which are constitutive conditions of autonomy is that they secure the individual's entitlements to the necessary conditions of self-determination against any such preferences or prejudices. Autonomy-constituting institutions necessarily embody the principle that individuals are entitled to institutional protection from subordination by the more powerful. The *scope* of such institutions therefore cannot, in all consistency, be fixed according to the quite contradictory principle that the preferences of the powerful should decide who is to enjoy autonomy and who is not.

This is not to say that the members of a political collectivity which does not take upon itself the task of securing the conditions of autonomy on a global scale are irrational and therefore non-autonomous. It is not arbitrary to distinguish, for different purposes, between intimates and non-intimates, neighbours and those further away, those who inhabit the same legal jurisdiction and those who do not, those with whom we have extensive economic relations and those with whom we do not, and so on. The point of the argument is to show that each autonomy-valuing person must intrinsically value the institutional conditions of autonomy for some largish collectivity. What are to count as non-arbitrary boundaries around that collectivity is then a proper subject for debate amongst such autonomous persons. This debate will sometimes be largely empirical (where, as a matter of fact, does the domain of this institution end?), sometimes more obviously political (who is to count as a member of this collectivity for the purpose of political decision-making?).

When we come to reflect on the grounds for extending the scope of rational concern for autonomy across state boundaries, it seems clear that one very obvious reason for doing so is when political cooperation with other states is required for the provision of contingently collective goods, for example, industrial and commercial projects needing intense economic cooperation, and environmental goods. If we intrinsically value the forms of political decision-making which constitute the exercise of our autonomy, we shall want nascent international political processes to be of such a kind. Collectivities which are internally non-autonomy-supporting because they are non-democratic, or because their members are desperately poor or illiterate, have no basis for conceiving of political processes as other than Hobbesian. They lack grounds for seeking agreement through rational debate, and hence negotiate by the use of threat advantages. They are therefore profoundly undesirable political associates for autonomy-valuers, who are compelled by such Hobbesian others to have recourse to the same strategic methods. We therefore have reasons to help to secure the autonomy of those with whom we interact, or expect to, in order to improve the quality of the interaction. We do not thereby treat these collectivities instrumentally, as long as, *ceteris paribus*, we prefer non-Hobbesian modes of political interaction with them to domination over them. For autonomy-valuers, domination of another collectivity is a rationally preferable alternative to such interaction only if the former's autonomy would otherwise be threatened by the latter.

The final section of this chapter is, as its title admits, a mere sketch of a theory of justice. But it suggests, I hope, a way of thinking about just social institutions which can provide a basis for a dynamic account of the scope of justice. The scope of justice alters because changes in the concrete modes of interaction between collectivities alter the moral status of boundaries. By emphasising that the reasons we have to protect the autonomy of others are relative to our actual material relations with them, the theory retains one of the chief virtues of Hobbesianism: realism. By placing inherently collective goods at the very foundation of justice, it avoids Hobbesian's worst vice: a conception of practical reasoning and of the basis of human interaction which can provide the basis only of cynical and exploitative human relations.

NOTES

1 For an excellent discussion of the failings of neo-Hobbesianism, see Barry (1989).
2 For an example of neo-Hobbesianism, see Gauthier (1986); for a modern Kantian theory, see Rawls (1972); for Rawls's later 'Kantianism', see Rawls (1980) and Rawls (1985); for communitarianism, see MacIntyre (1981), Sandel (1982) and Walzer (1984).
3 There is not, I think, a sharp dividing line between constructivist and transcendental arguments.
4 For a fuller defence of the good of autonomy, see Fitzmaurice (1993).
5 Raz (1986, p. 205) makes similar remarks regarding the value for the autonomous individual of a community in which plural modes of life flourish.

BIBLIOGRAPHY

Barry, B.M. (1989) *Theories of Justice*, Hemel Hempstead: Harvester-Wheatsheaf.

Beitz, C. (1975) 'Justice and international relations', *Philosophy and Public Affairs* 4(4): 360–89.

Fitzmaurice, D. (1993) 'Liberal neutrality, traditional minorities and education', in J. Horton (ed.) *Liberalism, Multiculturalism and Toleration*, London: Macmillan, pp. 50–69.

Gauthier, D. (1986) *Morals by Agreement*, Oxford: Oxford University Press.

MacIntyre, A. (1981) *After Virtue*, London: Duckworth.

Rawls, J. (1972) *A Theory of Justice*, Oxford: Oxford University Press.

Rawls, J. (1980) 'Kantian constructivism in moral theory', *Journal of Philosophy* 77(9): 515–72.

Rawls, J. (1985) 'Justice as fairness: political not metaphysical', *Philosophy and Public Affairs* 14(3): 223–51.

Raz, J. (1986) *The Morality of Freedom*, Oxford: Oxford University Press.

Sandel, M. (1982) *Liberalism and the Limits of Justice*, Cambridge: Cambridge University Press.

Singer, P. (1977) 'Famine, affluence and morality', in W. Aiken and H. LaFollette (eds) *World Hunger and Moral Obligation*, Englewood Cliffs, NJ: Prentice-Hall.

Walzer, M. (1984) *Spheres of Justice*, Oxford: Blackwell.

Williams, B. (1981) *Moral Luck*, Cambridge: Cambridge University Press.

3 Structural rationality, democratic citizenship and the new Europe

Julian Nida-Rümelin

INTRODUCTION

The breakdown of the communist regimes in eastern Europe was at least partly due to the world-wide renaissance of democratic ideals such as self-government and individual self-determination. Systems based on an institutionalized paternalism have crumbled and most of the remaining anti-democratic systems will probably lose a desperate fight. Possibly there will be some exceptions under the reign of Islamic fundamentalism. But the general tendency of world policy during the last two decades of the century has been and probably will be democratisation.

Obviously there is another renaissance: that of nineteenth-century nationalism. But the nation is not the only prevalent collective identity. The political development of eastern Europe shows that at present there are two main collective identities competing with one another: the ideal of the (ethnically and culturally homogeneous) nation-state and the ideal of European re-integration, which for the most part is viewed as identical with westernisation.

Similarly, in the western parts of Europe a discussion has begun about the long-term perspectives of the European Union which focuses on basic questions of European citizenship. Should and can European citizenship become a supplement to national citizenship and is European citizenship in a region with a multitude of languages compatible with democracy, if one considers as minimal requirements the existence of a common public discourse and some kind of collective actor constituted by an institutionally mediated aggregation of citizens' preferences?

This chapter tries to sketch a normative theory of democratic citizenship based on the idea of structural rationality which avoids the dilemmas that seem to be inherent in 'supra-national', e.g. European, citizenship. I will begin with some foundational questions of practical rationality, introducing the notion of structural rationality, then I will give an account of democratic citizenship based on the notion of structural rationality and, finally, I will discuss some implications of this account of citizenship for the idea of the new Europe.

STRUCTURAL RATIONALITY

At least in the English-speaking scientific community the predominant view of practical rationality is a consequentialist one. Underlying this view are two quite firm grounds. The first is the intuitive notion of being responsible for the consequences of one's actions and the notion that responsibility concerning actions is nothing else but responsibility for actual or probabilistic causal consequences of actions. Treating behaviour as a matter of personal action corresponds to the responsibility for the consequences of this behaviour. To a certain extent this intuition is incorporated in the legal system.

The second ground emerges from the paradigmatic core of modern decision theory.[1] Modern utility theory seems to yield a neutral framework which allows us to reconstruct all kinds of rational action as consequentialist. Modern utility theory is indeed neutral regarding axiological presumptions. Rational action maximises some subjective value function, but the question whether this is to be interpreted as representing the well-being of the person acting or the well-being of other persons, or whether well-being plays a role at all, can be left open.

Decision theory in the broader sense (including game theory and public choice) has developed instruments of analysis which have already advanced ethics and normative political theory and which will be of major relevance in the future. But there is a tendency to combine an inadequate, consequentialist theory of individual and collective rationality with these disciplines. Indeed, in one respect, the situation seems quite paradoxical: it is exactly those research projects – at least implicitly – devoted to a consequentialist theory of rationality that have led to results which undermine this theory. For this reason the impossibility results in social choice theory not only challenge our pre-theoretic conception of democracy, but can be seen as a general argument in favour of a non-consequentialist theory of rationality.

The consequentialist paradigm emphasises acting as some way of changing the world. If a person had not acted in this way, the world would look different. Thus a rational person cannot act without – at least implicitly – exposing some subjective rank-order within the class of possible worlds. As a consequence, the ideal type of practical rationality results in a complete ordering of possible worlds and their lotteries. Philosophically, however, there is a conceptual problem, because if one allows for any way of describing these worlds, the consequentialist view becomes trivial. If, for example, I refrain from doing *a* because I do not want to defect from the rule to tell the truth, and if 'in world *x* person *p* has lied' is one of the predicates that can be used describing worlds, then every kind of deontologically orientated behaviour can be conceptually transformed into consequentialist behaviour. But there is an intuitively clear-cut difference between rule conformity as an action guide and consequentialist optimising as an action guide, even if it is not easy to render this difference conceptually explicit.

Since there are many different axiological attitudes, personal motives and dispositions, there is a multitude of interpersonally different rank-orders giving rise to problems of coordination and cooperation in society. From a consequentialist point of view it is the task of an institutional framework to provide some basic restraints in order to make these differences compatible. This is done by establishing sanctions which change the outcomes of strategies and motivate consequentialist actors *in statu civile* to change their previous (*in statu naturale*) strategies. But there is a well-known shortcoming with this kind of Hobbesian theory of democracy: it cannot explain how this structural framework can ever be stable.

I now want to introduce a conception of practical rationality which, on the one hand, gives an account of institutional stability and which, on the other hand, constitutes a conception of democratic citizenship which defines the role of the nation-state in a way compatible with supra-national, e.g. 'European', citizenship. It will not be the task of this chapter, however, to develop the theory of structural rationality in detail. It should be sufficient to give an exposition of some central elements of structural rationality thereby revealing some shortcomings of a purely consequentialist conception of practical rationality.

In the history of ethics several alternative approaches to practical rationality have been discussed of which the Kantian has become paradigmatic.[2] Yet the theory of practical reason which Kant developed is not a general theory, it is confined to moral behaviour. Following the moral law and following hypothetical imperatives are two different accounts of action, both of which are based on the general idea of universal lawful causality, but practical reason adds the idea of laws which are chosen by the actor herself (i.e. autonomy). In the realm of moral behaviour the approach of autonomous action of course contains an essential element for understanding moral action, but I think it is inadequate to have a twofold theory of practical rationality. The Kantian conception is not a unified theory of practical rationality, since practical reason with its categorical imperative expressing the autonomy of rational beings and maximisation (with its technical and pragmatical imperatives) are not integrated. Only morality (the good will) expresses autonomy, whereas all other motives of action reveal human beings as part of nature governed by heteronomous deterministic laws. This dichotomy of two types of action (even to the point of confining action to the realm of morality) is not convincing. It does not take into consideration the complex structural inter-relations of universal and personal viewpoints which guide our decisions and which, from my point of view, should guide the decisions of the perfectly rational person as well.[3]

There are good reasons for trying to establish a unified theory of practical rationality. In the following I will sketch some central elements which, in my opinion, should be part of such a theory. To introduce the idea I use a fictitious biological example: a society of ants gradually gaining consciousness.

An ant-society is governed by a complex system of interaction and cooperation. The individual ants follow these behavioural rules non-intentionally. General conformity to these rules is based on the genetic constitution of the ants and there is no intentionality involved.

Now let us add some fiction. Let us assume that one particular ant gains consciousness. She begins to realise what she is doing, and after a while she acquires the ability to act freely (first assumption). Now the question arises whether she will still act in conformity to the rule system, guiding the behaviour of ants. For the sake of the argument we assume that the established system of rules of behaviour is optimal for the ant-society and that this fact is obvious to the 'conscious' ant: she knows that the established system of rules of behaviour is optimal (second assumption). We can leave it open which criteria there are for optimality in ant-societies.

Adding the further quite plausible assumption that it is not always in the personal interest of the ant to follow the rules (she might sometimes prefer to rest when no other ant is watching or when no other ant will sanction such shirking behaviour), it follows that the ant will not always act in conformity to the rules if she is a self-orientated maximiser.[4]

Let us suppose the conscious ant continues to conform to the rules. In this case there are different possible 'rational accounts' of such behaviour:

1 She develops a certain disposition to follow the system of rules shortly after gaining consciousness, probably under the influence of the

second assumption,[5] that is combining practical reason (in fostering an optimal system of rules) with constraining free choice. Having a disposition here means being no longer free to perform an act not in conformity to the rules of the system. There might be a certain range of free choice determining which disposition to acquire (the ant might, e.g., decide to attend a school teaching moral behaviour).

2 Now let us assume the ant remains free, i.e. she can always freely decide whether to perform a conforming or a non-conforming act. If the ant now decides to act in a conforming manner (well aware that this is not always in her personal interest) because she adopts the structure of ant-behaviour established by the rules as optimal, then this would be an example of what I will call structural rationality.

Thus we can establish the following characteristics of structural rationality:

1 'Structurally rational' is a predicate to be applied to (individual) actions (token), that is, to the primary objects of decision.

2 An action can be structurally rational only if it is the object of free choice, that is, it may not be dispositionally or otherwise determined.

3 A structurally rational action reflects positive valuation regarding the structure by the actor. 'Valuation' here is not meant necessarily in an axiological sense. The actor might foster or preserve a structure for deontological reasons, too.

4 Intentionality. The act is chosen with the motivating intention to conform with the structure.

There are certainly many conceptual and philosophical problems to be solved in order to make the idea of structural rationality more explicit. To mention just some of them: the descriptive relativity of actions causes problems with the concept 'conformity'; on the other hand, conformity cannot be defined for action tokens, but for action types; only in some cases is it adequate to establish a binary code of conformity, in others one needs degrees of conformity; the probabilistic aspects of structural rationality; the extension of structural rationality to group decisions; and, most important, problems of under- and overdetermination. But these problems are not peculiar to the concept of structural rationality, and we will not solve them here. Instead, I want to focus for a moment on the question how acting s-rationally could be motivated.[6] Two possible attitudes seem to be plausible in the ant-example:

1 Solipsistic attitude. The ant regards herself as being the only person around, the other ants are perceived as a kind of functioning machines. It seems that acting s-rationally under this condition could

be motivated by altruism only. Altruism in this context might result in attributing an inherent worth to the rules that constitute the conditions for coordinative behaviour.

2 We-attitude. Despite the difference in consciousness, the one conscious ant might feel a part of an ant-society with a common good. This allows for a weak form of we-attitudes: the conscious ant might think: 'The established system of rules of behaviour is good for all of us, it is collectively good, good for our society of ants,[7] so even if I am the only one to decide freely, I want to foster that common good, and so I participate in our projects by conforming to the rules which constitute our collective behaviour.'

We-intentions in the stricter sense, however, require more than one conscious actor:

A member i of a collective K we-intends to do a if and only if:

1 i intends to do her part of a, given that she believes that every (fully-fledged and adequately informed) member of K or at least that a sufficient number of them, as required for the performance of a, will (or at least probably will) do her part (their parts) of a.
2 i believes that every (fully fledged and adequately informed) member of K or at least that a sufficient number of them, as required for the performance of a, will (or at least probably will) do her part (their parts) of a.
3 There is a mutual belief in K to the effect that 1 and 2.[8]

We-intentions of this kind presuppose other conscious actors. So let us now assume that all ants gain consciousness. Thus, we can make the following assumptions:

1 The established system of rules of behaviour is optimal on the basis of the given first-order intrinsic preferences.
2 There is a common knowledge concerning 1.
3 There are we-intentions concerning different ant-projects (valuable on the basis of the ants' preferences).

If there are we-intentions of this kind, it follows that every ant has a motivation to conform with the established system of rules of behaviour, that is, to act in a structurally rational way.

STRUCTURAL RATIONALITY AS CONSTITUTING DEMOCRATIC CITIZENSHIP

Let us turn to a society of human beings. Everybody knows that without some elements constraining individual optimizing many projects essential for the well-being of everybody cannot be realised and the advantage of cooperation in general is reduced. For human actors a rigid, binary system of rules precisely governing behaviour seems to be inadequate. Structural rationality must be based on a less rigid system of constraining conditions, and this can be provided by a structural concept of collective rationality. To the extent that such a structural concept of collective rationality is applied in the theory of democracy, it can be based on a concept well known from the legal theory of H.L.A. Hart, the concept of secondary rules.[9]

Primary rules prohibit and command; they grant members of a legal community rights and impose duties on them. Secondary rules, on the other hand, determine which procedure is to be implemented in a legitimate generation of primary rules. The line demarcating primary rules from secondary rules is not hard and fast. Because the law of contract determines in which way new legal obligations are generated, Hart subsumes it under the category of secondary rules. Moreover, because (continuing with this example) the generation of rules that direct the correct completion and fulfilment of contracts is itself again bound to secondary rules not as determination of an absolute, but rather as a formulation of a relative difference, primary and secondary rules cannot be understood as two separate, disjunct set of rules. The difference between them can better be formulated in the following way. One specific rule (or one specific set of rules) is secondary *in relation* to another specific rule (or another specific set of rules), and so on. Accordingly, the rules emerging from a legal contract are secondary to a legal obligation that implies concrete contractual conditions, certain rules given by a political constitution are secondary to the system of rules by the legal contract, etc.

The classical version of legal positivism does not distinguish any obligation that is more than coercion by means of penalties. But a legal rule differs from a simple command in so far as it is normative. This means that a legal rule contains a claim on its addressees that is valid as such, not simply in virtue of the penalties to which it is linked. Validity does not mean just being supported by penalties. The validity of a legal rule can, on the one hand, be based on its content, which means that it is accepted as such as a certain rule of conduct (primary validity). On the other hand, its validity can be based on the fact that it has emerged out of an already accepted set of secondary rules (secondary validity). Societies that only know primary rules do not have, in Hart's opinion, any legal system. In Hart's concept of rights, secondary rules are constitutive.

To reveal the meaning and the status of this distinction, let us assume the following situation. At a given time t a person P has made another person Q a promise that obliges P to carry out a certain (generic) action a. In the meantime (at the time t') P has come to the conviction that it would be better for Q if he (P) abstained from doing a – always assuming that this would not harm any other conceivable interests. It is P's firm conviction that ~a would definitely have better consequences for Q. Moral intuition tells us that in no possible case in which P could have such a conviction should he abstain from doing a. Beyond this there can be even situations in which such conditions (of which P is convinced of) are fulfilled – but still P's decision for ~a would violate an individual right of Q. P's decision for ~a could even be a violation of rights, although ~a could be shown to be perfectly permissible in the moral sense. Even in possible cases in which P could have good reasons to believe that in the meantime (at the time t') Q himself has come to prefer ~a, it is not at all evident that P would now be allowed to decide, in breach of the promise at time t, to do ~a. Q could say: 'Even if at the time t I really had come to prefer ~a, it would still be high-handed of P to abstain from doing a without my explicit authorisation for doing so.' There is, in this example, a direct conflict between the Pareto-criterion on the one hand, and individual rights and duties on the other hand, as constituted by a given promise.

Rules of interaction, whether they are institutionally supported or just embedded in moral and conventional everyday normative patterns, generally emerge out of a long historical process. It is usually assumed that in a historical process rational decisions only play a subordinate role. Nevertheless, the tradition of normative contractualist theory persistently clings to the fiction of a rational choice of institutional structures. Yet in modern contractualism the Kantian version of the contractualist argument has become dominant.[10] In this version the contract constitutes a criterion of the right only, it is not a ground of obligation. The appeal of the contractualist idea for political philosophy can be explained by the specific role existing institutional or conventional regulations play in the context of the moral orientation of human action. Moreover, these institutional or conventional rules are generally conceived – ignoring times of revolution or situations such as a civil war – as secondary rules: they constitute the ground of validity of primary rules of first-order decisions. These judgements are made

more or less independently of the question of how these concrete institutional and conventional rules were developed, that is, independently
of the question of whether they are the product of human inventive-
ness or of historical and cultural evolution. In the example above, the
'conferring' of an individual right on *a*, which as a result of the promise
of P belongs to Q, is a primary rule; and of course the duty of P to do *a*
also is a primary rule. But, on the other hand, and it is important to see
the difference here, the institution of the promise itself possesses the
status of a secondary rule. Under normal circumstances we are simply
obliged to keep promises.

There are many cases in which, on the basis of a decision, secondary
rules can attain the character of a ground of validity. Let us first discuss
an example that does not, as parliamentary proceedings of legislation
do, presuppose the existence of formal institutions. Let us suppose a
group of persons plans a hike through the mountains together. As they
are all experienced mountaineers, they know that on such trips one
always has to reckon with sudden changes in the weather and, sub-
sequently, with dangerous situations. Planning their trip they decide
that in case of such a situation one of them – let us name him John –
would take over the task of deciding for the whole group what has to be
done. Later, on the trip, such a dangerous situation actually occurs.
John decides that in order to get back to the valley as quickly as possible
they should take the shortest route and descend off the face of a pre-
cipitous steep. Peter, another member of the group, is convinced,
beyond any doubt, that this decision is the wrong one, because the
implied risks are in fact much higher than those of the alternative solution which would be to take the route back slowly and cautiously on the
northern side of the mountain, even though this would cost them much
more time and would not allow them to arrive at the valley until late in
the night. Assuming that our group of mountaineers has sufficient solidarity not to leave any of its members alone, Peter could succeed in
forcing that whole group to follow him just by obstinately refusing to
submit to the decision of John. Yet, it seems that Peter has not the right
to do so.

There is obviously a great difference between a situation in which the
members of a group have already earlier agreed on a certain collective
decision-procedure, as in the one of the mountaineers, and a situation
in which this is not the case. In a cultural context predominantly characterised by democratic values a group of persons would, assuming
they had not already earlier agreed on a different kind of a decision-
procedure, apply the rule of majority vote. But this must also be
regarded as a secondary rule. If in our example there was not such a

secondary rule (the earlier agreement on the decision-procedure that referred the task of making the necessary decision to John), Peter would not only be morally allowed, but may be even morally obliged to evoke, by means of his refusal to submit to the decision of John and by appealing to the sympathy of the other members of the group, what in his eyes is the best collective decision. But in the case where there is already a (commonly accepted) secondary rule, Peter in general is simply obliged to accept this as a structural constraint. Only strong and extraordinary reasons might morally allow Peter to refrain from the established secondary rule. Certainly primary rules are capable of subverting secondary rules in some restricted cases. If Peter is indeed totally convinced that the descent John prefers will inevitably lead to the death of the whole group, then he may even be obliged to torpedo the collective decision made by John – notwithstanding the fact that the torpedoed decision was based on a collective decision-rule which sprang from an earlier common and unanimous agreement.

Democratic legitimacy is a feature of collective decisions that accord with certain secondary rules. It is difficult to say in abstract terms which secondary rules are constitutive for a democratic system. As the theory of comparative government shows, the empirically realised variety of such secondary-rule systems in parliamentary democracies is very wide. The family resemblance between all different kinds of democratic systems involves, on the one hand, a minimal measure of formalised control by the political decision-makers and, on the other hand, a constitutive role for an informal normative consensus. While the first of these elements manifests itself in rules of common, fair and free citizens' elections guaranteed by constitutions and internal democratic structures within the respective system of political institutions, the second element of a democratic system is essential for the specific normative character of its political decision-procedures: the decisions made in these procedures depend on the presupposition of being at least fundamentally capable of achieving common consensual agreement. Citizens' consensus – even if never in fact realised – is indispensably *intentio recta* for primary rules issued by the legislator. Legislative projects are universalistically justified with normative arguments like the common interest, political justice, economic efficiency, etc.

The universalistic justification of primary rules is essential in a democratic polity. The claim of universal justifiability of primary rules – a claim towards which every kind of communicative political acting in a democratic order must necessarily be orientated – does not mean a claim for a *de facto* common agreement on them. A dissent over primary rules, typically appearing in different cognitivistically formulated opinions about the adequacy of specific (universalistically intended) normative criteria, cannot, as a rule, be eliminated by a democratic decision-procedure. This is simply due to the fact that a democratic system is based on a common consensus of a higher order, and this common consensus itself refers to the acceptance of secondary rules. At the level of primary rules common agreement is *in intentio recta* only. At this level, however, *de facto* common agreement cannot be realised.

Another type of common agreement is not *in intentio recta*, but *praesumptio indirecta* of a democratic system. Let us explain this with the help of an elementary example. Let us suppose that a group of persons has to decide on *x* or *y* – whatever these alternatives might be (presidential candidates, legislative drafts, decisions in foreign policy, etc.). Let us further suppose that one person of this group, the person A, prefers *x*. When it finally comes to the vote – evoked by application of the rule of majority vote – the group decides for *y*. Now this does not necessarily change A's opinion about *x*: she might still be perfectly convinced that *x* is better than *y*. Now let us imagine that A had the power to decide which of the two alternatives, *x* or *y*, finally was going to be realised, and let us for this case, to keep the example as simple as possible, suppose that *ceteris paribus* is realized in its widest sense (no other social consequences of *x* and *y* than those already inherent in their full characterisation, no personal disadvantages for A, etc.). In this case there are now two possibilities: A could either decide for *x*, as she is still convinced that *x* is better than *y*, or she could decide for *y*, backed by the argument that the whole group of electors had (in a legitimate democratic decision-procedure) in fact voted for it. We cannot of course here go into the problems of the revealed-preference concept. But it should be quite clear that A, if she actually decided for *y* on the basis of the given reasons, would not in any way have to give up her conviction that *x* is better than *y*. An election or a vote in general – ignoring cases in which it serves as a parameter in the process of judging possible alternatives – does not provoke any change in the individual's first-order preferences. A's decision (if she decides for *y*) is motivated by preferences of a higher order, i.e. by criteria of structural rationality that refer to how individuals' first-order preferences should be realised collectively.

Even a wrong collective decision, if it does not violate the structure, is thereby legitimate and can oblige. None the less not all wrong collective decisions are obliging. Legal positivism of the normative type maintains that a legitimate collective decision is always obliging, either because there can be no wrong legitimate decisions, because there does not exist any independent criterion of the right beyond a system of secondary rules, or because of the fact that an independent parameter in the sense of a 'relative' natural law simply cannot be obliging at all. Normative legal positivism represents one extreme on a scale whose opposing extreme consists in the idea that secondary rules are totally irrelevant. Consequentialism and existentialism unite in their mutual rejection of secondary rules – a rejection explicit in existentialism and only implicit in consequentialism, here as a logical consequence of its specific concept of rationality.

Citizenship in democratic systems is constituted by a basic social consensus concerning the structural framework of secondary rules which determine under which constraints and with which procedures individuals' first-order preferences should be realised. Structural features of interaction and collective decision constrain individual optimisation. Only *within* the structural framework which constitutes democratic citizenship is there room left for – not necessarily self- or group-oriented – optimisation. Optimisation is constrained by structural features of a democratic order even if optimisation is itself oriented towards universalistic normative goals, e.g. political justice. Only where the democratic character of a social structure as such becomes dubious will the obliging character of its constitutive structural traits (secondary rules) also be questioned.[11] In this case the criterion of optimisation becomes dominant, and a Hobbesian *bellum omnium contra omnes* (in terms of either conflicting interests or conflicting normative orientations) will only be prevented by achieving a new basic consensus on the fundamental features of the social structure as a whole.

Democratic citizenship should not be based – *qua* aggregation – on the reductionist constitution of a collective actor,[12] but on structural features of interaction, constituted above all as secondary rules including the features of democratic decision-procedures. But for the establishment of structural rationality a system of formal rules of interaction and collective decision secured by means of penalties can never be sufficient. Structural rationality as a personal guideline of *praxis* is indispensable as a normative and motivationally effective element in order to constitute citizenship as the *corpus politicum* of a democratic order.

IMPLICATIONS FOR THE NEW EUROPE

For the emerging new Europe it is even more obvious than for the old that the idea of a European nation-state is unfeasible. The model of the United States as melting pot forming a new nation out of different national elements is not transferable to a region with its well-established traditions, cultures and identities like Europe. And even if it were feasible, one cannot wish its realisation (in fact, the US is not a melting pot, but it was in the past and mostly still is an integrationist model of marginalising cultures diverging from the predominant white Anglo-Saxon tradition). In fact the idea of a European nation-state in the traditional sense was not feasible for the EC of the six original states, all of which were highly industrialised and had similar social and political traditions and institutions, still less for the former EC of twelve states with its southern members like Spain and Greece. It is certainly not a sound model for the new Europe. The nation-state in the traditional sense presupposed the unified triad of territory, state and people. It presupposed a collective actor constituted by a common public, by a highly developed integrational orientation and the decay of all other competing collective identities. It could be realised at a European level only if the multitude of collective identities, cultural backgrounds, languages, religious and *weltanschauliche* orientations could be marginalised or reduced considerably.

The competing point of view is more realistic. On this view the new Europe cannot be more than a loosely connected *foedus pacificum* in order to coordinate international relations in Europe and in order to establish forms of multilateral economic (and possibly social) aid. The young states which evolved out of the Soviet Union are obviously in favour of this second line of thought. Citizenship on that account is confined to the nation-state. Each nation-state is constituted by a dominant cultural tradition, a dominant official language and an identity which is at least partly constituted by the emphasis on differences from neighbouring states, peoples and cultures – the history of Europe during the last two centuries and the present developments are bloody demonstrations of this aspect.

The project of the nation-state consequently carried out in the new larger Europe will result in a long series of conflicts – wars during the formation process and internal social conflicts within the nation-states as a side-effect of establishing the people constituting the state's 'legitimate citizenship'. But there is the alternative of a new understanding of democratic citizenship which allows for combining regional and cultural identities with 'supra-national' identities like European citizenship. In theory there is an alternative to the traditional view on citizenship constituting the nation-state and constituting, *qua* institutional decision-procedures, the state as a collective actor. In fact this alternative, at least partly, exists in more than a theoretical form.

If we understand citizenship as constituted by we-intentions of a certain kind backed up by individual rights of participation in collective projects within the framework of a legal system defining constraints which guarantee individual liberties, citizenship no longer constitutes a single collective actor (the nation-state), but instead there evolves a structural context of interaction on different levels. This interaction has two essential elements: the first element consists in a basic normative consensus on the institutional conditions and the second element consists in an orientation of individual behaviour to a certain extent towards structural rationality, preserving institutional conditions, and allowing for participatory democratic citizenship.

In this sense European citizenship is compatible with a multitude of individual we-intentions ranging from little communities like family or friendship groups to larger ones like associations and corporations, regionally defined communities like city or *Land*, cultural, political, religious and *weltanschauliche* communities. A well-developed concept of democratic citizenship, though, will always lay emphasis on an individualistically understood citizen's status. The rights *qua* citizen are predominantly individual rights, not rights which anybody gets *qua* being a member of whatever community. Citizenship is not constituted by groups, but by citizens interacting to a certain extent *as citizens* with specific we-intentions. That is, they are acting on the basis of structural rationality, while at the same time also acting as Lockean optimisers within commonly accepted structures of interaction, including structures of conflict resolution between different collective identities in Europe.

There is something tragic in the present development in Europe, as the victory of democracy has at the same time encouraged the re-establishment of the long obsolete idea of the nation-state. The new Europe has the chance to restrain the destructive potential of the new nationalisms in establishing institutional structures as a core around which the normative underpinning of a European citizenship can develop.

NOTES

1 This theoretical core is common to the main decision theoretic conceptions, e.g. those of Savage (1954), Jeffrey (1965), Fishburn (1970).
2 'Kantian' here with capital K, i.e. the theory of practical rationality which Kant developed in *Kritik der praktischen Vernunft*. The theory of structural rationality has indeed some characteristics which justify to call it a kantian (with small k) conception in so far as rational persons are thought to act intentionally in conformity with structural constraints (without mediation *qua* dispositions or sanctions *in foro interno*).
3 See Nida-Rümelin (1993a).
4 It might be questioned whether this assumption is compatible with the

second assumption, but Harsanyi's version of rule Utilitarianism shows that it is compatible, cf. Harsanyi (1979).

5 Gauthier's *Morals by Agreement* (1986) rests, at least implicitly, on the assumption that a rational person can decide to adopt a certain disposition. So we could interpret this first account as the Gauthier-solution. I discuss the relation of rationality, maximisation and disposition in Nida-Rümelin (1993b).

6 's' for 'structural', 'structurally', etc.

7 Whatever criteria are used to decide on the collective good: Kantian, Pareto, Average Utilitarian, Sum-Utilitarian, Rawlsian, Varian, etc.

8 Cf. Tuomela (1984), Chapter 4.

9 Cf. Hart (1961), especially Chapter V.

10 Explicitly in Rawls (1971), but true as well for other modern contractualist theories, e.g. Gauthier (1986), Buchanan (1975), Nozick (1974); cf. Nida-Rümelin (1987, 1988).

11 The right to resistance, the right to civil disobedience and to objection out of conscientious reasons within the realm of a democratic (to put it as Rawls puts it, in a 'nearly just') society cannot be an argument against this theses, because it is actually a specific feature of civil disobedience that it does not subvert the structure. It, rather, takes its position explicitly within the context of the democratic system itself.

12 The impossibility results of collective choice theory give further reason to refrain from any theory which identifies democracy with some kind of con-stituting a collective actor. This seems to me the most important insight of the theorems of Arrow (1963), Sen (1970), Gibbard (1973, 1974) and Satterthwaite (1975); cf. Nida-Rümelin (1991).

BIBLIOGRAPHY

Arrow, K. (1963) *Social Choice and Individual Values*, 2nd edition, New Haven and London: Yale University Press.

Buchanan, J. (1975) *The Limits of Liberty: Between Anarchy and Leviathan*, Chicago/London: Chicago University Press.

Fishburn, P. (1970) *Utility Theory for Decision Making*, New York: Robert E. Krieger.

Gauthier, D. (1986) *Morals by Agreement*, Oxford: Clarendon Press.

Gauthier, D. and Sugden, R. (eds) (1993) *Rationality, Justice and the Social Contract*, New York/London: Harvester Wheatsheaf.

Gibbard, A. (1973) 'Manipulation and voting schemes: a general result', *Econometrica* 41: 587–601.

Gibbard, A. (1974) 'A Pareto-consistent libertarian claim', *Journal of Economic Theory* 7: 388–410.

Harsanyi, J.C. (1979) 'Bayesian decision theory, rule utilitarianism and Arrow's impossibility theorem', *Theory and Decision* 11: 289–318.

Hart, H.L.A. (1961) *The Concept of Law*, Oxford: Clarendon Press.

Jeffrey, R. (1965) *The Logic of Decision*, London: McGraw-Hill.

Nida-Rümelin, J. (1987) 'Der Vertragsgedanke in der politischen Philosophie', *Zeitschrift für Politik* 34: 200–7.

Nida-Rümelin, J. (1988) 'Plädoyer für eine kontraktualistische Philosophie der Politik', in P. Koller, A. Schramm and O. Weinsberger (eds) *Philosophie des*

Rechts, der Politik und der Gesellschaft, pp. 51–7, Wien: Holder-Pichler-Tempsky.

Nida-Rümelin, J. (1991) 'Zur Philosophie der Demokratie: Arrow-Theorem, Liberalität und strukturelle Normen', *Analyse und Kritik* 13: 184–303.

Nida-Rümelin, J. (1993a) *Kritik des Konsequentialismus*, München: Oldenbourg.

Nida-Rümelin, J. (1993b) 'Practical reason, collective rationality and contractarianism', in D. Gauthier and R. Sugden (eds) *Rationality, Justice and the Social Contract*, New York/London: Harvester Wheatsheaf, pp. 53–74.

Nozick, R. (1974) *Anarchy, State, and Utopia*, New York: Basic Books.

Rawls, J. (1971) *A Theory of Justice*, Cambridge, Mass.: Harvard University Press.

Satterthwaite, M. (1975) 'Strategy-proofness and Arrow's conditions: existence and correspondence theorems for voting procedures and social welfare functions', *Journal of Economic Theory* 10: 187–217.

Savage, L. (1954) *The Foundations of Statistics*, New York: Wiley.

Sen, A. (1970) *Collective Choice and Social Welfare*, San Francisco: Holden-Day, Inc.

Tuomela, R. (1984) *A Theory of Social Action*, Dordrecht: Reidel.

4 Justice vs. culture: which comes first?

Ryszard Legutko

The process of European integration has made possible at least two distinct and mostly divergent ways of theoretical reflection. To simplify, one may say that the first type concentrates on the problem of European culture while the second takes, as the primary concern, the problem of justice. What is important is that those two approaches seem to ignore each other and it is rather unlikely that any common ground between them can be found.

DILEMMAS OF EUROPEAN CULTURE

We and They

The question of how to identify and to evaluate the culture of Europe has been with us since time immemorial. In recent decades most of the analyses of the unity of this culture were influenced by the existence of the Soviet Empire. The communist menace, no doubt, made this task easier. When the totalitarian regimes seemed at the peak of their power, it was almost self-evident to draw the line between the Free World and the Soviet Block, the distinction represented by various political categories, Karl Popper's (1971: 169–201) dichotomy of the closed and open societies being the best known. The last (to my knowledge) eloquent statement of this position was Robert Conquest's book with a telling title *We and They*, published in 1980. The date the book came out is also significant because it was exactly in this year that the first anti-communist mass movement in eastern Europe emerged, the movement which in the coming decade was to lead to the liberation of the Soviet-dominated countries, the tearing down of the Berlin Wall, and finally to the disintegration of the Soviet Union itself. Robert Conquest argues in this book, as its title suggests, that there were two distinct forces in the modern world being in a permanent clash – the consensual tradition (European culture) and the despotic tradition (totalitarian societies). His characterization of both echoes, to some degree, Karl Popper's distinction:

> Ours ... usually involves an attachment to ancient rights on a piecemeal, and even sentimental, basis not easily amenable to rationalization. But it also contains the element of debate and argument, as well as a feeling of deeper and less conscious needs, even if these have not been susceptible to adequate verbal elaboration. Despotism contains within itself all the elements of a more extreme irrationality: the elimination of real debate and criticism and the idolization of premature political perfectionism. In fact, the backwardness of modern despotisms resides not merely in the parallels which may be seen between them and the bureaucratic empires of the past, but also in the factors thought to constitute their modernity.
>
> (Conquest, 1980: 47)

The resemblance to Popper's dichotomy is striking, though the differences are no less significant. Conquest's characterisation is definitely more conservative, putting alongside the dialogic rationalism some pre-rational loyalties. The critical and self-critical mind would not thus be, on these grounds, a sufficient factor to account for the specificity of open society in general and for Western civilisation in particular. In short, Conquest's position is that there is something more in the Western tradition than openness to arguments and to rational debate.

Even during the time when the Soviet Union was still a superpower Popper's distinction provoked several important doubts, including among the most outstanding adversaries of totalitarianism. Alexander Solzhenitsyn dismissed it altogether, pointing out that communism was not an offshoot of the Eastern or Asiatic culture but came from within the heart of the West European tradition of openness. Milan Kundera, generally hostile to the despotic heritage of Russia, raised the issue of Mitteleuropa, an area whose cultural identity had been usually ignored by the Western defenders of the spiritual unity of Europe. Several voices were heard to the effect that all talk about this unity smells of cultural imperialism, arrogance and a sense of superiority towards non-Western cultures; it was also added that the processes which had shaped European identity consisted in the adaptation and assimilation of non-Western influences. People and ideas that reached this continent as a result of decolonisation as well as a change in the European attitude being now more open towards other cultures, make it urgent, it was argued, to re-evaluate and, in the long run, to revise the image of Europe as a spiritual unity which has been bequeathed to us by past generations. Finally, the decline of the Soviet Block convinced many anti-communists, even before the actual collapse of the empire, that the mere antithesis between open and closed societies need not provide a sufficient ground for identifying the essence of Europe. In fact, the existence of the powerful adversary, which always provokes excessively defensive and apologetic reactions from the other side, may have been an obstacle in arriving at an accurate and positive depiction of the nature of European culture as well as of its current dilemmas.

The questions thus were the following. What positive substance does the notion of an open society carry? Do its constituents – rationality, piecemeal social technology, self-criticism, etc. – provide an adequate response to the modern challenges? Do they amount to a set of identifiable ideas which may stand for the cultural unity of Europe? Can all their consequences, even the negative ones, be dealt with by the means which are at the disposal of an open society? The author of the distinction, Karl Popper, sustained all his claims in an article published a few years ago. Whatever the current problems and symptoms of a crisis, whatever the gloomy predictions of various prophets of doom, the Western mind, according to Popper, will find, sooner or later, some sort of solution to most of the predicaments. Human creativity provides an inextinguishable source of energy. The crises, if they exist at all, have thus to be viewed as temporary phenomena and not as something that should make us look for fundamental revisions (Popper, 1989).

In search of a European mystique

Other responses were more cautious and at the same time more substantive. Hugh Seton-Watson, the late English historian, also decided, in his last article published posthumously, to defend the viability of Europe's culture as a distinct phenomenon (Seton-Watson, 1985). He tried to qualify his answer by taking into account most counter-arguments: he emphasised the importance of multiculturalism and the positive effects of non-Western influences, he did not dismiss the Eastern provinces of the continent, he did not regard the Iron Curtain as a sign of the cultural division between 'Us' and 'Them'. He was well aware of all destructive and centrifugal tendencies within the European tradition, but he was convinced, like Popper, that one of the major characteristics of this tradition was a remarkable ability to come to terms with all those tendencies. 'There is still a European culture and it is one embracing the people of the north-west peninsula of Asia and their offshore islands, and also many individuals outside it, in the Russian land mass and beyond the oceans' (Seton-Watson, 1985: 16).

This Europe is not confined to politics. It is not only a set of political and economic institutions or a network of international relations. Underneath them prevails 'a European mystique' which emerged from the idea of Christendom and which unites all Europeans and distinguishes them from non-Europeans. It is this mystique that makes possible a movement for European economic and political unity. Can the first, he asked, exist without the second? 'It did not for more than 200 years', was his answer. But can the political and economic unity exist without a sense of spiritual unity? 'It can but at great cost, and perhaps not for very long' (Seton-Watson, 1985: 13).

This last reply is of utmost significance because it shows where lies Seton-Watson's and other like-minded people's real interest when they talk about European integration. When there is no consensus in culture, no common 'mystique', they imply, the political and economic processes of unification will probably not succeed. What constitutes this mystique is difficult to say because Seton-Watson was not sufficiently explicit. It is certainly something more than Karl Popper's openness, rationality, self-criticism and piecemeal technology, i.e., something more than a way of solving problems; but it is perhaps something less than a coherent *Weltanschauung*. Seton-Watson mentions Christendom – a community of peoples as contrasted with Christianity as a religious faith, the latter being clearly on the wane in Western Europe. He nevertheless admits the importance of Christian religion, in his words, 'still a powerful force' in sustaining the European idea. The difficulty in identifying this idea in more positive terms than the Popperian ones is, I believe, not accidental and it should by no means be interpreted as carelessness on Seton-Watson's part. Any concretisation would most certainly be highly controversial, which would undermine the very purpose of seeking the essence of the cultural consensus. But at the same time this impossibility strengthens the arguments of those who have serious doubts about the viability of the European idea, who find disquieting the plausible hypothesis that after the decline of Christianity no positive spiritual unity can be arrived at, and who at the same time are not satisfied with the, for them, unfounded optimism of the Popperians.

In short, the difficulty in coming to a common understanding of what constitutes the nature of the European mystique may lead us to a conviction that either most Europeans have lost a sense of this unity or they have lost interest in seeking it and arguing about it. In either case, one would be tempted to draw a conclusion that Western culture is undergoing a crisis. Such opinions have accompanied the history of Europe for a long time, mainly voiced by conservatives of various persuasions. Nowadays, I think, one should listen to those opinions more carefully than before; even if only partly true, they have more weight during the era of integration than at the time when Europe consisted of separate nation-states, some of which could resist the crisis which shook the foundations of the remaining part of the continent (like Britain during the 1920s and 1930s when most of the countries turned to authoritarianism and totalitarianism). The borders, political, economic and cultural, could sometimes neutralise the influence of destructive ideas. But since they also could neutralise the spreading of those ideas which contributed to the highest achievements in European culture, the overall balance is hard to calculate. It would certainly be absurd to conclude that the nation-state structure somehow secures the development of culture whereas the political integration is inimical to it.

The weariness of the European spirit?

Those who nowadays take up the notion of crisis and analyse it in a cautious and responsible way, not aspiring to a rather easy role of a prophet, do not reject the basics of the Popperian position. No-one says that the European self-criticism, openness and rational debate are to be dismissed as self-defeating prejudices or that they have become outmoded. No-one denies that the European culture may contain within itself the means to overcome the current problems, serious as they are. Yet what comes to the fore are fears and warnings rather than a sense of confidence. Attention is drawn to the exhaustion of some fundamental ideas which until the triumph of modernity provided the metaphysical background for philosophers' political optimism, also for the Popperian type of self-corrective rationalism. To a certain degree the tone of many writers resembles that of Edmund Husserl who in his famous lecture 'Philosophy and the Crisis of European Man', delivered at the University of Prague in 1935, complained about the 'weariness' of the European spirit (Husserl, 1965: 192). The successes of scientific and technological thinking, he claimed, had undermined the philosophical self-assertiveness of European man, turning away his real interest from the *Umwelt* to nature, from the ultimate questions to short-term practical issues, limited to a particular time and place. This attitude made man impotent to discover the larger, universal purpose of this spiritual unity which is called Europe.

Modern fears similar to those of Edmund Husserl were voiced during the meetings organised by John Paul II at Castel Gandolfo in 1985

(Institut für die Wissenschaften vom Menschen, 1986; 1988). Among the participants were: Leszek Kolakowski, Edward Shils, Robert Spaemann, Ernest Gellner, Charles Taylor, and others. Although not all of them were sympathetic to Husserl's type of universalism or particularly happy about the notion of crisis applied to modern times, they shared a feeling of anxiety. While not questioning the belief in the self-corrective mechanisms of European culture and not rejecting the general notion of openness as its constituent characteristic, they nevertheless seemed to agree that what we observe today is a process of exhaustion of certain principal ideas which have animated European culture. Of these, two were specifically mentioned. The first is a sense of, to use Robert Spaemann's expression, the unconditional; the second is historical collective consciousness. The first, it was argued, relates to universalism which until recently presupposed all reflections on European culture and which had its roots in the Christian idea of transcendence irreducible from non-Western cultures, the universalism of science and technology which at the same time failed not only to export but also to retain on its own cultural territory the universalism of metaphysics – a belief in the unconditional grounding of truth. Instead, the philosophy of cultural relativism has begun to take root. The acknowledgement of multiculturalism and an intellectual openness to new inspirations ceased to be initial assumptions of a student of European culture and turned into the ultimate conclusion: Europe does not offer much in terms of culture that would be valid outside its boundaries. The triumph of Western science and technology has also undermined a sense of historical belonging to a continuity of collective experience. For science and technology to develop and to spread, it was argued, it becomes natural that such loyalties be considerably weakened and the traditional communal bonds become less binding, which also, sooner or later, results in cultural relativism. In other words, it was claimed that there is a possibility that Seton-Watson's European 'mystique' will slowly disappear from the European mind. When the theory of open society was formulated, it did not reflect the actual experience of Europe which, having a definite spiritual identity, could not be entirely open. The alleged openness was then possible because of the persistence of traditional universalist metaphysics (Hellenic and Christian in origin) whose importance was ignored, or not fully realized, or, at best, taken for granted by the advocates of openness and whose effect still lingered partly as a defensive reaction to the menacing presence of the totalitarian empire. To use Robert Conquest's expression, the contrast between 'Us' and 'Them' helped to save some elements of the metaphysics on which this identity was based. Now the openness is gradually becoming a fact, or at least, fears are expressed that such a process might be under way which will confront European man with a completely new situation whose consequences are at present hard to predict and even harder to evaluate.

Does this diagnosis entitle us to be sceptical about, and to look with distrust at, all forms of organisation that are emerging in the new Europe? The answer must be emphatically in the negative if it were to mean that no principles of organisation are viable unless their cultural background is put in order. Any such suggestion would be unfounded. The diagnosis is nothing more than an attempt to draw attention to the now somewhat opaque processes which accompany European integration but which may in the future affect our lives in a no less decisive way than the changes in the sphere of the political and the economic. Seton-Watson's remark that political unity without a sense of common mystique is bound to thwart this unity need not be a prediction in the strict meaning of the word but a warning. One cannot exclude the possibility that an attitude of openness will evolve, as for some it is already evolving, into a philosophy of neutrality which in turn will change the notion of Europe from a cultural entity to a geographical entity. If that happens, all basic concepts which legitimise the integration of the European order will probably have to be redefined.

JUSTICE COMES FIRST

The razor of analytical philosophy

The second trend of reflection generated by the process of European integration develops within the framework of and is inspired by analytical philosophy. Differences between the two approaches are evident but still worth noting. Most of the problems that interested Seton-Watson or the Castel Gandolfo scholars fall outside the analytical philosophers' sphere of interest, largely for methodological reasons. The metaphysics of the unconditional or a decline of the historical collective consciousness in the Western world cannot be grasped by the conceptual tools of this philosophy. The methodological razor, characteristic of the whole modern current of thought which directly or indirectly derives from Wittgenstein and his predecessors, ignores or, which virtually comes to the same, refuses to take a position on a wide range of fundamental philosophical problems. Thinkers like Rawls and Nozick are concerned with different and undoubtedly more modest questions, using a method of analysis glaringly unsuitable for dealing with such prophetic issues as the spiritual crisis of the modern world, or with those which, like the metaphysics of the unconditional, are less prophetic but still have a sweeping scope. This, of course, does not mean that this philosophy has nothing to offer to the illumination of the ongoing civilisational processes. Employing its own mythological apparatus to decipher the meaning of concepts and expressions it may help to reinterpret the basic notions through which the process of European integration is being articulated, such as citizenship, sovereignty, etc.

The essential difference between the two approaches goes, however, far beyond the question of methodology. The analytical philosophers have promulgated a certain way of looking at reality and a certain way of thinking about political order. Even in Rawls's *A Theory of Justice* and Nozick's *Anarchy, State, and Utopia* – the books which do not contain any explicit or implicit allusion to the integration of the Western world – one can find a type of thinking which could be easily applied to the integrational processes. At least, there is nothing in these books which would prohibit the extrapolation of the political theories they contain to the relations between states and communities in the new Europe. The most conspicuous characteristic of this thinking is emphasis on the question of rules that regulate the coexistence of individuals and communities. To use Rawls's language, one can say that their primary concern is justice which, as he put it, 'is the first virtue of social institutions, as truth is of systems of thought' (Rawls, 1971: 3). In other words, those philosophers are trying to construct blueprints for a well-ordered society or to clarify the principles on the basis of which such blueprints can be constructed. They are manifestly not interested in analysing what for other philosophers preceded and in fact conditioned such blueprints, namely, the cultural and, in the ultimate instance, the metaphysical presuppositions of a political order. Thus Husserl's 'weariness of the European spirit' would have been an inconceivable and useless notion for the Rawlsians and the Nozickians.

Culture and the original position

This is not to say that the analytical philosophers see no role for culture (and metaphysics) in a political order, though some of their critics raised such an objection. Allan Bloom, for example, tried to ridicule Rawls for allegedly speaking 'to men with the souls of tourists' (Bloom, 1975: 659), which meant that the imaginary people inhabiting the Rawlsian world do not need and in fact are not expected to have any deep attachment to a definite hierarchy of values or to a certain metaphysical interpretation of reality. Bloom's phrase may be unjust when taken literally – Rawls is not against people whose convictions are more profound than those of tourists and who are therefore committed to serious philosophical views – but it indicates an important characteristic of Rawls's (as well as of Nozick's) approach. In their point of departure they bracket, as it were, culture and metaphysics, which are considered unsuitable for playing the role of the principles of order. It is thus believed that when we start constructing a blueprint for a well-ordered society, we have to suspend our philosophical and cultural attachments. We cannot proceed from the assumption of being Europeans, or of belonging to the Western civilisation, or of subscribing to the Hellenic-Judaeo-Christian tradition, or of an intuition of a collective mystique. Such a starting-point is untenable – and this is important – not because all these notions are ambiguous and may lead to endless controversies about the essence of the European idea, of the Hellenic tradition, etc. They are untenable as such, regardless of their degree of ambiguity, and the reason is that they are inherently one-sided.

In order to create a just system one has to proceed, to quote Rawls's expression, 'under a veil of ignorance' which separates us off from the influence of cultures, philosophies, moral systems, traditions, etc. Otherwise, the argument runs, we would violate the principle of fairness, without which no rules could be accepted by all the parties involved. To achieve justice we thus have to be neutral, and to be neutral we have to deprive ourselves, at least temporarily, of certain crucial characteristics which we may consider of essential importance for our cultural identity but which can be unacceptable for others and therefore potentially or actually bring advantage to some and disadvantages to others: Christians will thus put aside their Christianity, businessmen their greed, etc. Only when stripped of these layers of identities can they meet in a situation where the just rules of conduct will be set down and they will have a chance to be honoured in the future by all the parties who make the contract.

The construction of a blueprint for a well-ordered society does not then start from experience but from a hypothetical situation (which Rawls calls 'the original position'). A similar procedure is taken by Nozick who contemplates a no-order situation (anarchy) as potentially the most appealing and to test this hypothesis he invokes John Locke's state of nature, which is another form of the original position (Nozick, 1974: 3–25). This initial suspension of collective experience will, it is hoped, pay off in the future by making it possible for us to set up the conditions in which our cultures will flourish. Both Nozick and Rawls seem to believe that the initial arrangements made by the individuals and groups purged, voluntarily, of their cultural attachments will result in a framework which, in the long run, will bring more opportunities to pursue their 'life-plans', 'utopias', 'cultures', 'social unions'. Only within such a framework, based on a culture-free sense of justice, can conflicts between various ideologies and philosophical orientations be minimised. The trouble with culture or, to be more precise, with cultures as there are always many of them, is that being one-sided, they are divisive. Culture is thus not a solution, not a groundwork for political institutions; it is a problem which has to be solved by creating a structure which would neutralise the disintegrating consequences of unavoidable differences between various orientations. This, in turn, should lead to a richer growth of cultures, freed from antagonising struggles for domination. To put it briefly, a well-ordered society is a society of a well-ordered system of cultures.

Putting culture in a secondary position – partly, let us make it clear, in order to secure its further development within a neutral and fair framework – presupposes, however, a certain patronising attitude towards it. Although culture in this interpretation does not have a distinct meaning, it is certainly something that cannot be trusted with giving us an answer to fundamental questions about the political order. It may be socially and existentially useful, it may stabilize the order that has been created, illuminate it, but it cannot provide us with a philosophical point of view from which we can effectively judge the selection of the original principles. It is hard to resist the feeling that culture in this interpretation resembles more a hobby or a harmless pastime to which we can devote much time and energy but only after our basic work has been done. Bloom's quoted remark about people with the souls of tourists is thus in a way justified: cultural and metaphysical preoccupations in the Rawlsian and Nozickian worlds are not serious. Or, if they are serious, it is not clear how they can have no effect on the choice of the initial rules of order. Either I accept what follows from the rules established 'under the veil of ignorance' and then I treat the great dilemmas of European culture and metaphysics as private intellectual questions with the seriousness they deserve or I refuse to act 'under the veil of ignorance' in discussing the initial conditions of a well-ordered society. Rawls and Nozick do not seem to see this alternative.

The culturally neutral blueprint created by the analytical philosophers is, of course, an open society, at least in a particular sense of the term. This might potentially lead to some sort of a common ground between those who would consider the problem of European integration from the point of view of the shared culture and those who would start from the concept of justice in the state of nature. But the similarity is superficial and the open society in one sense has little in common with the open society in the other sense. The first group, it will be recalled, referred to the Popperian meaning and suggested that what it implied, namely, (self-)criticism and piecemeal social technology, pre-supposed a cultural consensus which in turn could become gradually undermined by the permanent exposure to the politics of openness as well as by the unfounded belief in the spontaneous reproduction of the spiritual preconditions which have made the open society possible. The analytical philosophers, on the other hand, rejected any notion of pre-existing cultural consensus and by this procedure they hoped to secure the relatively harmonious coexistence of cultures, freed in this way from the inconclusive and conflict-generating struggle for the dominating voice in the setting up of the initial principles of justice.

The most vivid and the extreme version of this approach is in Nozick's *Anarchy, State, and Utopia* where he envisages a society which is open to such a degree that any group subscribing to any set of ideals is admitted on the sole condition that it respect the general liberal framework; this framework stipulates that the groups will not impose their cultures either on other groups or on the rules of coexistence (Nozick, 1974: 297–334). This is a far-reaching stipulation: Popper's dialogic rational-ism – that pillar of an open society – virtually disappears being now replaced by the rule of non-interference. If we apply Nozick's precept to the process of European integration, we will have what some might call genuine pluralism while others would call it virtual disintegration of European unity. The latter qualification seems more convincing: it is hard to imagine how one can comply with dialogic rationalism and at the same time not interfere with other people's cultures. Nozick's pattern effectively precludes any dialogue. Every ethnic, religious or political community will be free to pursue its ideals, but it will have to refrain from any attempt to draw wider practical conclusions from the notion of the unity of European culture: such conclusions, one might fear, would be offensive to other groups who see this notion differently, and they would violate the rules of the initial contract. The distinction between 'Us' and 'Them' which was vital for the Popperians would not apply here either, as Nozick's openness guarantees admittance also for 'Them' provided 'They' comply with the principles of the framework. And this expectation seems rational for Nozick since, as the reasoning demonstrates, all groups will be better off within the libertarian frame-work than without it where they are sure to find themselves if they try to bend the rules of justice to their particular purposes. Such consistent openness, as is easy to see, results in the actual abolition of the distinction between 'Us' and 'Them': all 'life-plans' and 'utopias' are morally equal as long as they do not deviate from the principles of the contract.

The original position and consociational democracy

The blueprint does not have only a hypothetical value. Although it remains an open question to what extent it can be translated into actual political practice, one may nevertheless find its imperfect renderings in the empirical world. Of all models, the one that seems closest to the libertarian blueprint is a model of consociational democracy formulated originally by a Dutch political scientist, Arend Lijphart.[1] The analogy is not perfect, but it may have some explanatory power.

The model describes a society of segmented pluralism where different groups (also referred to as blocks or pillars) are distinctly separated from one another and where it is still possible to maintain a high degree of political stability and efficiency. The key to the functioning of such a system is the politics of accommodation which is defined in the following way:

> The term accommodation is here used in the sense of settlement of divisive issues and conflicts where only a minimal consensus exists. Pragmatic solutions are forged for all problems, even those with clear religious–ideological overtones on which the opposing parties may appear irreconcilable, and which therefore may seem insoluble and likely to split the country apart. A key element of this conception is the lack of a comprehensive political consensus, but not the complete absence of consensus. There must be a minimum agreement on fundamentals. . . . The second key requirement is that the leaders of the self-contained blocks must be particularly convinced of the desirability of preserving the system. And they must be willing and capable of bridging the gaps between the mutually isolated blocks and of resolving serious disputes in a largely nonconsensual context.
> (Lijphart, 1968: 103–4)

The similarity between consociational democracy and the Nozickian world is that in both we have a minimum of consensus among self-contained groups; the cultures that constitute the identities of those groups practically do not exert their influence on the rules and mechanisms which animate the overall system. The representatives of the blocks who conduct the policy of accommodation refrain from imposing their values on their rivals: they try to establish the rules of coexistence which are maximally neutral with respect to all the parties to the agreement. Accommodation, as Lijphart describes it, has therefore little to do with the actual dialogue between different blocks: it is a purely pragmatic approach to secure a minimum of cooperation on the basis of non-interference. The situation is somewhat similar to the international relations where rival states of different political and ideological systems may establish rules of coexistence without any state being forced to adopt the internal solutions of its adversaries.

The differences between Lijphart and Nozick are, however, equally significant. Lijphart did not depict a hypothetical model but tried to give a conceptual representation of the Dutch political experience. Although this might provide empirical evidence for Nozick, otherwise absent in his work, it will necessarily be of limited character. There will always be a question how many different groups the segmented pluralism can tolerate in actual political systems and under what conditions a minimum of consensus indispensable for consociational democracy can be preserved with the number of blocks increasing. Clearly, the supporters of the consociational model believed that it can be applied as a solution to many societies, especially those which are characterised by deep cleavages (e.g. South Africa and Northern Ireland). Although this solution, which is worth noting, did not claim to represent the value of justice, it was burdened with performing its function, i.e. with creating the rules of the coexistence of different groups and organisations within one political structure. Another difference between Lijphart and Nozick is that the model of consociational democracy is elitist: it assumes a high degree of deference of the masses *vis-à-vis* their leaders. Only then can the leaders expect that the effects of their politics of accommodation will be accepted. The elitist character of this model is hard to reconcile with the original positions of Rawls and Nozick, both insisting that justice would guarantee a free choice of individual 'life-plans'; it would be difficult for them to accept the assumption that the functioning of justice must presuppose the hierarchical discipline based on strong communal feelings.

Does the concept of consociational democracy provide Rawls's and Nozick's culture-free blueprints with the empirical content? Does it prove the possibility of its existence? The answer, even if we disregard the obvious incongruences between the two models as well as their mutual relative untranslatability, must be generally in the negative. While it is true that something similar to those blueprints existed in reality, it is equally true that this is now a thing of the past. Consociational democracy, as one of the critics put it, 'has become a historical phenomenon' in Dutch political life (van Schendelen, 1984: 25). This is admitted even by the author of the conception himself who had to rewrite the new edition of his works by changing the present tense into the past tense. How far the model which had developed most fully in Holland could be recreated in other societies under different cultural circumstances remains a debatable point. Since the Dutch model of consociational democracy has collapsed, any claim to its more universal relevance must be looked at with serious scepticism.

What is interesting is that the model lost its applicability at the time of growing pluralism, i.e. precisely at the moment when, according to the authors of the culture-free blueprint, it was most needed; in fact it was uniquely intended to cope with such a state of affairs, all other institutional patterns being considered inadequate. With the decline of traditional clear-cut communal boundaries and the increasing complexity of social cross-divisions (accompanied by political instability and by the disappearance of social deference), a genuine pluralism that emerged put an end to the model of segmented pluralism.[2] The interpretation of what happened is, of course, difficult and requires more than one perspective of analysis. But it is clear that the model turned out to be unable to reproduce the conditions of its own existence. In other words, the system of segmented pluralism ceased to exist because it did not have the power to preserve the blocks as major elements of the social structure. To put it yet differently, it could not avert and neutralise the centrifugal processes of diversification that were going on in society. The stability of consociational democracy depended on a certain cultural stability, and the protection of this cultural stability could not be secured by the means that the system had at its disposal. It might of course be argued that such cultural changes were unavoidable but this does not alter the fact that the system of accommodation failed to respond to the challenge.

It might be noted that this explanation of the failure of Lijphart's model finds some support in a counter-argument that some critics raised against Rawlsian and Nozickian blueprints. They pointed out that the blueprints, as Michael J. Sandel put it, failed 'to account for certain indispensable aspects of our moral experience'.[3] By this Sandel meant something not very dissimilar to Allan Bloom's 'souls of tourist' argument. Human beings, he maintained, have certain moral and spiritual attachments which are stronger and more fundamental than justice and from which they cannot distance themselves at will. History and commonality shape, in a decisive way, human character and public environment. Justice is necessary, but it comes later. Its importance grows with the decline of commonality. In other words, the whole project of a culture-free blueprint is misconceived because living in a culture (moral, historical, metaphysical, etc.) – 'an indispensable aspect of our moral experience' – determines the horizon of possible political solutions; whoever hides this horizon behind a veil of ignorance turns a political reflection into 'an exercise in arbitrariness'. The cultural openness and the neutrality towards the notion of good are thus deontological fantasies which appear only in non-existent deontological republics.

Translated into the context of consociational democracy, this argument means that Lijphart's model cannot be treated as a blueprint for an open and pluralistic society. What made it once work was a certain experience of commonality and a shared understanding of the common good (however slim and precarious), which are precisely the aspects of public life that the authors of the pluralistic blueprints want to distance themselves from. The fact that the consociational system did not survive the growing pluralism seems therefore a natural outcome.

The original position and socialism

The bracketing of cultural and metaphysical assumptions led Rawls and Nozick to the acceptance of the orders which are essentially, though each in a different way, liberal. The question arises if some more elements cannot be hypothetically suspended in the original position and if, once this is done in the name of justice, some other order, not necessarily a liberal one, might be a possible consequence. An affirmative answer to this question can be found in the theories of the analytical philosophers of a socialist persuasion. G.A. Cohen, to give the best-known example, has put forward an argument that in the initial position private property does not exist (Cohen, 1986; 1989). The world is originally owned by everyone; private property appears later, always through an illegitimate act of grabbing. In short, private property is theft, to use Proudhon's famous title. This hypothesis goes much further than the initial statements formulated by Rawls and Nozick who did not question the legitimacy of private property. The fact that Cohen's starting-point for building a political blueprint was the introduction of socialism into the original position certainly made the justification of his radical political programme easier. But at the same time, the original position became more arbitrary; if Rawls's world was considered philosophically too arid to be compatible with the notion of the human character and human culture, is not such a charge more substantiated with respect to a philosopher who additionally wants to deprive an individual of his right to private property?

About Cohen's hypothesis two points seem particularly worth noting. By delegitimising private property he dealt a further blow to the role of culture in the making of the political order. To declare that what is owned by individuals comes from theft is to question the moral basis of vast areas of culture which have been historically and politically related to the institution of private property. Whatever reservations are made by those who approve of this hypothesis, the world morally deprived of everything connected with private property would be hard to imagine. It would be culturally a far more deserted place than the one posited by Rawls or Nozick. Once we eliminate private property for philosophical purposes, we will probably be unable to reintroduce it later in an acceptable way as the hypothetical world would certainly be too remote from reality. One can compare it to the error of Descartes who, having applied his consistently sceptical method to mathematics and physical reality, could bring them back only through a most dubious device which was the ontological proof of the existence of God. The result was that in his philosophy physical reality and mathematics never regained the status they had before.

The second point is the consequence of the first. When so much of cultural substance is excluded, the philosopher who constructs a blueprint for a political order is likely to ignore or to play down the important historical and cultural evidence. If the essential element of socialism is already in the original position, why should we consult the evidence of social reality? Cohen's hypothesis leads to the rejection of capitalism and to the defence of complete public ownership of the means of production in the real world. The reasoning is, of course, logical once we accept the assumption: if private property is not a primary fact, then only such a property system must be accepted that accords it as little a role as possible. In this way public ownership of the economy which many thought discredited in the light of historical experience becomes a hopeful solution. This, of course, does not mean that historical experience offers absolute criteria of evaluation: public ownership cannot be automatically treated as an absurd notion like a square circle in geometry. It would be more proper to say that the burden of the proof lies with the defenders of public ownership of the means of production, not with those who reject it. Yet having said this, one cannot pretend that the historical evidence does not carry any weight; it is therefore inadmissible to deduce the legitimacy of public ownership from the concept of the world 'originally owned by everyone'. And it is precisely because the concept is so remote from reality that it loses much of its theoretical relevance. The original position, when pushed too far, might lead us astray: a too thick veil of ignorance is likely to turn into ordinary ignorance.

CONCLUSION

To summarize: the divergent character of the two possible approaches to the political processes of integration manifests itself in the following antitheses:

- The 'cultural' approach could result in pessimism, in a fear about the viability of the European spirit, in a feeling of a cultural crisis. The analytic approach, which abstracts from culture, is generally optimistic in its search for the blueprints and may be even hyperoptimistic by flirting with those forms of socialism which have unmistakably failed in the past.
- The first approach deplores the decline of universal metaphysics and the emergence of cultural relativism; the second approach considers universal metaphysics and cultural absolutism politically divisive and therefore harmful to the process of the rational choice of the just order.
- The first approach put emphasis on the role of the unity of culture; the second approach started from the assumption that such a unity is impossible and that therefore a more important objective is political non-interference of cultures.
- The representatives of the first approach interpreted the concept of open society in the light of the 'Us'-and-'Them' distinction but gradually became more and more cautious in using it. The liberal representatives of the second approach rejected the distinction, but resurfaced, somewhat paradoxically, among the analytical socialists who reanimated the idea of public ownership of the means of production. This idea, let us remember, had been for the authors of the distinction a major characteristic of a closed society. The paradox is that now 'We' has become 'Them' and 'They' has become 'Us'.

The important question is whether one can make any judgement about which of the approaches is preferable and on what grounds. There are many possibilities of making such a comparison but I would like to propose one: how much the acceptance of one approach influences the value of the other approach. The question is then the following: if we were to bridge the gap between those two lines of argumentation, which would necessitate the modification of the other?

It seems obvious that if we accept the analytical approach, we are not compelled to make any concession to the first approach. The speculations on various conceptions of justice and the constructing of different systems of coexistence of cultures and communities have little import on whether or not we believe in the unity of European culture, whether or not this culture undergoes a crisis, and whether or not this crisis can be overcome. When accepting the analytical approach we do not automatically make any stand on the cultural approach. The reverse, however, is not true. Once we are faced with the diagnosis of the European spirit, we cannot trust the verdicts of analytical philosophy and its proposals for a just order. As Alasdair MacIntyre argued, this philosophy is a philosophy of use, not of meaning; it would be therefore unable to diagnose a crisis of culture even if the crisis were a profound one (MacIntyre, 1984: 1–22). The culture-free attitude may reproduce and transmit both good and bad aspects in culture, without making us realise that the distinction between those two categories is essential. To all those who think of European integration in terms of fundamental metaphysical and moral questions this would be an unacceptable perspective. The problem is then ultimately to what extent we can talk about European integration ignoring those fundamental questions.

NOTES

1 Lijphart (1968). See also Daalder (1984); Dahl (1971).
2 Van Schendelen (1984: 24–5). See also van Mierlo (1986).
3 Sandel (1982: 179). See also Gray (1989: 249–54); Legutko (1990).

BIBLIOGRAPHY

Bloom, A. (1975) 'Justice: John Rawls vs. the tradition of political philosophy', *American Political Science Review* 69: 648–62.
Cohen, G.A. (1986) 'Self-ownership, world ownership, and equality: part II', *Social Philosophy and Policy* 3: 77–96.
Cohen, G.A. (1989) 'On the currency of egalitarian justice', *Ethics* 99: 906–44.
Conquest, R. (1980) *We and They*, London: Temple Smith.
Daalder, H. (1984) 'On the origins of the consociational democracy model', *Acta Politica* 19: 97–116.
Dahl, R.A. (1971) *Polyarchy: Participation and Opposition*, New Haven, CT: Yale University Press.
Gray, J. (1989) *Liberalisms*, London and New York: Routledge.
Husserl, E. (1965) *Phenomenology and the Crisis of Philosophy*, translated by Q. Lauer, New York: Harper Torchbooks.
Institut für die Wissenschaften vom Menschen (1986) *Über die Krise*, Vienna.
Institut für die Wissenschaften vom Menschen (1988) *Europa und die Folgen*, Vienna.
Legutko, R. (1990) 'Society as a department store', *Critical Review* 4: 327–43.
Lijphart, A. (1968) *The Politics of Accommodation: Pluralism and Democracy in the Netherlands*, Berkeley and Los Angeles, CA: University of California Press.
MacIntyre, A. (1984) *After Virtue*, Notre Dame: University of Notre Dame Press.
Mierlo, van, H.J.G.A. (1986) 'Depillarisation and the decline of consociationalism in the Netherlands: 1970–85', *West European Politics* 9: 95–119.

Nozick, R. (1974) *Anarchy, State, and Utopia*, New York: Basic Books.

Popper, K. (1971) *The Open Society and Its Enemies*, vol. I, Princeton, NJ: Princeton University Press.

Popper, K. (1989) 'Creative Self-Criticism in Science and Art', *Diogenes* 145: 36–45.

Rawls, J. (1971) *A Theory of Justice*, Cambridge, Mass.: Harvard University Press.

Sandel, M.J. (1982) *Liberalism and the Limits of Justice*, Cambridge: Cambridge University Press.

Schendelen, van, M.P.C.M. (1984) 'The views of Arend Lijphart and collected criticisms', *Acta Politica* 19: 19–55.

Seton-Watson, H. (1985) 'What is Europe, where is Europe? From mystique to politique', *Encounter* 65(2): 9–17.

5 Political pluralism and European citizenship[1]

Elizabeth Meehan

INTRODUCTION

The argument of this chapter is twofold. It is suggested here that, despite criticisms that European citizenship is cosmetic, the rights associated with citizenship are no longer regulated or guaranteed exclusively by the institutions of nation-states but have, in addition, an increasingly significant European dimension. This is not to say that citizenship as we have known it is being relocated to a new 'state' called Europe. Rather, there is a greater plurality of formal and informal channels through which people may participate, attempt to have needs met and seek redress or change. The second aspect of the chapter is that the protection of citizens' rights may depend upon institutional pluralism and human diversity and not, as sometimes is argued in order to minimise the prospects of European citizenship, on political and social homogeneity.

This approach to citizenship and European integration contrasts with conventional ways of thinking about citizenship as we have known it – which appear to rule out European citizenship. During the last two centuries, the notion of citizenship has come to be so closely associated with nationality that the two words are often used interchangeably. This rests upon a sometimes unspoken assumption that such a link is universally true over space and time. Thus, in the early days of the European Community,[2] commentators were often convinced that there could be no such things as 'European citizens' (notably, Aron, 1974). And, even now that certain citizens' rights do exist at the European level, they are often assessed as 'cosmetic' (e.g. O'Leary, 1995). Politicians sometimes argue that the prospect of the further development of European citizenship is either impossible or undesirable. Citizenship depending as it does, in their view, upon cultural or national homogeneity, either cannot emerge under a regime composed of diverse nation-states or it would require an imposed uniformity.

In the two decades intervening between Aron and O'Leary, however, notions of citizenship, such as Aron's, have been attacked. In competing accounts of citizenship, it is argued that the link between citizen, nationality and nation-state is contingent, not necessary (e.g. Gardner, n.d.; Leca, 1990). Both the territorial scope of citizenship and the content of the values and rights associated with it have varied according to political, historical and cultural contexts.

Legal and political rights have been guaranteed in territories ranging from city states to empires and aspired to in a theoretical cosmopolis. More than one political authority guaranteed rights in periods during the Roman Empire. People of different nationalities within the one empire could appeal to either local or imperial systems justice (Heater, 1990). Conversely, even in today's world, some people of different nationalities may be able to exercise the same political and legal rights enjoyed by nationals in whose state they are living. That the allegedly strong overlap between nationality and citizenship rights is not reflected systematically in practice is clear from a survey of eleven European states (Gardner, n.d.). Lawful residence – or place (Weiner, 1995) – as much as nationality may activate legal, political and social entitlements.

The content of values and rights of citizenship also varies. Aron's nationality-based conception of citizenship encompasses legal and political rights. He defines socio-economic rights as human, not citizenship rights, which may be able to be regulated by bodies other than national governments (Aron, 1974). But, even if social rights are accepted as part of citizenship, it can be argued that it is practicable to link them, like legal and political rights, with nationality. The solidarity needed for raising resources to meet needs may be easier to achieve when a sense of common 'belonging' can be appealed to, such as shared nationality (Miller, 1993). In contrast to Aron, others have argued that the history of citizenship in a variety of institutional and territorial contexts reveals a persistent tendency for a social dimension to be included, conviviality and distributive justice serving as sources of a sense of 'belonging' (Jordan, 1989; Heater, 1990; Weiner, 1995). Sometimes, the inclusion of a social dimension may stem from a sense that it is proper to promote individual well-being, sometimes in connection with beliefs about the existence of, or aspirations for, a common moral order (Jordan, 1989). Both these bases appear in the social policies of the European Union.

Before making the case that a more pluralist and complex conception of citizenship is emerging along with the changing political context of European integration, the chapter begins by setting out the philosophical and practical arguments for scepticism about the possibility of European citizenship. Thereafter, the chapter deals with developments in European policies which support the views of those for whom the meanings of citizenship are both broader and variable. In the following section on 'the constitution of institutions',[3] the chapter draws attention to the political pluralism through which these rights are exercised. Here, it is suggested that this pluralism is not one which simply maintains the diversity of fifteen nation-states but is one which may not entirely reassure the defenders of that state sovereignty which enabled Aron to argue that only states were in a position to guarantee legal and political rights. In conclusion, it is suggested that political and human diversity, far from being problematic to integration and European citizenship, may actually be better preconditions than homogeneity for the protection of citizens' rights.

THE SCEPTICAL ASSESSMENT OF EUROPEAN CITIZENSHIP

Aron's sceptical predictions in 1974 for the prospect of European citizenship were based on his distinction, noted above, between human rights and the rights of citizens. Though he thought that a single belief – in the natural equality of human beings – justified both sets of rights, he also argued that they were of a different order from one another. Human rights, in Aron's view, stem from participation in economic or civil society by property owners, as in eighteenth-century political thought and practice, or from the twentieth-century belief in the rectitude of relieving socio-economic deprivation. Citizens are distinguished by the status conferred upon them in rules about the administration of justice and political participation. Human or economic rights may be recognised or denied, irrespective of political status. Citizenship rights may be denied on socio-economic grounds but they cannot be guaranteed except in the context of nationality and the state – a so-called nation-state, even if it is a state where a single legal nationality embraces more than one ethnic or cultural identity.

In making his case that European citizenship would be logically and practically impossible, Aron noted that national and Community authorities then provided rights of a different order to one another. Bringing about European citizens' rights would entail a transfer of legal and political powers from the national to the European level (similar to the transfer of Scottish and English rights to a set of British entitlements). He saw no popular demand (political 'spill-overs' in the language of neo-functionalism) for the European federation that would be necessary for the transfer of citizenship to a political authority responsible simultaneously for legal and political rights and economic regulation. In so far as he saw dissatisfaction with the treatment of submerged nationalities or about social inequalities, he also discerned popular cynicism that such domestic problems could be resolved by regulation at a more remote level. Moreover, there was every sign in 1974 that national governments intended the Community to remain a regime in which participants in economic society cooperated in the absence of a common political society.

Hardly was Aron's pen dry, however, when a new momentum began towards the achievement of an 'ever closer union', reaching peaks in the Single European Act (agreed in 1985, effective from 1987), the Treaty of Maastricht (signed in 1991, ratified in 1993), and building up again in the 1996 Inter-Governmental Conference. From the mid-1970s, this momentum carried with it the idea of European citizenship (Weiner, 1995). This was reflected in the Adonnino Report (Commission, 1985) on political symbols and participation (see pp. 76–77) as well as in various draft treaties on closer union. It can also be seen in the growth of 'soft policy' initiatives and new entitlements which followed the Single European Act as the 'social dimension' of the Single Internal Market. The Maastricht Treaty 'constitutionalised' the 'Citizen of the Union' and set out some common political rights for the new form of citizen. These include access to information and redress of grievance. The Treaty also requires agreement to be reached to allow citizens living in member states other than their own to vote and stand for office in municipal and European Parliamentary elections. It also provides for citizens living outside the Union to be protected by the diplomatic and consular services of member states other than their own. In addition to specifying some individual rights, the Treaty institutionalises the collective right of citizens inhabiting sub-state regions to be represented in a new body at the centre – the Committee of the Regions.

Nevertheless, weaknesses and defects in these rights cause many commentators to remain as sceptical as Aron about the transfer or adaptation of national political rights. All critics note the exclusion of general elections, making the point that it is general elections which most closely relate to sovereignty and the prerogative of states to confer the ultimate in voting rights (e.g. Closa, 1995; O'Leary, 1995). They also draw attention to potential derogations from the provisions for municipal and European elections. These are possible where there are specific problems, particularly those which may jeopardise national identities, as in Luxembourg where the proportion of residents from other member states compared to the indigenous population is much

larger than elsewhere (Closa, 1995). O'Leary (1995) shows that the new
voting rights are little more than reciprocal arrangements which could
exist, and sometimes do (as shown in Gardner's survey, n.d.), irrespective of union; and that it will be difficult in practice to use the right to
diplomatic and consular protection by other member states. She also
argues that the direct legal link between individuals and the centre is
slight. Curtin and Meijers (1995) argue that the ostensible intention to
enhance rights to information is hypocritical, except on the part of the
Netherlands and, to some extent, Denmark. The Committee of the
Regions is also noted for its paucity as an innovation, though it is also
argued that it has been in existence for so short a time that little can be
said yet about it (Kennedy, forthcoming).

However, it is perhaps less important that the innovations are small
than that they are breaches in normal conventions. In a much shorter
time-scale than it took to establish universal legal, political and social
rights within states, a pattern, of which these breaches are a part, is
coming about of more horizontal avenues and a more plural set
of institutions through which citizenship, as both entitlements and
'lived' experience, may be realized. The expansion of European citizenship, as paradigm and practice, is the subject of the next section.
It is important to remember my opening remarks: that, in drawing
attention to such developments, it is not my intention to suggest that
citizenship of the traditional nation-state is being transformed into
citizenship of a new 'state' and that my purpose does not go beyond
illustrating modifications to our customary ways of thinking and
acting.

EUROPEAN LEGAL, SOCIAL AND POLITICAL RIGHTS

The elimination of national barriers to a European economy is in some
ways analogous to the abolition of the impediments of feudal relations
to national modernisation. Both sets of changes are about liberalisation through the reform of legal status and both have political and
social consequences which follow, though in a different order from one
another in the two arenas (see Dahrendorf (1988) on the domestic con-
nections and Meehan (1993) for a fuller discussion of European developments). Aron's ideas that the different roles of socio-economic actor
and political participant can be kept distinct and that nation-states are
the sole determinants of legal status have to be modified in the light of
developments in the European Union, particularly since 1974 (his time
of writing).

While it is true that a 'citizen of the Union' is someone who is a national of one of the member states and that conferring nationality remains the prerogative of states, the literature is unanimous in arguing that the European Union (or, more accurately for present purposes, European Community; see note 2) is a new legal order which involves some transfers of sovereignty (e.g. Lasok and Stone, 1987; Usher, 1981). It is precisely because of that legal federation that the consequences of being a Community national or Union citizen are not wholly within the control of member states. As a result of judicial interpretations of the Treaty of Rome, individuals had a distinctive European status for twenty years before the creation of the new creature, the citizen of the Union. And judicial rulings have brought about legal and social rights that go beyond the limits to which member states may have thought they had agreed (Arnull, 1990; Steiner, 1985). Moreover, the relationship between the well-being of individuals and the processes of integration has fostered a 'spill-over' of legal and social rights into the political sphere.

Even if it were true, and this is disputed, that member states always wanted to confine supra-national regulation to a free market, narrowly defined, they have not been able to do so without ceding some control over the legal status of citizens. Alleged hopes among the first generation of employers that the goal of the freedom of movement of labour in the Treaty of Rome gave them the right to move labourers around was quickly laid to rest by the view that the Treaty gave labourers themselves the right to choose to migrate. Of more long-term significance is an early ruling in the Court of Justice of the European Communities (ECJ) which announced that the legal status of the nationals of member states had changed as a result of the Treaty of Rome. The Treaty was more than a compact among states and conferred rights upon individuals. In arguing that nationals had a right to expect states to conform with Community law (and a duty to use their legal rights to ensure that this occurred), the ECJ transformed the peoples of Europe, for some purposes, into a people of Europe.[4] ECJ rulings on national interpretations of Community rules about social protection, conditions of employment and sex equality (which covers both employment and social security) have also affected legal status in ways perhaps not anticipated by member states. In many cases heard in all these spheres, the Court has expanded the legal definition of workers for Community purposes beyond what may be laid down in national laws. The Court has also argued that, in some circumstances, unmarried partners or divorced couples may count as family members for certain Community purposes, effectively, if not formally, in the case of unmarried partners. A new category, service consumer, has been identified as arising from

Treaty provisions for service providers, which has created new entitlements in the administration of justice.

Social policy in the European Union does not involve material redistribution at the common level, except through the structural funds, but generally regulates national systems of distribution and entitlements in the social field and at work. In so doing, European Community institutions, as well as national governments, affect not only legal status, but also substantive entitlements. Insistence by the Court of Justice that the freedom of movement of labour means that workers and their families must be able to move without suffering disadvantage has led to a construction of social protection and some conditions of employment as 'fundamental rights'. Moreover, the Court has said that social well-being must be interpreted broadly. Almost any national discrimination in the application of rules about social security, social assistance or 'advantage', employment (except where there is a clear public interest), and vocational training is unlawful. And this has had unanticipated effects on national budgets (Steiner, 1985), the setting of which was thought indubitably in the 1970s to be a proper part of domestic competence.

Thus, the detailed coordination of different national social security systems, the practical implementation of abstractly expressed common social rights in different states and a review of these by the ECJ brings about scrutiny of and changes to national legal and political systems. In addition to instruments patently aimed at the liberalisation of a European market from national protection and discrimination, other areas of life have been touched upon; for example, matters relating to immovable property, family law, residence conditions, border controls, the conduct of a fair trial (especially in relation to language), remedy for treatment that is unlawful under Community rules, and compensation under national rules about criminal injury.

Though these new dimensions of legal status and substantive entitlements arise from disputes in the sphere of Aron's human rights, they clearly impinge upon the exclusive competence of nation-states to define and guarantee the relationship between themselves and their nationals. Such developments make it difficult to maintain that a *cordon sanitaire* can be drawn around nationality, nation-state and legal or political rights, on the one hand, and socio-economic or human rights and international bodies, on the other. Moreover, the discourse of social rights and integration embodies both the individualistic and collective features of social citizenship, mentioned earlier. It is the language of expediency that appeals to governments trying to come to terms with the new developments – the free market will not work without a 'human face' and if there are disincentives to mobility among workers and service providers. But the preambles to the instruments of Community social policy and recent consultation documents (especially Commission, 1993) on its future embody a modern version of classical aspirations for a common moral order of conviviality; referring to the intrinsic needs for common standards of living, harmony and social cohesion. Jacques Delors's insistence that a social dimension to the Single European Market was essential stemmed not only from the expedient need to avoid 'social dumping' but also from his ethical commitments.

There is some responsiveness on the part of national citizens to the possibility of participating in a transnational moral order. In the last two decades, there has been a rise in transnational associations of voluntary organizations, women, trades unions and specialists in social policy, industrial relations and education (Mazey and Richardson, 1993). Since the Single European Act, there has been a spectacular growth of activity by people in sub-state regions who operate both at the centre of the Union and in direct cooperation with regions in other states (Mazey and Mitchell, 1993). Though it can be argued that the spur to circumventing national institutions is self-interest on the part of groups and regions that are dissatisfied with domestic policies, transnational links bring about the cross-fertilisation of ideas about standards in a wide range of issues; for example, health and safety, child care, vocational training, environmental protection, local economic regeneration, transport, and so on.

The spread of activity by civil organisations beyond national boundaries has a political dimension. Prior to the establishment of the primary political rights outlined in the previous section, the practice of recognizing the secondary rights of consultation and participation became increasingly normal. In the 1960s, the European Commission maintained links with employers and trade unions, although controversially (Holloway, 1981). As the social and regional funds became consolidated into concerted programmes of regeneration and development, it became obligatory for policy formation, implementation, monitoring and evaluation to be based upon full involvement by the 'social partners' and the 'local and regional partners'. Increasingly, such consultation brings in the voluntary and community sectors, including women's groups, now acknowledged in the 1996 Social Forum as the 'civil partners'. The new primary political rights, even they are open to the criticism of being cosmetic, represent a further step in a process of bringing about rights to participate in debate about the future of integration which began, according to Weiner, in the 1970s, was recommended most explicitly in the Adonnino Report (Commission, 1985) of 1984 and found an alternative expression in the Social Dialogue.

As in the case of social rights, developments in political participation can be construed either as expedient or as an aspect of creating a common moral order. The Commission's espousal of consultation can be explained on the basis that, as an important player but small and unelected, it needs to consult in order to secure legitimacy and outside expertise. Citizens who support the idea of wider political opportunities may be thought of as looking for a bigger arena within which to play out self-interests; if loss of social 'advantage' is a disincentive to mobility, the same must be even more true of the loss of political rights. But, as in the case of the social policies again, Pietro Adonnino's recommendations about the symbols of politics, such as flags and anthems, and his language of the need for tangible rights and arguments for social dialogue also indicate a recognition of the need for a regime, not of uniformity, but in which there can be elements of a common sense of belonging. The same is true of the 1996 Social Forum and the arguments of non-governmental groups about the need to ensure that citizenship is not excluded from the agenda of the 1996 Inter-Governmental Conference on what still needs to be done after the Maastricht Treaty. It is also argued by the Commission that policies will both meet real collective needs and be effective only if they are based on the first-hand knowledge of people 'on the ground'.

The fact that there are several interpretations of the significance of such innovations may be a circumstantial illustration of Weiner's thesis that it is when there is a confluence of policy imperatives and the presence of key policy actors with ideas that are not entirely conventional that breaches occur in paradigms and practices of citizenship. There are, however, two dimensions of European citizenship which risk a continuation of traditional, exclusionary aspects of citizenship. First, the fact that European Union citizenship necessarily rests upon a Treaty based principally on economic objectives makes it defective for women, who are rarely in similar socio-economic circumstances to men (Meehan (1992) reviews the literature on this, though she also thinks this argument can be overstated, see Meehan (1993)). Second, the status of non-nationals is precarious. Though there are some means (judicial rulings in certain specific cases and non-binding general agreements) through which non-nationals may enjoy some of the rights of Community citizenship, the abolition of internal frontiers is causing governments to agree upon rules which make it more difficult for non-nationals to enter the Community. These rules are being brought about under the inter-governmental pillar of the Maastricht Treaty and are not open to the channels of scrutiny and review that exist for Community, as distinct from Union, policy (Curtin and Meijers (1995); see also note 2). If Weiner is right, however, that place and lawful residence are becoming triggers for the exercise of citizens' rights, the rulings and recommendations mentioned above might be the precursors of a more secure position for those non-nationals who are allowed to enter.

The fact that member state governments have retained for themselves the right to confer nationality and have ensured that immigration is a matter for inter-governmental, not common, policy-making indicates that fears of an enforced homogeneity may be misplaced though the pluralism that is emerging is not one that will comfort the holders of traditional views about state sovereignty. Such political pluralism is the subject of the next section.

TOWARDS A 'CONSTITUTION OF INSTITUTIONS'

In addition to fifteen different sets of rules about who is a national and hence qualifies as a citizen of the Union, the content of their Community rights is mediated by other forms of pluralism. To a substantial extent, this is the pluralism of a confederation of relatively autonomous nation-states – 'l'Europe des Patries'. But there are also signs of a kind of pluralism in which citizens use the opportunities of a new range of institutions for their own purposes which may not conform with state conceptions of national interests.

From the point of view of states in a confederation, it should be noted that the common legal order has different legal instruments which reflect the variety of the component parts. Regulations are directly applicable in member states, as they stand and without further action by governments. But regulations about social security and assistance reflect the existence of national diversity in methods of identifying income and need and in systems of redistributing resources. Thus, these regulations, despite some controversy in the 1960s (Holloway, 1981), allow the continuation of different systems and provide coordinating rules to ensure that migrants are not disadvantaged by being subject to two or more schemes. Many common policies are implemented through directives. Directives are addressed to governments, 'directing' them to take further action to bring about a common objective, expressed fairly abstractly and without detailed instructions. This form of intervention acknowledges the existence of a plurality of legal and enforcement institutions, practices and procedures of the different member states.

To some extent the ECJ has limited the freedom of national governments and courts to determine the details of how directives are implemented when it finds that national procedures diminish the effectiveness of the common purpose or when individuals have been denied rights because they are expressed more narrowly in national than in Community law. Thus it is that areas thought to be within the policy competence of member states can be brought under the ambit of Community regulation; for example, variations in the provision of remedy for breaches of the law, the scope of exemptions relating to death and retirement in equality legislation, and education where it can be shown to overlap with vocational training. Nevertheless, non-incremental, new directions in the distribution of policy competencies cannot take place without amendments to the Treaty of Rome and without the consent of the Council of Ministers, a body which is more pluralistic or inter-governmental than supra-national.

The strength of and attachment to diversity amongst the member states were evident in disputes about majority voting in the Single European Act and the Social Charter. In both cases, unanimous voting remains over the question of workers' rights, a sphere in which there are very different traditions in the United Kingdom, France and Germany. And this is reinforced in the Social Protocol of the Maastricht Treaty, which exempts the United Kingdom, and in about forty other exceptions based on recognition of distinctive national traditions. It is also there in the provisions for policy-making through inter-governmental negotiation in Justice and Home Affairs and for Foreign and Security Policy.

Likewise, limits to common regulation are set in the principle of subsidiarity. Though this may mean all things to all people (Harden, 1991), its formulation in the text of the Maastricht Treaty appears to protect the plurality of interests among fifteen member states by obliging the Commission to demonstrate convincingly that proposals for common action meet certain tests. These are that there is a common problem and that, by its nature, it cannot be solved except by common action. All other matters remain the responsibility of individual governments, to be pursued according to different national interests (Commission, 1991).

But both the institutional set-up and the principle of subsidiarity can be read as a means of greater popular power below the level of states. It is quite plain that groups in the United Kingdom who do not share the government's view that social rights are contrary to the national interest view the ECJ more benevolently than 'Euro-sceptics'. For example, there are statutory duties on the Equal Opportunities of Great Britain and Northern Ireland to review the workings of equality laws and to make recommendations for amendments to them and related legislation. Recommendations for change since 1979 have fallen upon deaf ears. In that time, it has been possible to try to correct anomalies or to begin to tackle strategic issues only through individuals seeking referrals of their cases to the European Court of Justice (Collins and Meehan, 1994). The same channel has been used to review the meaning of employment in connection with 'acquired rights', in situations of the transfer of activities, so as to bring protection for local authority workers affected by compulsory competitive tendering. At a more general level, it has been the ambition of labour movements and 'civil partners' since the mid-1980s to bring about a 'bill of rights' for Community citizens, not merely Community workers, which would be entrenched and justiciable. This aspiration remains an important part of the agenda of such groups, as well as of the participants at the 1996 Social Forum and members of the Social Affairs Committee of the European Parliament, in their efforts to influence the 1996 Inter-Governmental Conference.

Though an alternative understanding of subsidiarity to that which protects the nation-state from above is that it provides a justification for European centralisation (Adonis, 1991), a more widespread competing interpretation is that subsidiarity may disperse power downwards. Advocates of sub-state regional interests and nationalists, speaking for nationalities submerged within the current state structure, look to the preamble of the Maastricht Treaty where it appears to mean decentralized democracy, entrenching the practice of social, local and regional partnership. As mentioned earlier, these partners are actors in a common regime where some of their activities circumvent and others include the nation-state. It has been suggested (e.g. Siedentop, 1990) that the propensity of UK governments to understand federalism and centralisation as synonymous, instead of seeing federal or quasi-federal arrangements as a defence against European centralisation, lies in the risk of exacerbating opposition to domestic concentrations of power. And, indeed, the regions of the United Kingdom have notable presences among the plethora of regional offices in Brussels in order to remedy communication defects that they find in the hierarchical channels of a centralised domestic system (Bew and Meehan, 1994; Mazey and Mitchell, 1993).

Constitutionally speaking, such offices are channels of routine information, not official agencies of representation. But it would be unrealistic to assume that alternative understandings of the 'national' interest remain concealed amongst people who are in daily contact with one another in the Brussels policy and social networks. In addition, regionalists and nationalists in the United Kingdom, and elsewhere, have made every effort to use the rules about partnership in decisions about structural funds to ensure that local and regional voices are heard (Bew and Meehan, 1994; Mazey and Mitchell, 1993). Similar activity takes place in the voluntary sector in Great Britain (Baine *et al.*, 1991). Using new opportunities for even more radical change can be seen among the 'social' and 'civil partners' in both Northern Ireland and the Republic of Ireland. In both places, such groups have taken part in the creation of new domestic institutions, under the pretext of Europe, in which consultation is transformed from a cosmetic exercise into 'negotiated policy-making' over a range of policies which may not originate entirely from the European Union (NICVA, 1996; the phrase is O'Donnell's, 1995).

It is as a result of the British fear of the word 'federal' as perceived by 'Euro-sceptics' in the United States of America that the Maastricht Treaty simply refers to 'union'. It seems plain that the transformation that is taking place will make the European Union analogous neither to an empire nor to the United States. The central institutions are not the army of an imperial power; they are the creatures of their constituent parts – the member states. And the member states are far more firmly established than the thirteen former colonies that ratified the American Constitution. Nevertheless, the history of the debate in eighteenth-century America does have some bearing upon the argument that European citizenship would either require some pre-existing homogeneity or the coercion of diverse peoples into a false uniformity. Indeed, American ideas turn modern fears upon their head.

SOCIAL DIVERSITY

Lord Jenkins once told an audience at the Queen's University of Belfast that, even though he ardently supported European integration, he could hardly envisage the day when the French, Italians, or other nationals of the European Union would describe themselves in Japan as European as Texans would say that they were American. But it should be remembered that George Washington and James Madison thought of themselves as Virginian. They saw no tension in being both Virginian and American and were unusual in this, their contemporaries identifying themselves by their state (Marshall, 1991). Two centuries later, pride in state remains strong (Parish, 1991) and millions of citizens identify themselves dualistically, not only by state and legal nationality, but also in hyphenated ways such as Black- or Afro-American, Hispanic-American, Irish-American, Italian-American, and so on. Within the British part of Europe, the Scots and English united under the same king nearly four hundred years ago and the same parliament a century later, yet remain recognisably distinct from one another. Until the last twenty years, most Scots were like Washington and Madison in taking for granted a dual identity – Scottish and British.

A wide range of literature indicates that identities, even national identities, both depend upon and vary with political context (see Delanty (1995) on the first creation of 'Europe' and 'Europeanness'); hence the hyphenated Americans and recent cavilling in Scotland that the term British is too readily used as a 'cover' for English. There is some evidence that, though people would not substitute 'European' for other labels they apply to themselves, they are increasingly willing to add 'European' on to other means of self-identification (Meehan, 1993; Smith and Corrigan, 1995).

Perhaps more fundamental even than showing that identities are empirically variable is to draw attention to the theoretical significance of diversity to the American federalists. The existence of human diversity was a *sine qua non* for republican federalism. It was as essential as the existence of a myriad of civil associations and multiple levels of power and authority for different policy functions and for avenues of redress (Beer, 1993). The converse was also true; far from being a pre-condition, homogeneity would have been the enemy of their republican enterprise because it would have eliminated debate, atrophied political competition and encouraged monopolies of power. The existence in Europe of more levels of authority and channels of influence below, above and crossing states involving interaction amongst groups of people with differences, as well as similarities, amongst their traditions and outlooks means that, in Tassin's words, the European Union can be a 'public space' where a 'plurality of wills, feelings and interests' are not amalgamated but can come 'face to face'.

NOTES

1 I should like to thank the Nuffield Foundation for the grant that initiated this work and the European Consortium for two special sessions at Forli and Rotterdam where early versions were presented. Readers should also note that, as a result of publishing delays, this chapter now draws upon, rather than pre-dates, my other publications: principally, *Citizenship and the European Community*, London: Sage, 1993; 'The debate on citizenship and European union', in P. Murray and P. Rich (eds) *Visions of European Unity*, Boulder, Col.: Westview Press, 1996; and 'European integration and citizens' rights: a comparative perspective', *Publius*, special edition, forthcoming.

2 The common policies that are the main focus of this chapter stem from what is still, legally, the European Community. The European Union, introduced

by the Maastricht Treaty, has two other 'pillars', dealing with Justice and Home Affairs and Foreign and Security Policy, where matters are dealt with through inter-governmental agreement and not subject to the same procedures of policy development, through the European Commission and the Council of Ministers, and judicial review in the Court of Justice of the European Communities.

3 The phrase is used by Johnson (1976) about the United Kingdom but it seems felicitously suitable for the same range of considerations in any polity.

4 The principal case was *van Gend en Loos v. Nederlandse Administratie der Belastingen*, Case No. 26/62, [1962] ECR 1. See earlier reference to O'Leary's criticism that link created here is slight. On the one hand, she is vindicated by a ruling in the German Constitutional Court: *Manfred Brunner and others v. The European Treaty*, Cases 2 BvR 2134/92 and 2159/92 [1994] 1 CMLR 57. This is discussed in Harmsen (1994). But, on the other hand, *van Gend en Loos* has also been treated as a significant breach in established conventions.

BIBLIOGRAPHY

Adonis, A. (1991) 'Subsidiarity: theory of a New Federalism?', in P. King A. Bosco (eds) *A Constitution for Europe: A Comparative Study of Federal Constitutions and Plans for the United States of Europe*, London: Lothian Foundation Press, pp. 63–73.

Arnull, A. (1990) *The Individual in Community Law*, Leicester: Pinter/Leicester University Press.

Aron, R. (1974) 'Is multinational citizenship possible?', *Social Research* 41(4): 638–56.

Baine, S., Bennington, J. and Russell, J. (1991) *Changing Europe: Challenges Facing the Voluntary and Community Sectors in the 1990s*, London: National Council of Voluntary Organizations/Community Development Foundation.

Beer, S.H. (1993) *To Make a Nation: The Rediscovery of American Federalism*, Cambridge, Mass.: The Belknap Press of Harvard University Press.

Bew, P. and Meehan, E. (1994) 'Regions and borders: controversies in Northern Ireland about the European Union', *Journal of European Public Policy* 1(1): 95–114.

Closa, C. (1995) 'Citizenship of the Union and nationality of member states', *Common Market Law Review* 32: 487–518.

Collins, E. and Meehan, E. (1994) 'Women's rights in employment and related areas', in C. McCrudden and G. Chambers (eds) *Individual Rights and the Law in Britain*, Oxford: Clarendon Press/The Law Society.

Commission of the European Communities (1985) 'A peoples' Europe' (Adonnino Report), *Bulletin of the European Communities Supplement 7/85*, Luxembourg: Office for Official Publications of the European Communities.

Commission of the European Communities (1991) *Background Report: Briefing Note on the Agreement of the European Council at Maastricht*, London: Jean Monnet House, ISEC/B33/91. 18.12.91.

Commission of the European Communities (1993) *European Social Policy Options for the Union*, Green Paper, Brussels: Commission of the European Communities, Directorate-General for Employment, Industrial Relations and Social Affairs.

Curtin, D. and Meijers, H. (1995) 'The principle of open government in Schengen and the European Union: democratic retrogression', *Common Market Law Review* 32: 391–442.

Dahrendorf, R. (1988) *The Modern Social Conflict*, London: Weidenfeld and Nicolson.

Delanty, G. (1995) *Inventing Europe: Idea, Identity, Reality*, Basingstoke: Macmillan.

Gardner, J. (ed.) (n.d.) *Hallmarks of Citizenship: A Green Paper*, London: The Institute for Citizenship and the British Institute of International and Comparative Law.

Harden, I. (1991) 'The Community budget, national budgets and EMU: a constitutional perspective', in J. Driffill and M. Babor (eds) *A Currency for Europe*, London: Lothian Foundation Press.

Harmsen, R. (1994) 'Integration as adaptation: national courts and the politics of Community law', paper presented at the Annual Conference of the Political Studies Association of Ireland, October, 1994.

Heater, D. (1990) *Citizenship: The Civic Ideal in World History, Politics and Education*, London: Longman.

Holloway, J. (1981) *Social Policy Harmonisation in the European Community*, Farnborough: Gower.

Johnson, N. (1976) *In Search of the Constitution*, Oxford: Pergamon Press.

Jordan, B. (1989) *The Common Good: Citizenship, Morality and Self-Interest*, Oxford: Basil Blackwell.

Kennedy, D. (ed.) forthcoming. Proceedings of a Conference on the Committee of the Regions at the Institute of European Studies, the Queen's University of Belfast. To be published in a special edition of *Regional and Federal Studies*.

Lasok, D. and Stone, P. (1987) *Conflict of Laws in the European Community*, Abingdon: Professional Books, Ltd.

Leca, J. (1990) 'Nazionalita e cittadinanza noll l'Europe delle immigrazione', in WAA (Italian for various editors), *Italia, Europa e Nuove Immigrazione*, Turin: Editioni della Fondazione Giovanni Angelli, pp. 201–60.

Marshall, P. (1991) 'The ratification of the United States Constitution', in P. King and A. Bosco (eds) *A Constitution for Europe: A Comparative Study of Federal Constitutions and Plans for the United States of Europe*, London: Lothian Foundation, pp. 343–52.

Mazey, S. and Mitchell, J. (1993) 'Europe of the regions: territorial interests and European integration; the Scottish experience', in S. Mazey and J. Richardson (eds) *Lobbying in the European Community*, Oxford: Oxford University Press, pp. 95–121.

Mazey, S. and Richardson, J. (eds) (1993) *Lobbying in the European Community*, Oxford: Oxford University Press.

Meehan, E. (1992) 'European Community policies on sex equality: a bibliographic essay', *Women's Studies International Forum* 15(1): 57–64.

Meehan, E. (1993) *Citizenship and the European Community*, London: Sage.

Meehan, E. (1996) 'The debate on citizenship and European union', in P. Murray and P. Rich (eds) *Visions of European Unity*, Boulder, CO: Westview Press.

Meehan, E. forthcoming 'European integration and citizens' rights: a comparative perspective, *Publius: The Journal of Federalism*.

Miller, D. (1993) 'In defence of nationality', *Journal of Applied Philosophy* 10(1): 3–16.

Northern Ireland Council for Voluntary Action (NICVA) (1996) *Partners for Progress: The Voluntary and Community Sector's Contribution to Partnership-Building*, (Report commissioned from independent researcher, Christine Carroll), Belfast: NICVA.

O'Donnell, R. (1995) 'Modernisation and social partnership', in R. Wilson (ed.) *New Thinking for New Times*, Belfast: Democratic Dialogue, pp. 24–33.

O'Leary, S. (1995) 'The relationship between Community citizenship and the fundamental rights in Community law', *Common Market Law Review* 23: 519–44.

Parish, P. (1991) 'The changing character of American federalism in the 19th century', in P. King and A. Bosco (eds) *A Constitution for Europe: A Comparative Study of Federal Constitutions and Plans for the United States of Europe*, London: Lothian Foundation, pp. 361–8.

Siedentop, L. (1990) 'The EC and constitutional reform: Thatcher's inconsistency', *The Financial Times,* 7 November.

Smith, M. and Corrigan, J. (1995) 'Relations with Europe', in R. Breen, P. Devine and G. Robinson (eds) *Social Attitudes in Northern Ireland: Fourth Report 1994–95*, Belfast: Appletree Press, pp. 84–105.

Steiner, J. (1985) 'The right to welfare: equality and equity under Community law', *European Law Review*, Vol 10: 21–41.

Tassin, E. (1992) 'Europe: a political community?', in C. Mouffe *Dimensions of Radical Democracy: Pluralism, Citizenship, Community*, London: Verso, pp. 169–92.

Usher, J. (1981) *European Community Law and National Law: The Irreversible Transfer?*, London: University Association for Contemporary Studies/ George Allen and Unwin.

Weiner, A. (1995) *Building Institutions: The Developing Practice of European Citizenship*, Ottawa: PhD thesis submitted in the Department of Political Science, Carleton University.

6 A liberal view on a European constitution

Angelo M. Petroni

> The greatest problem for Europe is therefore to know: how one can restrain sovereign power without destroying it.
>
> Joseph de Maistre

INTRODUCTION

For the future historian of twentieth-century Europe it will be a difficult problem to explain why the very idea of European union became, all of a sudden, so popular among intellectuals and the public at large. Indeed, for decades the idea of a European union was merely an ideal and – what is more – a project shared by a tiny minority. As you would expect, this very large convergence on European union is made possible largely by the fact that there is no such thing as a reasonably unique concept of what this union should be. 'Europe' is becoming more or less by definition a good thing, irrespective of what people mean by it. Given that philosophy is, if anything, the discipline of analysing concepts, in this chapter I shall try to produce some analytical considerations relating to the very idea of a European constitution.

DOES A EUROPEAN CONSTITUTION EXIST ALREADY?

The problem of establishing (or *not* establishing) a constitution for Europe is hardly one of inventing a new text from scratch. It is one of the theses of this chapter that there is valid ground for affirming that a form of constitution has been developed (and partly implemented) by jurisprudence since the very origins of the EC institutions.

As is well known, from the legal point of view there is no such thing as an EC, but three Communities established with the Treaties of Paris of 1951 (the European Coal and Steel Community) and of Rome of 1957 (the European Economic Community and the European Atomic Community). It is on the basis of these treaties and how they have been interpreted and implemented that the problem of the present 'constitutional' situation in Europe has finally to be assessed.

Of course the Treaty of Union has represented a major event for

Europe. However, it is reasonable to say that the Treaty was – and is – a major *political* event but it has not substantially changed the juridical and constitutional framework of Europe as is showed by the fact that the European Parliament after the Treaty has called for a European Constitution (1993).

The main question to be addressed is whether the founding treaties of the EC (or EU) have to be considered as purely international agreements amongst sovereign states. The origin and the structure are of course that of multilateral treaties signed by representatives of the states and they have been ratified and empowered according to the principles of international law. However, both the content of the treaties, and in particular the treaty establishing the EEC, and the jurisprudence which has arisen from their implementation qualify them as something essentially different from the classical treaties between states retaining their national sovereignties. Let me recall here the two basic elements which justify this statement.

In the first place, contrary to the basic principles of international law, the Treaty of Rome endows the Community with powers which *apply directly* to the citizens of the states concerned. This is established, for example, by Article 189 of the Treaty. In this way the citizens of the member states are subject both to their national law and to Community law. By the same token, as Michel Massenet (1990: 11) writes, 'contrairement aux traités internationaux de type classique, les traités communautaires confèrent aux particuliers des droits que les jurisdictions nationales ont le devoir de sauvegarder'.[1] Individuals can protect the rights guaranteed by the Treaty by appealing to the Court of Justice. According to Article 187 of the EEC Treaty the sentences of the Court of Justice are valid *directly in the territory* of the member states. National authorities are obliged to enforce the sentences of the Court against their nationals without an *exequatur* (Art. 192). This also constitutes a strong element of difference between the Treaty of Rome and classical international treaties. (For example, neither the International Court of Justice at The Hague nor the Strasbourg European Court for Human Rights can be appealed to by individuals.)

Second, the jurisprudence elaborated by the Court of Justice in interpreting the Treaties has constantly ruled in favour of the pre-eminence of the Treaties over national laws. In the famous *Costa* sentence (1964) the Court ruled that

> By contrast with ordinary international treaties, the EEC Treaty has created its own legal system. ... By creating a Community of unlimited duration, having its own institutions, its own personality,

its own legal capacity . . . and, more particularly, real powers stemming from a limitation of sovereignty or a transfer of powers from the States to the community, the Member States have limited their sovereign rights.[2]

This limitation is *definitive*.

In another famous sentence the Court ruled that, 'It is not for the Court . . . to ensure that the rules of internal law, even constitutional rules, enforced in one or other of the Member States are respected.'[3] A *monistic* point of view (in the sense used by Hans Kelsen (1991)) is followed in the relationship between the Treaties and derived jurisprudence, on the one hand, and national laws, on the other. In particular, the national judge is obliged to apply Community law and to consider, on his own authority, as invalid any national law (be it past or future) which might conflict with it.

Are these characteristics of Community law sufficient for us to affirm that the Treaties (and their interpretation) represent a constitution? As you would expect in such cases, much (too much) depends on the content you attribute to the concept of constitution. If 'constitution' means an explicit agreement made by individuals upon the basic rules of their society, then obviously the Treaties are not a constitution, and Community/Union law is not a constitutional law. However, it is even truer that following this criterion there would be no 'true' constitutions around at all.

On the other hand, if – from the viewpoint of legal positivism – the constitution is taken to mean the highest law valid in a given territory, then the situation becomes more complex. Provided that member states have agreed to accept both the content of the Treaties *and* the interpretations of the Court of Justice, the Community/Union law *is* the highest law. Albeit in very different ways, all the highest legal authorities of the EC/EU states have accepted the supremacy of Community/Union law over their national law (see Isaac, 1990: 172–82).[4]

At the same time, Community/Union law is not the source of the validity of all the other laws enforced in the European states. If this logical dependence is considered an essential feature of a constitution, as it is in a contractarian view, or even in some legal positivism perspectives, then obviously Community law is not constitutional law. However, by this same token, would the American Constitution be a constitution? And would there exist at all any constitutional law in England? Note that, even if you consider nation-states with civil law systems such as Italy or France, it is very difficult to affirm that there is a strict logical dependence of the bulk of the law on the constitution.

Normally laws remain relatively unchanged when a new constitution is adopted, and the pre-eminence of constitutional law means that previous laws that conflict with it are abolished.

Some time ago Norman Barry stressed the difference between the traditional liberal meaning of 'constitution' as 'a set of substantive rules protecting a fully-fledged individualistic political morality, or as a set of neutral but rigorously strict procedural rules' and the 'mistaken idea of a constitution . . . prevalent in much of contemporary welfare economics'. The liberal constitution is not designed to implement the people's choice 'but to impose significant constraints on government, whatever form it takes (majority rule or otherwise)' (Barry, 1989: 270–1). In terms of this distinction, it seems to me that Community law is very close to the concept of a liberal constitution. It imposes constraints on national governments and majorities on the basis of *individual* freedoms (the 'four freedoms' stated in the EEC Treaty).

There is barely any need to stress that Community/Union law does not possess all the desirable features that a constitutional law should have to effectively contain governments and preserve individual rights. There is no list of individual rights in the EEC Treaty, and of course many points of the Treaties and of jurisprudence do not correspond to a liberal view. But this is no ground for denying that Community/Union law possesses a remarkable amount of the formal features of a liberal constitutional law.

BACK TO THE AMERICAN MODEL

Since its very foundation the United States of America has provided an endless source of arguments both in favour of and against the idea of a European union (for an overview, see de Rougemont, 1991).[5] The question has been revived by James Buchanan:

> Europe in 1990 finds itself historically positioned in a setting analogous to the United States in 1787. There are, of course, major differences as well as similarities, and analogies can always be overdrawn. But if attention is placed on the comparison between the unrealized opportunity that is (was) within the possible and the alternative future that failure to seize the opportunity would represent, the similarities surely overwhelm the differences.

> (Buchanan, 1990: 4)

The lessons of the American experience for the Europe of 1990 are clear. The citizens of the separate nation-states face an opportunity to enter into a federal union that can be an instrument for achieving the enormous gains of economic integration. In this respect, the parallel with the America of 1787 is direct. In the process of establishing an effective federal union, a central political authority must come into being with some sovereignty over citizens in all the nation-states.

(Buchanan, 1990: 6)

More or less the same words were used by Luigi Einaudi in 1947 about the reconstruction of Europe (Einaudi, 1948).[6]

Oddly, one of the fathers of European federalism shared a completely different view about Europe and America:

La situation n'était pas la même et le précédent n'est pas convaincant. Loin d'avoir derrière eux un long passé d'indépendence, ces Etats [the American States] venaient de s'affranchir . . . d'un régime colonial; ils étaient à la recherche d'une formule selon laquelle s'organiseraient leur cohabitation future et même cela n'allait pas tout seul, ni tout de suite. . . . L'Amérique était un pays neuf qui se donnait les institutions de son choix, sans avoir à remplacer les institutions antérieures, ni à rechercher une entente avec d'autres pays.[7]

Schuman re-echoed here a famous statement of de Tocqueville (1835: 176):

The circumstance which makes it easy to maintain a federal government in America is not only that the states have similar interests, a common origin, and a common language, but that they have also arrived at the same stage of civilisation . . . the difference between the civilisation of Maine and that of Georgia is slighter than the difference between the habits of Normandy and those of Brittany.

De Tocqueville concluded that it was easier for Maine and Georgia to federate than for Normandy and Brittany.

You will not find much more in the current anti-federalist views. For example, in commenting upon Buchanan's article, a prominent anti-federalist, Alan Sked (1990:1), writes that, 'The conditions which, according to Buchanan, determined America's position in 1787 do not apply to Europe today. The result is that his paper appears to be based on a completely false premise.'

In examining these matters the analytical level gets more or less inevitably mixed up with value judgements. Consciously designed institutional arrangements (be they constitutional or otherwise) are technologies, and technology is defined both by the existence of 'valid' scientific laws ('regularities') and by states of things which are wished to be produced ('ends'). 'Ends' are the difference between technology and scientific predictions of phenomena. Assuming that regularities are beyond possible change,[8] different ends will be produced by different arrangements of 'specific conditions'. Strictly speaking, you cannot assess the 'technological' rationality of an institution if the ends are not specified.

In proposing his constitutional view for Europe Buchanan's ends are quite clear: 'the achievement of widely recognized and shared object-ives, those of internal (intra-European) peace and economic prosperity, within political arrangements that ensure individual liberties and, at the same time, allow for the maximal practical achievement of standards of justice' (Buchanan, 1990: 2).[9] Buchanan thinks that these objectives can be attained by a European constitution envisaging: first, the right to secede from union 'upon agreement of some designated supra-majority within the seceding jurisdiction' (Buchanan, 1990: 7). The lesson from the American experience is that the formal rules of the constitution do not suffice to contain the powers of the central government or to avoid a 'federal Leviathan'; and second, rules ensuring *competition* 'among producers and consumers of goods and resources across the territory that encompasses the several nation-states' (Buchanan, 1990: 11). Of course, the problem of the possibility of implementing a federal consti-tution for Europe is quite different from the problem of whether the specific model proposed by Buchanan will produce the effects it is intended to produce. Let me start with the first question.

Is Europe today in a situation similar to that of America in 1787? Basically, it depends on what you consider the relevant elements to be. Having no universally valid general theory about the rise (or failure to rise) of federations, we have no objective rule for establishing what has to count as a 'relevant' element. Any answer will therefore hardly be a scientific one. My guess is that the parallel is not very useful in descrip-tive terms. We lost a long time ago the faith the Framers had in the possibility of looking at Greek or Roman history for deciding which political institutions would work and which would not.

Obviously we do have arguments, other than analogies with the fram-ing of the American Constitution, in favour of the possibility of implementing a federal constitution in Europe. If we assume that in democratic regimes, without external threats, citizens finally get the institutional arrangements they prefer, then there is wide scope for the possibility of implementing a sort of European union. Let me refer to the 1987 special edition of *Eurobarometer* 'Europe 2000'. About two-thirds of the interviewees declare themselves to be 'much in favour' or 'quite in favour' of the United States of Europe (23 per cent and 40 per cent respectively). Some 13 per cent are 'quite against' and 7 per cent 'strongly against'. For the six founding countries of the EEC, this figure rises to 70 per cent (83 per cent of respondents). To the question of when they would like to have a European government responsible for the economy, foreign affairs and defence, 9 per cent answered 'immediately', 21 per cent in the next ten years, 17 per cent in the next ten to twenty years, 11 per cent in the next twenty to thirty years, 7 per cent in several generations, 9 per cent said 'never', and 26 per cent gave no answer. Some 53 per cent of all the interviewees believe that in the year 2000 Europeans will vote on a European constitution proposed by a European Parliament; 25 per cent said they did not agree with this, and 22 per cent gave no answer (*Eurobarometer*, 1987).[10] There is obviously no reason to assume that opinion polls reflect the stablest and 'deepest' preferences of individuals and that these preferences will convert more or less directly into electoral preferences. Nevertheless, the overwhelming majority of politicians who declare themselves in favour of a federal Europe is a good indication of the fact that they believe this to be true.

Let us now turn to the second question. The advantages of federations in terms of the keeping of internal peace, providing defence and removing internal barriers to trade, are well known. There is not a great deal to be added to the classical theses of the *Federalist* or, more recently, of Lionel Robbins (1937, chapter 9, and 1963, chapter 7). However, we should not forget what recent experience has taught us: these advantages are *not* the result of federalism in its more general sense, namely, as a *technique* for creating new political entities out of pre-existing sovereign states by sharing sovereignty,[11] but of a mixture of federalism and liberal democratic institutions.

The real debate arises when we consider the problem of whether the federal Leviathan can be effectively tamed. In discussing this I think that we should carefully distinguish between two different questions: first, how to prevent a *Bundesstaat* from becoming an *Einheitsstaat*; and second, how to prevent the creation of a federal union from increasing the total amount of government over citizens. The two questions are historically and conceptually related, but are nevertheless distinct.

Let us consider the first point. The right to secede is the mechanism that, for Buchanan and for Peter Bernholz (1991) in his detailed constitutional project,[12] should ultimately guarantee that the federal government stays within its constitutional limits. I would like first to quote a passage from a 1969 article by Buchanan:

> The cost of making any change in structure from what was to what is has been borne *in past periods*. The cost involved in making a

change to something different must be borne *at the time of decision*. There is always a bias toward the status quo, toward continuing in existence the set of organizational rules that exist.

(Buchanan, 1977: 278)

Mutatis mutandis, this holds if we mean by 'rules', not constitutional rules but the actual, more centralised rules that the political federal process might produce. The real working of the right of secession as a guarantee of constitutional framing supposes that the cost of seceding is not too high. Is this a realistic premiss? We may notice that the higher the level of economic integration, the higher this cost will be – let alone for the 'regional' division of labour that the extension of markets will produce. We have neither theoretical nor empirical evidence that the corresponding cost imposed upon the union by the secession will result in bargaining situations which will tend towards the restoration of the constitutional rules, or towards a higher equilibrium. Depending upon unpredictable conditions, the threat to secede could be either ineffective in restoring the original framing, or ruinously disruptive of any cooperation.

Probably some suggestions could come from the history of the decline of the American federalism. Peter Aranson focused on the primary role of the Supreme Court in this process. Aranson distinguishes between 'constitutional' and 'contingent' decentralisation. The first 'is guaranteed as a matter of organic, constitutional law'; the second is the result of a government's decision, 'as a matter of prudential or political judgement' (Aranson, 1990: 20) of how much authority to devolve to the constituent units. Following a shift from doctrine to utilitarianism,

[the Supreme Court] soon gave way to a consequentialist juris-prudence. The Court thereby replaced its earliest understanding of federalism as contingent decentralization. The inevitable result of this shift has been the increasing centralization of the American polity along with the decline of federalism itself.

(Avanson, 1990: 25)

There is a contrast between this explanation and the explanation given by von Mises. For von Mises the centralisation of the United States was not the result of any deliberate attempt by Washington bureaucrats and lobbies to deprive the states of authority and to create a centralised government and can in no way be considered as unconstitutional. The equilibrium between the states and the federal government was disrupted because the new powers created by public intervention in the economy went to the federal government. And this was absolutely necessary for the unity of the internal market to be preserved. It was not possible to leave to each state the power to control the economy according to its own plans. Von Mises concluded that the autonomy of the states as guaranteed by the constitution was possible only if there was not public intervention in the economy. Voting in favour of governmental control over economic activities the citizens, implicitly, albeit unwillingly, voted in favour of higher centralisation (von Mises, 1983, section 2). From this point of view the shift in the intellectual doctrine of the Court does not represent at all the basic cause of the decline of American federalism (even if, of course, it may well be complementary, or even an induced consequence).

If von Mises's argument is correct, then federalists are faced with a very serious problem. As a matter of fact, it is scarcely credible that state interventionism in the economy will return to what it was in the nineteenth century, and the tendency of federations to become more centralised would be unavoidable.

Let us come now to the second point. In Buchanan's view, constitutionally guaranteed cross-national competition will ensure that

> particularised interferences with internal economic relationship within a single national unit will be policed with reasonable effectiveness. . . . Politically orchestrated regulatory activity will tend to be restricted to that which increases overall efficiency, *as this criterion may be defined by the preferences of citizens.*
>
> (Buchanan, 1990: 11, my italics)

This problem of cross-national competition is probably one of the main differences between the liberal view of federalism for Europe, and the standard 'federal' view which is today prevailing in Europe – and which Jacques Delors represents at its best. However, I think that we have to be careful in assessing the *constitutional* role of cross-national competition, *if* by constitution we mean 'liberal constitution'. There are few doubts of course that guaranteeing to citizens and firms of the states of the federation the right to free trade and free location within the federation, as well as free trade and free migration with foreign countries, is a way of limiting the power of the states over the citizens. But in order to avoid this 'efficiency' becoming compatible with a more or less unrestricted domination of the majority over the minority, the overall cost of relocation within the federation should be quite low. There are serious doubts whether this is so. The cost for 'exploited' minorities of resettling in another member state of the union is not comparable with the cost that an American has to bear in moving from one state to another. 'European differences' mean that for the great majority of citizens differences in language, legal systems and customs are very effective barriers.[13]

Of course, in arguing in favour of a European federal constitution we do not need necessarily to show that it will reduce the total amount of government over European citizens. All that we need to show, from a liberal point of view, is that this amount will not increase substantially. According to Sked, this is what liberal federalists are unable to do:

> It is more or less an axiom of government that the more levels of government that are provided for, the more government and bureaucracy one will get. The idea that government can be spread over more layers is proved false by all human history.
>
> (Sked, 1990: 6)

This is an important argument, which cannot be easily dismissed. Let me note some points. If we take Sked's thesis as one of comparative politics, it is obviously false in several instances. For example, Switzerland has more levels of government than France or Sweden, but it has less overall government. Therefore, a proof of Sked's thesis should consist in showing that an increase in government arose in the past as a consequence of *adding* more levels of government. This is not easy to do. If we consider modern and contemporary European history, the increase in government (and bureaucracy) has been the result of the formation of the nation-states, i.e. of the progressive weakening of 'lower' levels of government. We simply do not have the reasonably large and stable evidence which would be needed to support Sked's thesis. And going back in history to find random examples would prove – as ever – nothing at all. The example of the United States (and, perhaps, Switzerland) has therefore (again!) necessarily to be the basis for Sked's thesis. To draw conclusions, not to say 'axioms', from cases which are more or less unique is very difficult indeed. The risk is producing loose talk rather than scientific argument, given that we lack the relevant nomological (comparative) knowledge. There is no ground for denying that there would have been more government in America if no federation had been established.

OLD REASONS FOR A EUROPEAN FEDERATION, AND SOME NEW PROBLEMS

As I said before, the arguments in favour of a European federation which are currently presented are more or less the same as they have been since the 1930s. Since that time there have not been many cases around of successful federations, and therefore the evidence in favour of implementing a federation independently of the detailed structure that one might imagine for it needs perhaps some qualifications.

Let us start from federations as a means for keeping intra-European peace. The traditional idea that intra-European wars in this century have been the result of the concept of the absolute (unlimited) sovereignty of nations has been recently reaffirmed by Maurice Allais (1990: 17–18):

> Aujourd'hui la situation est claire: ou bien nous fonderons à nouveau l'organisation de l'Europe sur le dogme de la souveraineté nationale *illimitée*, et, tôt ou tard, les mêmes causes entraînant les mêmes effets, nous serons à nouveau amenés à nous affronter dans des conflits sans issue, et finalément à la décadence; ou bien nous fonderons notre avenir . . . sur des bases nouvelles.[14]

However, something new should supplement, and perhaps replace, this point of view. What the argument fails to consider is that the evidence we have today has considerably changed the nature of the problems. The basic fact is that liberal democratic regimes have never engaged in *mutual* war (even if they engaged in many wars with countries having different regimes).[15] Of course, from the point of view of the so-called realist theory, which is represented in our century by such people as Edward Carr, George Kennan, or Henry Kissinger, this would be more or less a coincidence, the causes of wars having little to do with the nature of the national regimes, and very much with the traditional geopolitical factors and the 'balance of power'. One virtually immediate consequence is that the problem of preventing intra-European wars is a legitimate one, if one shares the 'realistic' point of view, but not if one shares the point of view which considers the liberal and democratic nature of the European regimes. One could be tempted to argue that liberalism and democracy are not necessarily irreversible, and that a federation would therefore ensure a double security. The weakness in this argument is that there is no evidence that federations of undemocratic countries would be effective peacekeepers. Dramatic evidence of the contrary is provided in the present times.

It does not seem that any new perspective about keeping intra-European peace is likely to affect the perspectives for European external defence. As a matter of fact, for any reasonable future it seems quite unlikely that solid liberal and democratic regimes will be established in the east and in the south of Europe. However, the point at stake here is that arguments in favour of a European common external defence are not necessarily arguments in favour of a European union – be it federal or otherwise. A sufficient degree of protection from an external foe for a set of actors sharing a common set of vital interests can be provided, under a reasonably wide range of conditions, by collective action. Of course, there are good strategic and historical reasons for saying that the highest degree of protection will be attained by unifying the several actors as a single actor. But this highest degree of protection might be unnecessary, and a military alliance could suffice.

The experience of NATO as the guarantor of Europe's defence provides very mixed evidence. On the one hand, it could be seen as the proof that an effective protection from an external foe can be provided by an alliance of independent states. But the predominant role of the USA leaves very wide room for arguing that it has not been the alliance of independent states which has finally guaranteed their protection.

A very complex problem is represented by the arguments in favour of a central government as the sole effective guarantee of a free European market. One of the elements of the problem is that of assessing the necessity for such a central government against the historical experience of the EC. In 1959 Allais criticized the mode of integration which was implicit in the Paris and Rome Treaties and which dominated Community action for decades. As he put it, 'l'union politique doît précéder l'union économique. C'est là une condition fondamentale. Il faut absolument détourner l'opinion publique de la dangéreuse illusion suivant laquelle l'union économique peut préparer la voie à l'union politique' (Allais, 1960: 135–6).[16] This view has since then become extremely popular, especially among socialist and *dirigiste* supporters of a unified Europe. At first sight it might seem to be just a refuted prediction. Europe reached a relatively high degree of economic integration without a political union, and nobody could doubt that this economic integration is today the most solid basis for building a politically united Europe.

However, such a view would underestimate the role that EC institutions played. As I argued in the first section of this chapter, the Treaties and the subsequent jurisprudence represented a sharing of sovereignty between the nation-states and the Community/Union. It would therefore be one-sided to affirm that any form of political union – for good or for bad – was absent from the process of economic integration. The history of the EC and the EU is for a significant part the history of the taming of the attempts by nation-states to protect – directly or indirectly – their markets and their enterprises.

WHAT KIND OF A EUROPEAN CONSTITUTION ARE WE GOING TO GET?

One of the main areas of confusion in the current debate about the constitutional future of Europe is about the meaning of 'federalism'. If you claim, as Jacques Delors once did, that as a result of the move towards federal Europe, 'In ten years, 80 per cent of economic legislation, and perhaps fiscal and social, will have its origin in the Community', then the obvious conclusion is that the concept of federalism is employed in different and even contradictory ways, and that Delors's federal state is much closer to the classical European nation-state than to the federal state of the framers of the US constitution. The very concept of 'subsidiarity' would become not just somewhat vague, as it is anyway, but even empty, if it is assumed that the federal/central authority will be in control of the greatest part of the economic legislation.

The fear that the European institutions are destined to turn into a super-state is as old as the Community itself. Perhaps nobody expressed it better than Wilhelm Röpke; writing in 1958, he saw in the Community institutions the way towards generalised economic and political planning – a European Saint-Simonism – which would have been even more dangerous than planning at the national level (Röpke, 1958, chapter 5). Undoubtedly the Community, and now the Union, have always had two 'souls': one liberal, the other *dirigiste*. This is reflected in the EC Treaty, which contains several Articles which leave plenty of room for heavy state intervention in the economy. If one considers that the Treaty was written at the high point of intellectual and political support for planning, this is hardly surprising. As is well known, the Treaty of Union was written from a point of view much more favourable to the free market. However, it is easy to see that the two 'souls' are very well present even in this Treaty, as is shown by the 'Social Charter', which corresponds to a *dirigiste* ideology. In predicting that a European federal union 'will be established in the 1990s', Buchanan predicts also that it will not transform itself into a centralised state. The reason is twofold: first, the romantic myth of the benevolent and omniscient state that

> came to influence public perception of politics in application to the existence of the separately sovereign nation-states of modern Europe . . . has been substantially displaced in the public consciousness of the 1990s, and there are no longer philosophers around who promote its revival. Nowhere in the world, East or West, do we find, in the 1990s, the naive faith in collectivist nostrums that characterized both

intellectual and public attitudes for most of the 19th and 20th centuries.

(Buchanan, 1990: 18)

Therefore a European state could not be expected to command the same loyalties as nation-states in the last two centuries; and second, 'Cultural, linguistic, and ethnic homogeneity' will continue to exist in Europe, and this will oppose the possibility of the federal union's transforming itself into a nation-state (Buchanan, 1990: 17–18).

I believe that Buchanan's position is largely in conflict with the evidence at our disposal. Let me consider the first point. There are few doubts, of course, that the 'naive faith in collectivist nostrums' has faded away. But it was hardly faith in collectivism which was responsible for the progressive centralisation of states – be they federal or not – in the nineteenth and twentieth centuries. The tendency towards centralisation is much older than any popularly shared faith in collectivism. De Tocqueville was already able to write in 1835 that

> In the course of the last half-century Europe has endured many revolutions and counter-revolutions, which have agitated it in opposite directions; but all these perturbations resemble one another in one respect: they have all shaken or destroyed the secondary powers of government. The local privileges which the French did not abolish in the countries they conquered have finally succumbed to the policy of the princes who conquered the French. Those princes rejected all the innovations of the French Revolution *except centralization*; that is the only principle they consented to receive from such a source.[17]

(Tocqueville, 1835: 322)

We have to be careful in distinguishing between faith in collectivism and faith in the benevolent state. There is hardly any evidence that among the public at large this second faith has faded away. Even more relevant for our discussion is the fact that the public seems to prefer a benevolent European state to a benevolent national state. If we look at the *Eurobarometer* of June 1990 this statement is largely justified: 64 per cent of the interviewees considered the 'Community Charter of Social Rights' as 'a good thing', and only 4 per cent 'a bad thing' (75 per cent and 3 per cent in Holland, 60 per cent and 5 per cent in Germany, 67 per cent and 8 per cent in England, respectively). Some 92 per cent were in favour of EC regulations in health and safety work; 80 per cent were in favour of EC regulations on minimum income, 81 per cent were for worker participation, and 85 per cent were for job-related training, to quote just a few items (*Eurobarometer*, 1990, note 33).[18] The trend seems to continue without any major alteration.

As far as the second point is concerned, one cannot help but concur that attempts to develop a fully centralised European state will be hindered by Europe's variety. Here rest the main hopes of anti-federalists as well as of liberal federalists. The argument, however, should not be overstressed. The history of the making of nation-states shows that the centralistic states emerged from ethnic, cultural, and linguistic differences which were extremely strong (see Weber, 1976, in particular, chapter 7). And, of course, differences have a tendency to be reduced as economic and cultural exchanges increase.

ANOTHER WAY TOWARDS A EUROPEAN CONSTITUTION

If the arguments I have presented in the previous pages are sound, then I think that the most likely conclusion which we should reach is that if a European constitution is implemented, it will be 'federal' much more in the sense of Delors than in the sense of de Rougemont, Buchanan or Bernholz. The preferences of the majority of European citizens and of European politicians point very clearly in this direction. Given the unpredictability (practical, if not ontological) of the events of human history, there is not much difference between such a prediction and a prophecy. This has its consolations, of course, and leaves some (at least psychological) room for intellectuals to speculate about different possible worlds. Let me therefore return to the more ideological problem of what would be the right constitutional framing for Europe from a liberal point of view.

I believe that we have to start from historical and current evidence concerning the difference between the role of the political and bureaucratic bodies of the Community/Union, on the one hand, and the activity of the Court of Justice, on the other.

It is widely recognized that the decisions issued by the political and bureaucratic bodies are mostly characterized by two basic features: first, they are the result of a compromise of national interests; and second, they are strongly – and increasingly – driven by a *dirigiste* view of the economy. These features are remarkably insignificant in the decisions taken by the Court of Justice. As a matter of fact, the greatest and most influential part of its decisions ruled against national interests, and was a prohibition of any unjust conduct – defined as a violation of the Treaties. For firms and individuals the judgements of the Court have been by far the most effective way of preserving the four freedoms of the EC Treaty and, in consequence, of implementing a free market in Europe. Especially since the *Dassonville* judgement and the *Rewe-Zentral* judgement – better known as the 'Cassis de Dijon' judgement,[19] – the Court has increasingly discountenanced the direct or indirect attempts of the national governments to protect their markets, firms and interests.

Such outcomes are not the result of chance, of course. They were basically the result of the traditional judicial practice followed by the Court which considers the two opposed parties as being equal before the law. This allowed individual rights and free-market principles to prevail over wide *and* strong interests. You could scarcely expect a majoritarian democratic process to produce equivalent or better outcomes.[20]

Naturally, the difference between the decisions of the Commission and the Council, on the one hand, and the judgements of the Court, on the other, should not be overstressed. The decisions of the Commission and of the Council are themselves a fundamental source of the law that the Court of Justice is bound to enforce, and the Treaties, as I suggested above, impose many limitations on the exercising of the four freedoms. But, from a liberal point of view, the overall superiority that the jurisprudential way of creating a united Europe has had over the political and bureaucratic way as represented by the Council and the Commission seems to be reasonably clear.

If this evaluation is sound, then arguments can be produced in favour of a way of creating a European union which would distinguish itself from the mainstream. It consists in putting at the core of the process of 'unification' the development of a European Common Law protecting the civil as well as the economic rights of the citizens. This European law should not be invented from scratch, but should evolve from the existing jurisprudence and from a reform of the EEC Treaty and the EU Treaty, which should in turn be transformed into a full charter of rights in the liberal sense. The existing political institutions should be reformed in order to guarantee effective implementation of the system of rules created by the jurisprudence of the present Court of Justice, and of other judicial bodies which would have to be created.[21]

Probably this central role given to the law and to the judiciary is compatible with different forms of political institutions. But it is likely that it would be incompatible both with a pure confederal framework and with a centralised state. In the first case the incompatibility is more or less theoretical, given that a European Common Law would impose a limitation on the sovereignty of nations (or, more concretely, on the powers of their parliaments). In the second case, evidence from the past shows that the centralisation of political power is in contrast to a strong role for the judiciary and to a system of law which is not derived from legislation.

To put the law and the judiciary at the core of the constitutional process of Europe would also be consistent with its constitutional history. While the American Constitution was the result of a deliberate attempt to establish a political order guaranteeing peace and individual rights in the absence – after the revolution – of any absolute sovereign power to be tamed, the European constitutions were the result of a very long political and intellectual process of limitation of the power of the absolute monarchs. In the abstract terms of contractarian theory, the establishment of the American Constitution was a process very similar to a *pactum unionis*, while the constitutional history of Europe corresponded rather to the concept of a *pactum subiectionis* – of a 'new' pact between the subjects/citizens and the monarch.[22] The law and the judiciary played a major role in this process.

The substantial weakness of the Community's political powers allowed the judiciary to rise and acquire importance, within the process of European union. Having in mind liberal values and ends, and having evaluated the evidence available, I think that one should consider this as a fortunate coincidence. Consequently, its preservation and improvement should be considered as the essential element of a liberal constitution for Europe.[23]

NOTES

1 Translated as: 'in contrast to international treaties of the classical variety, the treaties of the Community confer on private persons rights that national jurisdictions have the duty to safeguard' (Massenet, 1990: 11).
2 Court of Justice of the European Communities, *Reports*, Flaminio Costa vs. ENEL, 15 July 1964, p. 593.
3 Court of Justice of the European Communities, *Reports*, Geitling vs. High Authority, 15 July 1960, p. 438.
4 The British Parliament (*European Community Act*, 1972) followed a way intended to preserve its sovereignty, but prescribed that judges respect the principles ruled by the Court of Justice – including therefore the primacy of Community law.
5 De Rougemont (1991) wrote extensively about federalism as decentralisation and as a protection of the rights of minorities.
6 See also the following passage written in 1954:

> Nella vita delle nazioni di solito l'errore di non saper cogliere l'attimo fuggente è irreparabile. La necessità di unificare l'Europa è evidente. Gli stati esistenti sono polvere senza sostanza. Nessuno di essi è in grado di sopportare il costo di una difesa autonoma.... Le esitazioni e le discordie degli stati italiani della fine del quattrocento costarono agli italiani la perdita dell'indipendenza lungo tre secoli; ed il tempo della decisione, allora, durò forse pochi mesi.
>
> (Einaudi, 1956: 89)

(In the life of a nation usually the mistake of not knowing when to grasp the fleeting moment is irreparable. The necessity of unifying Europe is evident. The existing states are powder without substance. None of them are able to support the costs of their own defence. . . . The hesitation and the dissension of the Italian states at the end of the fifteenth century cost the Italians the loss of their independence for three centuries; and then, the time of decision lasted maybe a few months.)

7   The situation is not the same and the precedent is not convincing. Far from having behind them a long history of independence, the American States had just rid themselves . . . of a colonial regime; they were in search of a formula according to which their future living together could be organised and even that would not take place on its own or immediately. . . . America was a new country that gave itself institutions of its own choice, without having to replace existing institutions nor look for an understanding with other countries.

From this judgement Schuman concluded:

It will not do to fuse states, to create a super-state. Our European States are an historical reality; it would be psychologically impossible to make them disappear. Their diversity is indeed a happy fact, and we do not want to level or equalise them.

(Schuman, 1963: 24)

8   I do not mean derivative regularities, i.e. regularities which derive from the union of more fundamental laws and some specific conditions, but regularities which cannot be further explained. The laws of human nature – if any – would be in this sense fundamental laws beyond possible change. Of course the problem here is *not* ontological. The relevant point is that the laws cannot be changed at will.

9   'Standards of justice' is not very clear indeed.

10 It is to be remarked that figures do not reveal a constant progress over the years toward more pro-European preferences. Except for England, there were more people in favour of the United States of Europe in 1970 than in 1987.

11 This technical, ideologically neutral aspect of federalism was stressed by Bruno Leoni (1958). See also Leoni (1962). This means that Aaron Wildavsky's (1990) claim that 'if there is anything essential to a vibrant federal system, it is competition' is either false or more or less tautological.

12 Bernholz's proposal gives the right to secede not just to the member states, but also to transnational regions of ten million or more of inhabitants from the nation-states.

13 These barriers will be far less effective for capital and firms, of course. But this could be insufficient to prevent majorities from creating a favourable legal and fiscal environment for capital and firms, and still imposing 'confiscatory' taxation upon minorities. This possibility would be independent from any collusion between states for avoiding competition. On this last point see Benson (1990). Benson shows also that the states use the federal offices to reduce the impact of competition. In particular, the deduction of

state and local taxes from federal taxes means that the cross-state variation in taxes is substantially diminished.

14 Today the situation is clear. Either we re-establish the organisation of 'Europe on the dogma of unlimited national sovereignty and, sooner or later, the same causes involving the same effects, we shall again be led to confront one another in irresolvable conflicts, and finally in decline; or we shall have to establish our future . . . on new foundations'.

15 Probably the most relevant analysis of these matters is given by Michael Doyle (1983).

16 'political union must precede economic union. That is a fundamental condition. It is absolutely necessary to disabuse public opinion of the dangerous illusion according to which economic union can prepare the way for political union.'

17 The italics are mine.

18 See *Eurobarometer*, 1990, note 33. See in particular the Appendix to volume I, pp. 19–22. These data seem to contrast with a more specific poll concerning alternative 'National or joint Community decision-making?'. Here a much lower support is given to the EC versus national decision-making. For example, 37 per cent of the interviewees are in favour of EC decision-making about workers' representation, and 49 per cent in favour of national decision-making (cf. ibid.: p. A23). A reasonable explanation is that in expressing their support for the Social Charter the citizens expressed more their preferences for welfare than their preferences for the Community in itself.

19 Court of Justice of the European Communities, *Reports*, Procureur du Roi vs. Benoît and Gustave Dassonville, 11 July 1974, and Rewe-Zentral AG vs. Bundesmonopolverwaltung für Branntwein, 20 February 1979, respectively. Contrary to widespread opinion, the 'Cassis de Dijon' sentence did not establish mutual recognition as a principle replacing harmonisation. It was, instead, a device for preventing the 'acquis communautaire' from being verified, in view of the fact that harmonisation – explicitly contained in the EEC Treaty – will take a long time to be accomplished.

20 I have examined the problem of the democratic status of the Community institutions from a liberal point of view in Petroni (1990).

21 This is exactly the contrary of the position of the former EC Commissioner Peter Sutherland, who claimed that 'Je le reconnais bien volontiers: le droit n'est que l'instrument d'une politique' (Sutherland, 1988: 15). (I freely admit it: the law is only the instrument of politics.)

22 On this distinction and its relevance for contemporary Contractarian theory see Petroni (1984: 850–63).

23 A detailed project for a liberal Europe was presented by a group of intellectuals in 1993, named the European Constitutional Group. The writer is a member of this group. In this project great attention was given to the problem of how to prevent the judiciary of EU from expanding its competencies in such a way as to represent in itself a drive towards unwanted (or unnecessary) centralisation of power. On these matters see also the special issue of *Biblioteca della libertà*, 'La via dell'Europa passa da Maastricht?', XXX(195): 129.

BIBLIOGRAPHY

Allais, M. (1960) *L'Europe unie, route de la prospérité*, Paris: Calmann-Lévy.
Allais, M. (1990) *La construction européenne face aux bouleversements d'Est*, Paris: Centre d'Analyse Economique.
Aranson, P.H. (1990) 'Federalism: the reasons of rules', *Cato Journal* 10(1): 17–38.
Barry, N. (1989) 'The liberal constitution: rational design or evolution?', *Critical Review* 3(2): 267–82.
Benson, B.L. (1990) 'Interstate tax competition, incentives to collude, and federal influences', *Cato Journal*, 10(1): 75–90.
Bernholz, P. (1991) 'Quale constituzione', *Biblioteca della libertà* 26(1): 29–38.
Buchanan, J.M. (1977) *Freedom in Constitutional Contract*, College Station, Texas A and M University Press (reprinting *inter alia*, 'Pragmatic reform and constitutional revolution', 1969).
Buchanan, J.M. (1990) 'Europe's constitutional opportunity', in J.M. Buchanan *et al.*, *Europe's Constitutional Future*, London: IEA.
Doyle, M. (1983a) 'Kant, liberal legacies, and foreign affairs', *Philosophy and Public Affairs* 12(2): 205–35.
Doyle, M. (1983b) 'Kant, liberal legacies, and foreign affairs', *Philosophy and Public Affairs* 12(3): 323–53.
Doyle, M. (1986) 'Liberalism and world politics', *American Political Science Review* 80(3): 1151–69.
Einaudi, L. (1948) *La Guerra e L'Unità Europea*, Milan: Comunità.
Einaudi, L. (1956) *Lo Scrittoio del Presidente*, Torino: Einaudi.
Eurobarometer (1987) Brussels: Commission of the European Communities, March.
Eurobarometer (1990) Brussels: Commission of the European Communities, June.
Isaac, G. (1990) *Droit communautaire général*, Paris: Masson.
Kelsen, H. (1991) *The General Theory of Norms*, Oxford: Clarendon Press.
Leoni, B. (1958) 'Attualità del Federalismo', reprinted in *Scritti di Scienza Politica e Teoria del Diritto*, Milano: Giuffrè, 1980.
Leoni, B. (1962) 'L'idea Federale e il significato effettivo della CEE per un'Europa unificata', *Il Politico* 24(3): 481–94.
Massenet, M. (1990) *Le droit de l'Europe*, Paris: Institut Euro 92.
Mises, L. von (1983) *Bureaucracy*, New Haven and London: Yale University Press.
Petroni, A. (1984) 'Contrattualismo', *Il Mulino* 33(5): 850–63.
Petroni, A. (1990) *L'Europe, la justice et la démocratie*, Paris: Institut Euro 92.
Robbins, L. (1937) *Economic Planning and International Order*, London: Macmillan.
Robbins, L. (1963) *Politics and Economics*, London: Macmillan.
Röpke, W. (1958) *Jenseits von Angebot und Nachfrage*, Erlenbach-Zürich: Eugen Rentsch Verlag.
Rougemont, D. de (1991) *28 siècles d'Europe*, Paris: Christian de Bartillat (originally published 1961).
Schuman, R. (1963) *Pour L'Europe*, Paris: Nagel.
Sked, A. (1990) *James Buchanan on Europe*, London: The Bruges Group.

Sutherland, P. (1988) *1er Janvier 1993: ce qui va changer en Europe*, Paris: Presses Universitaires de France.

Tocqueville, A. de (1835) *Democracy in America, Volume I*, ed. P. Bradley, New York: Vintage Books, 1945.

Weber, E. (1976) *Peasants into Frenchmen: The Modernization of Rural France, 1870–1914*, Stanford, CA: Stanford University Press.

Wildavsky, A. (1990) 'A double security: federalism as competition', *Cato Journal* 10(1): 17–38.

7 Pluralism, contractarianism and European union

Percy B. Lehning

INTRODUCTION

The central question in this chapter is to inquire what it means when we speak about 'European citizenship' from the perspective of political theory. It raises the question if it makes sense to use the concept 'citizenship' beyond the borders of the nation-state.[1] The concept 'citizenship' is an essential contested concept. It is therefore argued in the first place which concept of possible conceptions should be used in the context of a nation-state, and also which institutional structure the specified concept requires. Next it is argued that, when discussing 'citizenship' across the borders of a nation-state, a 'postnational' conception of membership, so to speak, the concept that has been developed for application *within* the boundaries of the nation-state should be extended when we talk about a more universal concept of citizenship or – at least – when we defend a normative conception of citizenship for the 'European Union'.

CONCEPTIONS OF CITIZENSHIP

Theorising about citizenship requires that one takes up questions having to do with membership, (national) identity, civic allegiance, and all the commonalities of sentiment and obligation that prompt one to feel that one belongs to *this* political community rather than *that* one.[2] Conceptions of citizenship always 'defines those who are, and who are not, members of a common society' (Barbalet, 1988: 1).

Modern discussions on citizenship tend to take the ideas developed by T.H. Marshall (1964) in his lecture of 1949, 'Citizenship and Social Class', as a starting-point. I will do the same, be it that his ideas will be used in the first place for a political theoretical discussion of citizenship, and not for an (empirical) political sociological one. Marshall noted that citizenship is captured by full membership of a community, where membership entails participation by individuals in the determination of the conditions of their own association.[3] Different types of political community give rise to different forms of citizenship. He differentiated between three layers of citizenship rights, civil, political and social rights, and the institutions which support them.[4]

There is, here, clearly a focus on equality: citizenship is about expanding and enriching the notion of equality by extending its scope through civil, political and social rights (to public education, health care, unemployment insurance and old-age pension).[5] These rights are, of course, the traditional components of a welfare state – confronting the risks of sickness, old age, invalidity, unemployment and poverty. By guaranteeing these rights to all, a welfare state ensures that every member of society can feel like a full member of society. When fully developed, it embodies an idea of social justice: everyone is to enjoy entitlements which stand apart from and to some extent conflict with the outcomes of a market driven by considerations of efficiency.[6]

But citizenship is not only a legal status, defined by a set of rights and responsibilities. It is also an identity, an expression of one's membership in a political community. Marshall, as well, saw citizenship as a shared identity that would integrate previously excluded groups and provide a source of national unity in British society.

The discussion on citizenship can be summarized by stating that the concept of citizenship has two constitutive elements: *rights* and *identity* (or *belonging*). Each of these elements must be experienced in a geographical context, regardless of the fact how this geographical context is defined. The function of citizen can be discharged at a multitude of levels, from local government and functional interest groups through to the cosmopolis (Heater, 1990: 318–19).

If 'citizenship' has to do with rights and identity, then clearly two dimensions are involved: a 'liberal' one and a 'communitarian' one. Citizenship is 'intimately linked to the ideas of individual entitlement on the one hand and of attachment to a particular community on the other' (Kymlicka and Norman, 1995: 283). In that sense, the debate on citizenship is closely linked to the political theoretical debate between liberals and communitarians.[7] For our purpose, the important point to note is that the alternative theoretical perspectives of citizenship seem to be:

• a liberal one in which individual identity is emphasised; and
• a communitarian one, emphasising the cultural or ethnic group soli-

darity. There is a conjunction of identity: it is a 'communalist' identity, nationalism being an example.[8]

The problem with this dichotomy is that both liberal and communitarian theories pose threats to the idea of citizenship, once we have stipulated that it has – at the same time – two aspects: rights and identity. Both perspectives, the liberal and the communitarian one, jeopardize the idea of political community that is neither reducible to an aggregation of individuals nor to a conjunction of identity-constituting groups. Noting this problem, Beiner points out the tension between the egalitarian element of shared citizenship, appealing to what is shared across divergent cultural or ethnic groups, which may be undercut by the emphasis upon *particularistic* identity (Beiner, 1995: 14, 11).

This is the core of the problem when developing a coherent and realistic conception of citizenship: How to cope with two competing visions: liberal universalism and illiberal particularism? This is the so-called dilemma of the 'universalism/particularism conundrum' (Beiner, 1995: 12). What synthesis, or 'third' conception of citizenship, would help us out of this conundrum?[9] Such a conception has, first of all, to take into account the increasing social and cultural pluralism of modern society. Due to this fragmentation there is less convergence or agreement between members of a specific society than there once used to be. The question has become one of identifying what 'draws a body of citizens together into a coherent and stably organized political community, and keeps that allegiance durable?' (Beiner, 1995: 1).

The classical answer is, as mentioned above, given by Marshall. It can, however, be argued that his view runs into difficulties once the idea of a common civilization, a national unity, is challenged by the emergence of increasing social and cultural pluralism. Despite the possession of common rights of citizenship, members may feel excluded.[10]

How, then, to revise current definitions of citizenship to accommodate increasing pluralism of modern societies, and how to ensure that citizenship can indeed provide a common experience, identity and allegiance for the members of those societies, if there is no longer a shared or 'common heritage', or 'way of life' by reference to which citizens' rights can be defined?[11] On what should 'a shared citizenship identity that will supersede rival identities based on ethnicity' (Kymlicka and Norman, 1995: 309) be based?

Beiner, for instance, opts for a conception of citizenship, which he calls 'republicanism', in which 'civic bonds' are emphasised. It is 'the requirement that all citizens conform to a larger culture, but this culture is national–civic, not national ethnic. It refers to *political*, not social allegiance.' Membership in the state is identified, not membership in civil society (Beiner, 1995: 12, 8).

Habermas's answer to the conflict between the *universalistic* principles of constitutional democracies, on the one hand, and the *particularistic* claims of commitments to preserve the integrity of habitual ways of life, on the other, is 'constitutional patriotism': an idea that is neither individualist nor communitarian, neither liberal nor anti-liberal. It is based on the changed meaning of the term 'nation' from designating a pre-political entity 'to something that was supposed to play a constitutive role in defining the political identity of the citizen within a democratic polity' (Habermas, 1992: 3). A nation of citizens does not derive its identity from some ethnic and cultural properties, but 'rather from the *praxis* of citizens who actively exercise their civil rights' (Habermas, 1992: 3). This republican strand of citizenship, 'completely parts company with the idea of belonging to a prepolitical community integrated on the basis of descent, a shared tradition and a common language' (Habermas, 1992: 3). It is the political culture that is shared and that is the common denominator in which the constitutional principles are rooted, and which is the base for constitutional patriotism. It also means that – although the political culture is shared – all citizens do not share the same language or the same ethnic and cultural origins. On the contrary: they are aware that they are a part of a multi-cultural society.

The important point to note here is that the normative content of citizenship is dissociated from national identity based on '*ethnos*'.[12] Or, formulated in another way, '*demos*' and '*ethnos*' are separated when discussing 'citizenship'. In the interpretation of citizenship which tries to cope with the 'universalism/particularism conundrum', cultural or ethnic pluralism is not denied. What is denied is that this kind of pluralism should play a role for national identity. Here we touch upon a fundamental principle that is commonly shared in modern liberal theories.

In a liberal political order the state and its laws should remain *neutral* with respect to the varying conceptions of the good life held by individuals. This principle of neutrality is an important aspect of liberalism because, once one acknowledges the fact that there exist pluralism and reasonable disagreement on the idea of the good life, it enables individuals to have the freedom to choose between those ideas.[13] Neutrality is seen as a political ideal: it governs state policies and institutions, the public relations between persons and the state, and not the private relations between persons and other institutions. Liberalism is in this view not seen as a philosophy of man, but as a philosophy of politics.[14] Thus the consequence of the fact of reasonable pluralism is the denial that effective citizenship requires the state, or the political culture, to advance a particular vision of the good.

In the following it will be argued that a 'liberal democratic conception of citizenship', based on the political theory of John Rawls, gives a political theoretical argument for citizenship that guarantees 'shared citizenship identity'; a conception that can cope with the fact of cultural and ethnic pluralism of modern societies, and can create a common identity.

A LIBERAL DEMOCRATIC CONCEPTION OF CITIZENSHIP

Rawls's interpretation of liberalism differentiates between personal and political ideals, between *homme* and *citoyen*.[15] His political theory is a theory about *citoyen*. It formulates a liberal democratic theory of citizenship.[16] It is developed in response to 'the fact of reasonable pluralism': the fact that 'the diversity of reasonable comprehensive religious, philosophical, and moral doctrines found in modern democratic societies is not a mere historical condition that may soon pass away; it is a permanent feature of the public culture of democracy' (Rawls, 1996: 36).[17]

This pluralism raises a fundamental problem. No general and reasonable comprehensive doctrine can assume the role of a *publicly* acceptable basis of political justice, or be the base of a shared conception of citizenship. The public role of a neutrally recognized political conception of justice, and with it a conception of citizenship, is, then, to specify a point of view from which *all* citizens can examine before one another whether or not their political institutions are just. The political conception of justice comprises the substantive principles of justice, worked out to apply to the basic structure of a modern constitutional democracy. It involves, so far as possible, no prior commitment to any wider doctrine, but is formulated 'in terms of certain fundamental ideas seen as implicit in the public political culture of a democratic society' (Rawls, 1996: 13).[18]

These ideas on political liberalism, and its related conception of political justice, help us to answer how a political order in which citizens are deeply divided by conflicting and even incommensurable reasonable religious, philosophical, and moral doctrines, nevertheless can be stable and just (Rawls, 1996: 133).

There are three possible bases of a political order: one based on a universal acceptance of some particular comprehensive moral doctrine, one based on a *modus vivendi*, and one based on an 'overlapping consensus'. The crucial question is: which will guarantee stability and social unity within that political order?

The fact of reasonable pluralism rules out the first base of social union. Such agreement would require state coercion incompatible with democracy. A second possibility would be a *modus vivendi* agreement on basic principles of cooperation between groups of individuals with differing comprehensive moral doctrines, adopted by each party on the basis of its self-(group) interest. Rawls does not deny that this basis is consistent with the demands of democracy. But he argues against such a conception because it is inherently unstable, given its dependence on 'happenstance and a balance of relative forces' (Rawls, 1996: 148).

The third possibility is the idea of finding an overlapping consensus around a political conception of justice. Justification, when arguing about the question whether or not political institutions are just, has to proceed from some consensus. In this process of justification, an overlapping consensus plays an essential role. It is independent of shifts in the distribution of power, in contrast with the stability of a *modus vivendi*. Unlike a *modus vivendi*, it is a moral commitment in social union and thus less prone to desertion when it is to one's party advantage. And unlike a comprehensive moral doctrine, it demands only limited moral commitment. It can be adopted by people with differing reasonable comprehensive doctrines and justified varyingly, according to those same doctrines. It eventually creates citizenship with a common legal and political identity.

There is, as mentioned earlier, a sharp distinction between how we understand ourselves as citizens within the political system and how we may regard ourselves in our personal affairs or within certain intermediate associations. That is the reason Rawls sees the members of liberal democracies as having a *double identity*, resulting in two kinds of commitments and attachments (Rawls, 1996: 30–2). In their personal or private capacity they are seen as holding a conception of the good, a view about what a valuable life consists of. This is their non-institutional identity. But they have also a public, or institutional, identity, or their identity as a matter of basic law. Citizens have usually both political and non-political aims and commitments.

Citizens' identities should take precedence over personal identities in the sense that people will agree to continue to confine the pursuit of their personal conception of the good within the bounds prescribed by the principles of justice. We think of ourselves as citizens first, and as citizens we implement only measures which we can justify to others who do not share our personal conceptions of the good.

A liberal democratic conception of citizenship acknowledges the equal ability of citizens to pursue in life an ideal of the good of one's own choosing. It implies the rejection of the idea that the state should or could be seen as a community, defined by a substantive ideal.

In answering, then, the question how to cope with the dilemma of the 'universalism/particularism conundrum', our conclusion is that the principle of neutrality should be strongly defended against communitarian arguments. The communitarian view is that the political order must subordinate justice to a higher, more substantive ideal than the conceptions of the good citizens have.[19] Those communitarian ideas, however, make freedom, the freedom of choice of one's own conception of the good, impossible. But at the same time it should be stressed that this idea of freedom of choice does not reject the importance of the idea of 'belonging', or a 'sense of community'. But it does, indeed, reject, for instance, Sandel's suggestion that we should give up the 'politics of rights' for a 'politics of the common good'.[20]

For our present argument it is not really important if the substantive principles of justice that are worked out by an overlapping consensus are the Rawlsian principles of justice, 'justice as fairness', so to speak, or other principles of justice, as long as we agree that the principles formulate liberal ideas of justice, similar to but more general than 'justice as fairness'. It should be, in any case, principles that are basic to any welfare state, and give a political theoretical argument for the rights Marshall thought were constitutive for citizenship.

We have claimed that the overlapping consensus that results in a political conception of justice, shared throughout a political community, does generate a shared identity, indeed, a shared citizenship identity that will supersede rival identities based on ethnicity. It should be stressed that this idea, especially the idea of a public, or institutional, identity, is of course based on the fact that Rawls's theory is a contractarian theory. The basic idea of the conception of liberal democratic citizenship is that the public or institutional identity of citizens is contractually founded. And this means that the political community is potentially inclusive of all those remaining on the outside, legally, socially and physically, or inclusive of those who, in their private or personal lives, have a specific conception of the good, or different, ethnic background.

'Double identity' is a basic element in the Rawlsian contractual reasoning, and in our conception of citizenship. If one would argue

that 'identities are founded morally and pre-contractually' which means that the political community is a 'community of character, historically stable, an association of men and women especially committed the ones to the others, and endowed with a specific sense of their common life,[21]

we would not have been able to step out of the communitarian or *Gemeinschaft* outlook in the first place, and would not have been able to argue for a conception of liberal democratic citizenship which is neither universalistic, nor particularistic, and that can cope with the diversity of modern multi-cultural societies.

CITIZENSHIP AND CONSTITUTIONAL DEMOCRACY

What kind of institutions of the basic structure of constitutional democratic societies support this conception of liberal democratic citizenship, and would generate the public, or institutional, identity, or the identity as a matter of basic law of citizens? The institutions of constitutional democracies should satisfy four conditions stipulated by Rawls: respect for the rule of law; the protection of fundamental freedoms; secure, though not constitutionally entrenched, property rights; and conformity to the principle of majority rule in the making of public policy (Rawls, 1971: 221–43).

The first three of these conditions stipulate the requirements of constitutional government, and the fourth condition stipulates that the constitutional government should also be democratic. To be 'democratic' can be specified more precisely. Dahl has formulated five criteria that fully specify the democratic process. When making binding collective decisions the following conditions should not be violated:

1 Equal votes.
2 Effective participation.
3 Enlightened understanding.
4 Inclusiveness: the *demos* must include all adult members except transients and persons proven to be mentally defective.
5 Citizens have to exercise final control over their own agenda.

Final control of the agenda by the *demos* means that the *demos* must have exclusive opportunity to make decisions that determine what matters are and are not to be decided by processes that satisfy the first three criteria (Dahl, 1983: 95; 1985: 59–60).

We would stipulate, following Albert Weale, three further assumptions.[22] The first of these is that the majoritarian principle implies *a representative assembly with decision-making powers* and not merely consultative powers. The second assumption Weale has formulated is that there is a burden of proof upon the anti-majoritarian. This assumption is *the democratic premiss* of this chapter, namely, that *accountability is normally essential to the exercise of political authority*:

> Whenever there are political institutions making authoritative decisions for a population, then those institutions should be accountable to the population in the form of a representative assembly from which a government is chosen based upon the support of a majority of the representatives.[23]

The third assumption is that arguments about how best to justify one set of political arrangements relative to others ought ultimately to make reference to the interests of individuals, and cannot stop at the interests of collective entities like cultures, churches, communities or languages. This individualist assumption is, of course, in line with the argument, given earlier, that we have to take into account the social and cultural pluralism of modern societies, and that from a liberal perspective citizens should have the equal ability to choose their own conception of the good. It is, in fact, a minimal democratic criterion: the interests of each person are entitled to equal consideration, and in the absence of a compelling argument to the contrary, an adult is assumed to understand his or her own interests better than another (Dahl, 1983: 107).

To recapitulate, we see that the second constitutive element of citizenship, identity, requires a democratic process with accountability, based on shared principles of democracy and social justice. With this description of liberal democratic citizenship, we have criteria to judge to what extent 'citizenship' is in fact realized within the borders of a nation-state. Are principles of political justice in place that are basic to a welfare state? And is, indeed, government based on political principles of accountability?

Our next question is: What are the implications of this conception of liberal democratic citizenship in a situation where we cross the boundaries of a nation-state, and step into a pan-national arena?

EUROPEAN CITIZENSHIP

When we discuss 'citizenship' across the borders of a nation-state, the concept of liberal democratic citizenship developed for a nation-state should be extended. The question becomes now: What are the implications, when we talk about a more universal concept of citizenship or – at least – when we give a political theoretical defence of a liberal democratic conception of citizenship for the 'European Union', of the two constitutive aspects of citizenship, *identity* and *rights*, and of the institutions and practices of political cooperation?

The argument is twofold. In the first place, there is no reason to think that across the boundaries of the nation-state the problem of cultural or ethnic pluralism will vanish. On the contrary, one would say! The conception of citizenship that can cope with the problems raised by pluralism *within* a nation-state should also be applicable in a situation *across* borders where there is probably even more pluralism.

Second, as has been argued, the liberal democratic conception of citizenship is 'liberal' for the following reasons. We may differ, but we are equally citizens, and it is as citizens that we advance claims in the political realm and assess the claims made by others. Equal citizenship is based on universalist liberal principles. And identity, so we argued, should be based on the democratic constitutional principles rooted in a political culture which serves as the common denominator. The consequence of these ideas is the denial that effective citizenship requires the state, or the political culture, to advance a particular vision of the good. It is hard to imagine that arguments for equal concern and respect for persons defended within a nation-state would vanish in any 'pan-national' conception of citizenship.[24] Thus, in a European context the minimal democratic criterion is still in place, with its democratic premiss of accountability.

What institutional structure, then, does the specified conception of citizenship require to be able to create 'shared citizenship identity', or to create 'constitutional patriotism' on a pan-national scale? And what can we say about 'European social rights'? Let us start with the assumption that 'federalism' will be the most adequate institutional form of government that fits the requirements of the liberal democratic conception of citizenship. What kind of political theoretical arguments, or 'good reasons', could be given to defend the choice of this form of government? Systematising the normative principles of federalism, we will use a social contract approach, because such an approach is useful for helping us to organise our moral intuitions and draw consistent inferences about principles and institutions. It allows us to abstract from arrangements that are the result of bargaining processes in real-world negotiating with its defects, 'such as short-sighted political expediency, lack of empirical and historical knowledge, and unfair bargaining strength' (Norman, 1994: 84).

Several additional arguments for using a social contract approach when defending a federal structure could be given. Remember that we have in a European context, just as in the case of the nation-state, to deal with the problem of pluralism. Let us also remember that in the context of the nation-state we argued for using Rawls's contractarian approach. The public or institutional identity of citizens is contractually founded, eventually leading to the idea of a 'double identity' that citizens have.

Let us add, broadening the scope to a European context, the following. Meehan has noted that through the construction of contractarianism,

> nationality and, hence, citizenship rights can be legally *acquired* through *ius solis* as in France and Italy. The second construction resembles the emphasis on nationality by descent, *ius sanguinis*, in Germany and the United Kingdom. If the modern association of citizenship with nationality rests on a legal or contractual view of communities, then it would not be too difficult to envisage a new form of it at the European level.
>
> (Meehan, 1993: 21–2)

And we can note the same as we already did in the context of citizenship within the nation-state: if citizenship is based on a communitarian or *Gemeinschaft* outlook, it would be much more difficult to envisage a new form of citizenship at the European level. Good reasons, then, to use a contractarian approach. But there is still another reason to support this choice. Habermas has remarked that:

> In a future Federal Republic of European States, the same legal principles would also have to be interpreted from the vantage point of different national traditions and histories. One's own national tradition will, in each case, have to be appropriated in such a manner that it is related to and relativized by the vantage points of the other national cultures. It must be connected with *the overlapping consensus* of a common, supranationally shared political culture of the European Community. Particularist anchoring *of this sort* would in no way impair the universalist meaning of popular sovereignty and human rights.
>
> (Habermas, 1992: 7; my italics)

Remember that we have already used the idea of an overlapping consensus in the context of the nation-state, to be able to cope with the problem of pluralism. Arguing for a specific institutional form, federalism, this idea of an overlapping consensus is used once again, but now in this broader context.

FEDERALISM, OVERLAPPING CONSENSUS, AND DEMOCRATIC AUTHORITY

In applying Rawls's contractarian approach for an argument for federalism we retain the key elements and motivations of his theory. Stability is not only a primary requirement for a well-functioning democratic nation-state, but also for a federation. And analogous to Rawls's three possible bases of political order within a nation-state, we suggest that there also could be three possible bases for types of federal commitment: one based on a '*modus vivendi*', one based on a universal acceptance of some particular comprehensive moral doctrine, and one based on an 'overlapping consensus'.[25] The question is, once again, which one will guarantee stability and social unity in a situation where we know that there are, not only within a nation-state, but also across the boundaries of nation-states, deeply dividing, conflicting conceptions of the good.

Let us assume that democratic states would not band (or remain) together in a federation if they did not perceive it to be to their mutual advantage. It does not follow, however, that federal relations are nothing more than a *modus vivendi*. In fact, for reasons parallel to those advanced by Rawls, it is reasonable to suppose that a federation based merely on a *modus vivendi* – one in which pan-federal identification, tolerance and solidarity do not develop – will remain inherently unstable: a partner that had for generations been a net beneficiary might defect the moment it felt called upon to be a net contributor.[26] At the same time, federations differ from unitary states because federal partners (and their citizens) did not want to relinquish all of their autonomy, sovereignty and identity. This is already a reason to believe that federal partners do not have to or wish to accept deep, monolithic conceptions of citizenship and identity as the basis of their union. We can go further and say that they do not all have to share the same reasons for accepting the federal union and their citizens do not have to identify with the federal state in the same way or to the same extent. Norman's conclusion is that the most suitable basis for a just and stable federal union will thus be 'some form of overlapping consensus that demands more of federal partners and their citizens than a *modus vivendi*, but less than a comprehensive, monolithic conception of shared identity and citizenship' (Norman, 1994: 88).

Rawls's idea that members of liberal democracies have a double identity is relevant here once again. In their personal or private capacity they have a non-institutional identity. But the public, or institutional, identity, or their identity as a matter of basic law, may be broadened now to encompass being a member of a federation, if that federation is based on an overlapping consensus.

We can be more specific about this overlapping consensus based on principles that are to serve as a stable basis for cooperation between federal partners, given the fact of reasonable pluralism. Just as in the case of one specific constitutional democracy, the overlapping consensus in this case should work out substantive principles of justice, which apply to the federation as a whole. And it is, once again, not really important if these principles are the Rawlsian principles of justice, or other ones, as long as they formulate liberal ideas of justice, similar to but more general than 'justice as fairness'; principles, in other words, that form the traditional components of a welfare state, but that now apply to the federation as a whole – confronting the risks of sickness, old age, invalidity, unemployment and poverty in all parts of the federation.

This overlapping consensus shared throughout a federation should generate a shared citizenship identity that will supersede rival identities based on, in the first place, national identities. And in this case, where we discuss a federation it may be necessary, more so than in the case of a specific constitutional democracy, to take measures to encourage development of a moral commitment to the federation to prevent a 'fall back' into an unstable *modus vivendi*. This moral commitment would positively consist of developing a sense of solidarity and tolerance among the citizens of the new federation to encourage the emergence of a new pan-national, shared citizenship identity, a 'sense of community'.

Norman points to the flip-side of this argument for a development of solidarity and shared identity. It may be more important to list factors that may have the potential to destabilise a pluralistic federation such as the perception of citizens of any sub-unit that it is unfairly disadvantaged, or that it is under-represented in key federal institutions, or that there is mutual distrust and a lack of mutual understanding (Norman, 1994: 91).

We have questioned the assumption that 'citizenship' necessarily adheres to the sovereign nation-state. The idea of an overlapping consensus in the context of a federal Europe, in conjunction with the idea of a 'double identity', leads us not only to the idea of 'belonging' that comes with the concept of national identity, but also to 'belonging' that goes with a number of different levels of social organisation: the neighbourhood, the town or city, the county, and the region, in addition to the nation.

The identity is, then, derived from the practice of citizens who actively exercise their rights. Just as in the case of citizenship within the context of a pluralistic, multi-cultural nation-state, it is the political culture that is shared and that, eventually, should lead to a shared citizenship identity. Once again, political allegiance is what counts, and 'a sense of community' should develop from that common denominator in which the constitutional principles are rooted. It would lead, in Habermas's terms, to 'constitutional patriotism' on a federal level.[27]

We would argue, then, that the second constitutive element of liberal democratic citizenship is, also at the European level, defined by a public, or institutional, identity, an expression of one's membership in a political community. We also stipulated how this 'shared citizenship identity' is constituted by the existence of certain institutions and practices of political cooperation on the European level. And, we add, just as in the case of a nation-state, it is defined by the requirements of a democratic process with accountability, based on shared principles of democracy and social justice.

CONCLUSION

Recapitulating the core elements of liberal democratic citizenship, we have argued that identity and rights must be experienced in a geographical context, regardless of how this geographical context is defined. Thus, they have also to be experienced in the context of the European Union. Arguing that members of liberal democracies have several identities, public identity can encompass being a member of the European Union. However, to be able to develop this 'shared citizenship identity', certain institutions and practices of political cooperation have to be in existence at the level of the European Union. It requires a democratic process with accountability, rooted in a political culture of the European Union, based on shared principles of democracy and social justice, which serve as the common denominator. The principles of social justice that should apply to the Union as a whole form the traditional components of a welfare state, confronting the risks of sickness, old age, invalidity, unemployment and poverty in all parts of the Union.

The fact that not only modern democratic nation-states are confronted with increasing social and cultural pluralism but the Union as a whole is also, means that all citizens do not share the same language or the same ethnic and cultural origins. On the contrary: they are aware that they are a part of multi-cultural societies. The normative content of the concept of liberal democratic European citizenship takes this into account. A European *demos* cannot be based on ethno-cultural terms, on an idea of ethnic homogeneity.[28] In fact, the concept of liberal democratic European citizenship parts company with (national) identity based on *ethnos*, and is a plea for solidarity and tolerance among the citizens of the European Union.

This description of the requirements of a liberal democratic conception of citizenship gives us, once again, but now in the context of the European Union, criteria to judge to what extent 'citizenship' is in fact realized. This chapter does not inquire about the match between the normative conception of 'European citizenship' defended here and the reality of the European Union. Offhand, however, it seems safe to say that the requirements that are formulated here to be able to speak of 'European citizenship' are presently not met within the European Union.[29]

NOTES

1 One should add that it would be surprising if arguments for or against 'citizenship' that go beyond those borders and deal with the 'European Union' would have no implications for an even wider application of the concept.

2 See also Beiner (1995: 19).

3 See also Barbalet: 'In the modern democratic state the basis of citizenship is the capacity to participate in the exercise of political power through the electoral process' (Barbalet, 1988: 2).

4 See Marshall (1964: 78).

5 See also King and Waldron (1988: 423).

6 We are not so much interested in our present discussion about the correctness of Marshall's empirical claim about the succession of rights, and that this has a universal pattern. Of course, in England he sees them as having taken hold in three successive centuries.

7 See, for instance, for an overview Mulhall and Swift (1992). See also Taylor (1989).

8 See for this distinction also Beiner (1995: 13–14).

9 See David Miller for another distinction of conceptions of citizenship. He labels them 'liberal, libertarian and republican'. The main lines of the liberal conception 'can be seen in the classic statement by T.H. Marshall. Citizenship should be understood as a set of rights enjoyed equally by every member of the society in question' (1995a, 435). Miller includes Rawls's theory in this liberal conception. An example of the libertarian conception of citizenship is to be found in Nozick's *Anarchy, State, and Utopia* (1974), according to Miller. The third conception is a republican conception of citizenship and is the one Miller underwrites.

10 See Kymlicka, 1989, especially Chapter 9.

11 Kymlicka and Norman (1995: 286).

12 See on the reasons why ethnicity cannot in itself be a basis for political association or, for that matter, for common citizenship also Barry (1991: 167–9).

13 The importance of this principle in liberal theory is recognised by many different theorists. See, for instance Larmore (1987), Rawls (1996), Sandel (1982).

14 Larmore (1987: 129).

15 See especially the publications of Rawls after 1985, culminating in his *Political Liberalism* (1996).

16 See also Hill (1993: 73).

17 Miller's critique of this liberal conception of citizenship is that it cannot deal with pluralism, in contrast to his own republican conception of citizenship (Miller, 1995a: 443). I have to admit that I cannot follow his argumentation with regard to this point. See also note 9.

18 The political conception of justice Rawls has in mind is, of course, his own conception: *justice as fairness*. It is intended to solve the fundamental question of political justice, namely, what the most appropriate conception of justice is for specifying the terms of social cooperation between citizens regarded as free and equal persons (Rawls, 1971; 1985: 234; 1987: 7; 1996).

19 In this chapter I discuss only what is called 'teleological communitarianism' as formulated by, for instance, Sandel and MacIntyre. I do not elaborate on non-teleological communitarian ideas as formulated by, for instance, Charles Taylor (1989; 1992).

20 See also Larmore (1987: 119) for stressing the importance of 'belonging'. Sandel's suggestion for a politics of the common good is to be found in Sandel (1984: 17). In 1996 he is still of the same opinion. See Sandel (1996).

21 See Meehan (1993: 22).

22 See for an extensive argument on these assumptions: Weale, 'Majority rule, political identity and European Union', Chapter 8 in this volume. My argument for the *democratic* requirements of 'liberal democratic citizenship' owes a lot to the ideas formulated in that chapter.

23 See Weale, in this volume, Chapter 8, p. 126.

24 But see, for instance, Goodin (1988); Miller (1995b). See also the debate triggered by Martha C. Nussbaum's essay 'Patriotism and cosmopolitanism', in Martha C. Nussbaum *et al.* (1996).

25 This idea of adapting and applying Rawls's idea of an overlapping consensus to the problem of federalism is recommend by Wayne J. Norman (1994). It should be pointed out that Rawls himself does not apply this idea to federalism. He does, however, apply his social contract theory to the 'law of peoples', that is to say, he asks how the law of peoples may be developed out of liberal ideas of justice similar to but more general than the idea of 'justice as fairness'. He is especially interested in the principles and norms of international law and practice. See Rawls (1993).

26 See also Rawls's explanation for rejecting the '*modus vivendi*' perspective when it is characterised as a treaty between two states whose national aims and interests put them at odds (1996: 147).

27 See also Habermas (1996). Compare also the arguments offered by Weale and Nida-Rümelin in their chapters in this volume.

28 See for several objections to the idea of a *demos* based on ethno-cultural terms Weiler *et al.* (1995: 9–24). See also Habermas's reaction to arguments that a European Union should require certain cultural homogeneity among its people (Habermas, 1996: 137).

29 See for an inquiry into the fit between the concept of liberal democratic European citizenship developed in this chapter and the actual situation in the European Union, the final chapter of this volume: 'European citizenship: a mirage?' by Percy B. Lehning.

BIBLIOGRAPHY

Barbalet, J.M. (1988) *Citizenship*, Milton Keynes: Open University Press.

Barry, B. (1991) 'Self-government revisited', in B. Barry, *Democracy and Power: Essays in Political Theory*, vol. 1, Oxford: Clarendon Press; pp. 156–86.

Beiner, R. (1995) 'Why citizenship constitutes a theoretical problem in the last decade of the twentieth century', in R. Beiner (ed.) *Theorizing Citizenship*, Albany: State University of New York Press, pp. 1–28.

Dahl, R.A. (1983) 'Federalism and the democratic process', in J.R. Pennock and J.W. Chapman (eds) *Liberal Democracy*, New York and London: New York University Press, pp. 95–108.

Dahl, R.A. (1985) *A Preface to Economic Democracy*, Berkeley, CA: University of California Press.

Goodin, R.E. (1988) 'What is so special about our fellow countrymen?', *Ethics* 98: 663–86.

Habermas, J. (1992) 'Citizenship and national identity: some reflections on the future of Europe', *Praxis International* 12(1): 1–19.

Habermas, J. (1996) 'The European Nation State: its achievement and its limitations. On the past and future of sovereignty and citizenship', *Ratio Juris* 9(2): 125–37.

Heater, D. (1990) *Citizenship: The Civic Ideal in World History, Politics and Education*, London and New York: Longman.

Hill, G. (1993) 'Citizenship and ontology in the liberal state', *Review of Politics* 51: 67–84.

King, D.S. and Waldron, J. (1988) 'Citizenship, social citizenship and the defence of welfare provision', *British Journal of Political Science* (18): 415–43.

Kymlicka, W. (1989) *Liberalism, Community and Culture*, Oxford: Clarendon Press.

Kymlicka, W. and Norman, W. (1995) 'Return of the citizen: a survey of recent work on citizenship theory', in R. Beiner (ed.) *Theorizing Citizenship*, Albany: State University of New York Press; pp. 283–322.

Larmore, C.E. (1987) *Patterns of Moral Complexity*, Cambridge: Cambridge University Press.

Marshall, T.H. (1964) 'Citizenship and social class', in *Class, Citizenship and Social Development*, New York: Doubleday. (The essay was first published in 1949.)

Meehan, E. (1993) *Citizenship and the European Community*, London: Sage.

Miller, D. (1995a) 'Citizenship and pluralism', *Political Studies* 43: 432–50.

Miller, D. (1995b) *On Nationality*, Oxford: Clarendon Press.

Mulhall, S. and Swift, A. (1992) *Liberals and Communitarians*, Oxford: Blackwell.

Norman, W.J. (1994) 'Towards a philosophy of federalism', in J. Baker (ed.) *Group Rights*, Toronto, Buffalo and London: University of Toronto Press, pp. 79–100.

Nozick, R. (1974) *Anarchy, State, and Utopia*, New York: Basic Books.

Nussbaum, M.C. *et al.* (1996) *For Love of Country: Debating the Limits of Patriotism*, Boston: Beacon Press.

Rawls, J. (1971) *A Theory of Justice*, Oxford: Oxford University Press.

Rawls, J. (1985) 'Justice as fairness: political not metaphysical', *Philosophy and Public Affairs* 14: 223–51.

Rawls, J. (1987) 'The idea of an overlapping consensus', *Oxford Journal of Legal Studies* 7: 1–25.

Rawls, J. (1993) 'The law of peoples', in S. Shute and S. Hurley (eds) *On Human Rights*, New York: Basic Books, pp. 42–82; 220–30.

Rawls, J. (1996) *Political Liberalism*, New York: Columbia University Press; paperback edition with new introduction.

Sandel, M. (1982) *Liberalism and the Limits of Justice*, Cambridge: Cambridge University Press.

Sandel, M. (1984) 'Morality and the liberal ideal', *The New Republic*, 7 May: 15–17.

Sandel, M.(1996) *Democracy's Discontent: America in Search of a Public Philosophy*, Cambridge, Mass., and London: The Belknap Press of Harvard University Press.

Taylor, C. (1989) 'The liberal-communitarian debate', in N. Rosenblum (ed.) *Liberalism and the Moral Life*, Cambridge, Mass.: Harvard University Press., pp. 159–82.

Taylor, C. (1992) 'The politics of recognition', in A. Gutmann (ed.) *Multiculturalism and the 'Politics of Recognition'*, Princeton, NJ: Princeton University Press, pp. 25–73.

Weiler, J.H.H. *et al.* (1995) 'European democracy and its critique', *West European Politics*, 18: 4–39.

8   Majority rule, political identity and European union

Albert Weale

The general purpose of this chapter is to inquire as to what help might be expected from the normative theory of constitutional democracy in the design of political institutions for an integrated Europe. Since this general problem is an impossibly large one for a single paper, I shall narrow down the range of inquiry by considering one particular element in the theory of constitutional democracy, namely, the principle of majority rule, and I shall consider how respect for the principle of majority rule might adequately be reflected in a European constitutional and political order. Indeed, I shall narrow the range of inquiry even further by considering one aspect of this question. I shall focus upon the issue of whether national political identity is so strong as to suggest that the future of Europe ought to be conceived in terms of political cooperation between independent nation-states, for which the idea of popular majoritarianism is an irrelevance, rather than a European union with an identity of its own for which the principle of majority rule would be an essential legitimating element.

I shall assume throughout the chapter that constitutional democracies are identified by the four conditions stipulated by Rawls (1972: 221–43): respect for the rule of law; the protection of fundamental freedoms; secure, though not constitutionally entrenched, property rights; and conformity to the principle of majority rule in the making of public policy. Roughly speaking, the first three of these conditions stipulate the requirements of constitutional government, and the fourth condition stipulates that the constitutional government should also be democratic. None of the conditions is unambiguous, of course. To take just one example, there is a persistent debate in politics and political theory as to whether the fundamental freedoms are to be construed positively or simply negatively. For the purposes of this chapter, I shall take the political theorist's privilege of bracketing difficult or refractory questions, and I shall assume that, however these issues are resolved, there exists a set of institutional forms whose elements bear sufficient family resemblance to one another for us to be able to distinguish constitutional democracies from other forms of government.

In discussing the problems with which I am concerned, I shall be making three further assumptions. The first of these is that the majoritarian principle implies a representative assembly with decision-making powers and not merely consultative powers. Frederick the Great of Prussia was once alleged to have said: 'My people and I have come to an agreement which satisfies us both. They are to say what they please, and I am to do what I please.' It is, of course, precisely the possibility that there may be constitutional freedoms without democracy that requires us to add the majoritarian condition to the others. Isaiah Berlin's (1969: 129–30) claim that in the Prussia of Frederick the Great, or in the Austria of Joseph II, persons of imagination, originality and creative genius as well as 'minorities of all kinds' were less persecuted and felt the pressure of institutions and customs less heavy upon them than in many an earlier or later democracy may or may not be true as an historical observation. The definitional point remains: constitutional democracies are a subset of constitutional governments more generally, and are distinguished from other members of the set by their adherence to the principle of majority rule in the formation of public policy or legislation.

The second assumption operates more powerfully in the background of the arguments I shall pursue here, and in this chapter I shall not attempt to justify it directly. It is that there is a burden of proof upon the anti-majoritarian. This amounts to something like the following principle: whenever there are political institutions making authoritative decisions for a population, then those institutions should be accountable to the population in the form of a representative assembly from which a government is chosen based upon the support of a majority of the representatives. My burden of proof assumption is merely what I shall call the democratic premiss of this chapter, namely, that accountability is normally essential to the exercise of political authority. There are, of course, many arguments about the strength of this burden of proof, and it is not my intention to examine these arguments here. I shall simply assume that legitimate government standardly has to take an accountable form, and that special reasons have to be adduced when political decision-making takes place without the benefit of mechanisms of majority rule.

I should say, in passing, that I take the relevant majority in this case to be a popular rather than a legislative majority. When talking about representative government based upon the majoritarian principle, it is crucial to distinguish between legislative and electoral majoritarianism.

This is not always done, even in sophisticated discussions of democratic institutions. Thus, Lijphart's (1984) categorisation of democracies in terms of a consensual or consociational model on the one hand, and a majoritarian Westminster model, on the other, entirely ignores the fact that legislative majorities in Westminster systems often rest on electoral pluralities. This is typically the case in the UK and New Zealand (Lijphart's prime examples of majoritarian systems); and within these systems legislative majorities may not even have the support of electoral pluralities, the most recent example being the 1978 victory of the National Party in New Zealand. As John Stuart Mill (1861: 302–25) pointed out, legislative majoritarianism may well be a poor expression of electoral majoritarianism, and one of Mill's arguments for proportional representation, in Chapter 7 of *On Representative Government*, was that it was only through proportional representation that electoral majoritarianism could be secured. It is not my purpose to pursue this line of argument in the present context, although it may provide one part of the account as to what the commitment to democratic majoritarianism involves.

My third assumption is also methodological, and it is that arguments about how best to justify one set of political arrangements relative to others ought ultimately to make essential reference to the interest of individuals, and cannot stop at the interests of collective entities like cultures, churches, communities or languages. Of course there may be all sorts of reasons why political systems take measures to protect cultures, churches, communities and languages, but I am going to assume that the ultimate justification will refer to the interests of individuals who compose these collective entities. This individualist assumption in part is intended to capture the broadly liberal point that in a pluralistic culture citizens cannot expect all other citizens to share their ends, although they ought to be able to expect them to respect their interests. It is also, I think, truer to the way that most arguments about democracy are conducted, since nowadays we think about representation usually in terms of individuals rather than, say, estates. The exception to the standardly individualistic assumptions on which the modern conception of representation rests is provided by territorial units within federal political systems. Typically in federal systems the constituent territorial units of the federation are represented in their own right within a broader system of representation. In subsequent sections, I shall be principally concerned with the theoretical justification of this exception. Suffice it to say for the present that my individualist premiss makes it harder, not easier, to provide a theoretical rationale for federalist practice.

In thinking about European union, the issues of institutional design that will be at the forefront of my concerns are those that pertain to the European Union (EU). This is not because I have a personal preference for 'deepening' rather than 'broadening' the EU, nor because I regard the establishment of flourishing constitutional democracies in eastern Europe as a secondary task. It is simply that my estimate would be that European union is most likely to arise from the evolution of EU institutions rather than some other body. Moreover, the problem of the 'democratic deficit' within the EU is one that has loomed large in public discussion, and, as I shall seek to show, the application of the majority principle is the central issue in conceptualising the problem of the democratic deficit.

MAJORITY RULE AND EUROPEAN UNION: A PRELIMINARY ARGUMENT

If we start from the democratic premiss that when political institutions make authoritative decisions for a population, then those institutions should be accountable to the population in the form of a representative assembly responsible for matters of government, we seem to have a simple, and yet effective, way of identifying the democratic deficit of the EU.

In seeking to conceptualise the notion of a democratic deficit, there are at least three dimensions of decision-making power and authority that need to be considered. The first is the *locus* of decision-making authority: which body or bodies have the power to make decisions? The second is the *scope* of authority: over what questions is decision-making power exercised? And the third is the nature of the *decision-rule*: what principle of aggregation do authoritative bodies use when they make decisions? These three aspects of locus, scope and decision-rule can be invoked in a variety of ways when criticising the democratic deficit of the EU. Thus members of the European Parliament claim that it is undemocratic that decision-making power is concentrated in the Commission or the Council of Ministers, rather than in the directly elected representatives of the people, and this is essentially a point about the locus of authority. Similarly, the democratic credentials of the EU can be questioned by reference to the scope of the issues that are subject to majority rule, or the nature of the decision-rule used, and these criticisms come together in the observation that reform of the Common Agricultural Policy is delayed because the policy sector is not one covered by the principle of majoritarianism.

How are these dimensions of locus, scope and decision-rule affected

by any arguments about the character of democracy and the extent of
the democratic deficit in the EU? It is clear that the present powers of
the EU are an exercise of political authority over citizens in the member
states. In other words, we have the conditions under which the majoritarian principle, reflecting the democratic premiss that I identified
earlier, would apply. Such a principle would seem to imply that a
directly elected representative European assembly should be the locus
of political power from which a government should be chosen reflecting
a majority of those voting. The appropriate decision-rule would also
appear to be that of majority voting within the representative assembly,
and the scope of the majority principle would only be restricted by the
need to protect the fundamental freedoms.

In other words, a straightforward application of majoritarian principles would yield an irreversible shift of decision-making power and
competence away from bodies like the Commission and the Council of
Ministers, which do not discharge their democratic accountability by
retaining the confidence of representatives of a majority of the electorate, to the European Parliament, a majority of whose representatives
would then become the locus for the governance of Europe.

Many would not find this conclusion puzzling or unexceptionable,
but surely it moves too quickly from premiss to conclusion. Those who
favour an increased pace of European integration invariably conceive
the future of Europe in terms of federalism. That is, they conceive that
a European government would necessarily involve the sharing of power
between different levels of government, each representative of different
interests. Yet, the structure of the argument that I have outlined yields
only a rationale for a unicameral legislature; it does not yield a rationale
for the sort of federal regime that even the most passionate integrationist has favoured in recent debates over political union. Surely, when
political theory is so out of accord with political practice, something is
amiss. This is not to say that unreflective political conviction is right, or
that one should be necessarily dazzled by the prospect of a single-
chamber legislature operating under majoritarian principles elected by
constituencies as diverse and far-flung as Copenhagen and Calabria or
Bangor and Berlin. Unreflective political conviction may be wrong and
novelty in political institutions soon wears off. On the other hand, I am
persuaded by the intuition that says that a European union would have
to have a federal structure if it were fully integrated, and I should like to
explore the problem further.

There are, I think, two broad responses possible to the claim that
federalism is a necessary feature of democratic European institutions.
The first is to say that the existence of federalism ultimately reflects the

facts of political power, and that principled political argument simply has to yield to pragmatic institutional considerations. After all, there are long-standing and well-established national governments within the EU, and the politicians who have established their reputations and political capital in those systems are not going to wish to give up the advantages they currently enjoy, unless they can see compensating advantages (as is arguably the case for some political leaders in the Low Countries, who could expect to have much more influence on the world stage in an integrated Europe than in their own countries). Moreover, it is possible to erect a whole theory of federalism on these pragmatic considerations, as William Riker (1964) showed when he accounted for the existence of federalism in terms of a political centre that wished to secure territorial borders, but lacked the military power to impose itself on outlying districts. On this account, federalism becomes a second-best solution to full political integration across the territory of a state, and legitimate authority is divided because, for military reasons, it cannot be brought under one command. Analogously, we can say that there is no locus of political power within Europe that is capable of holding down by the simple weight of force the diversity of political communities that currently exist.

This pragmatic response is undoubtedly a possible one, and for many people the issue will just end there. But I am inclined to think it inadequate, largely because it neglects or underplays the issue of legitimacy. An essential element in the exercise of political authority is the belief in the legitimacy of that authority, and legitimacy, as David Beetham (1991) has shown, inevitably involves the giving of reasons. Can we find some force of argument, rather than simply an argument of force, that would help us discern a principled basis to a democratic European federalism?

When we find that a political theory is significantly out of accord with political practice, there are a number of possible responses. One is to say, as Sidgwick (1901: 473–8) said of his own version of 'reflective equilibrium', that we require a theoretically coherent statement of principles to provide a critical component to our political thinking and to challenge our unreflective intuitions. In the present case I have already conceded, however, that this response is implausible, since federalist convictions seem so fundamental to the understanding of those who favour European union. A second response is to identify a mistaken assumption or principle at the foundations of our reasoning and to amend our premises. Yet the democratic principles that I sought to identify at the beginning of this chapter would seem to be the minimum necessary to provide an account of the legitimacy of the modern democratic state. We must therefore find an alternative way of accounting for the discrepancy between theory and intuition, and in the present case I suggest that the culprit is the tacit assumption that lies behind much thinking about the nature and scope of political power, namely, that a political community requires an identity grounded in something other than the practice of politics. This assumption, I shall argue, is characteristically present in the reasoning of otherwise divergent accounts of democracy, and in the next section I seek to show how this assumption operates in one classical argument about the allocation of power in federal regimes.

MAJORITY RULE AND POLITICAL IDENTITY

It is sometimes suggested that discussions on EU political union should consider the parallel of the American states before the constitutional convention of 1787. In this case we have thirteen loosely confederated states, ultimately driven towards union by the demands of external defence, and the economic advantages of integration – or at least the brilliant intellectual interpretation of these trends offered by the federalists, most famously in the *Federalist Papers*. There are, of course, many disanalogies, as well as analogies, in this comparison, but let me explore it for what it is worth in the words of one elegant piece of political analysis:

> It was the wish of one party to convert the Union into a league of independent states, or a sort of congress, at which the representatives of the several nations would meet to discuss certain points of common interest. The other party desired to unite the inhabitants of the American colonies into one and the same people and to establish a government that should act as the sole representative of the nation, although in a limited sphere. The practical consequences of these two theories were very different.
>
> If the object was that a league should be established instead of a national government, then the majority of the states, instead of the majority of the inhabitants of the Union, would make the laws; for every state, great or small, would then remain in full independence and enter the Union upon a footing of perfect equality. If, however, the inhabitants of the United States were to be considered as belonging to one and the same nation, it would be natural that the majority of the citizens of the Union should make the law.
>
> (Tocqueville, 1835: 122)

In this passage de Tocqueville counterposes the idea of a league of independent states with the idea of one and the same people, each idea forming independent and antagonistic principles of political cooperation. As de Tocqueville points out, with characteristic wryness, the two principles were supported by different interests and, although incompatible, they were in fact combined in the principles of representation embodied in the Senate and the House of Representatives: 'the result was that the rules of logic were broken, as is usually the case when interests are opposed to arguments' (Tocqueville, 1835: 122–3).

De Tocqueville's contrast between a league of independent states and a unified people seems to me to be central to the problems involved in applying the principle of majority rule to the institution of a united Europe. Is political union to be conceived in terms of inter-governmental cooperation or is it to be thought of as the creation of an integrated political system? Is such a union to be conceived as an association of states, or at least entities with some political independence, or is it to be conceived as a representative of a single people? Are we talking of a union of collectivities or a society of individuals? Thus, in terms of the EU, the most radical way to conceptualise the problem of the democratic deficit would be to shift the locus of authority away from the Council of Ministers operating under unanimity or weighted majority voting towards the Parliament, operating under simple majority voting. The most conservative way to conceptualise the problem would be to argue that there really is no problem of the democratic deficit so long as the governments that are represented at the Council of Ministers are accountable to their domestic parliaments. One way to make sense of this dispute is to see it as an example of a dispute about the nature of political identity that is presupposed in the principle of majority voting.

As a rule of social choice the method of majority decision has the interesting and, by comparison with other rules of social choice, unusual characteristic that it is the subject of a formal existence theorem. May (1952) was the first to identify the necessary and sufficient conditions for the method of majority decision, showing that the method could be characterised in terms of four properties: anonymity, issue neutrality, positive responsiveness and universal domain. The key conditions here, for our purposes, are anonymity and issue neutrality.

The method of majority decision works by counting preferences and making that alternative the winner in a pair-wise choice that has a higher number of preferences in its favour than the alternative that it is confronted with. In this process, no attention is paid as to who holds which preference. Since the rule depends only upon the numbers of persons who favour one alternative relative to another, the identities of the individuals holding the preferences will not make any difference to the result. In this sense the method of majority decision is anonymous. It is also issue neutral. Since it is only the number of persons who favour one alternative over another that counts, the content of the preferences being weighed can also make no difference. The method of majority decision will count preferences for war against peace in just the same ways that it counts preferences for whether dog owners are required to hold licences or not. Note, in particular, that anonymity and issue neutrality are defining conditions of the method of majority decision, so that these features are not incidental to the operation of the majority principle, but are essential characteristics of its operation.

If the members of a political community find that they can operate satisfactorily with the method of majority decision, this is likely to be in part because these features of anonymity and issue neutrality are unproblematic for them. Since anonymity means that no special relationship holds between any particular issue and any particular individual, a community in which the method of majority rule operated over relevant issues is one in which individuals are deprived of a decisive say in particular questions. To highlight the significance of this, contrast a community operating with the majority principle with a community operating a system of rights. A system of rights is simply a way of tying the choice about what to do about certain issues to the decisions of a particular subset of persons within a political community. Thus, within a system of rights, the principle of anonymity does not hold: we always need to know who has the right to decide. The property of issue neutrality means that this anonymity will hold throughout the whole set of issues that come within the domain of social choice.

When de Tocqueville identified the terms of the constitutional dispute over the articles of confederation, he assumed that it would be natural for members of 'one and the same nation' to adopt the principle of majority rule, based upon the representation of individuals. In essence, de Tocqueville was assuming that a common national identity made the adoption of the principle of majority rule unproblematic, and this in turn expresses a Rousseauian view that, in the appropriate circumstances, majority voting expresses an underlying identity of interests: 'The first man to propose them [laws] merely says what all have already felt, and there is no question of factions or intrigues or eloquence in order to secure the passage into law of what everyone has decided to do' (Rousseau, 1762: 247).

The converse of this view is that where, again to use de Tocqueville's phrase, 'separate interests and peculiar customs' exist, then the appropriate unit of representation should not be individuals operating according to the principles of majority voting, but the collectivity constituted by the individuals who share an identity. This was of course the argument notoriously developed by Calhoun (conveniently ignoring the conflict between slaves and slave-owners) in connection with the 'peculiar' institutions of the South. Calhoun's argument was that the existence of local interests that were antithetical to the interests of American society at large should be protected by a system of concurrent majorities, in which the decision-rule would be to take

> the sense of each interest or portion of the community which may be unequally and injuriously affected by the action of the government separately, through its own majority or in some other way by which its voice may be fairly expressed, and to require the consent of each interest either to put or to keep the government in action.
>
> (Calhoun, 1853: 20)

Both de Tocqueville's observation that the rules of logic were broken in the formation of the US Constitution and Calhoun's insistence that the only logical way to respect distinct interests and customs rest upon the same premiss: that distinct political communities, with their own identity, should be protected from the unrestrained operation of the principle of majority rule, and this premiss in turn is merely the converse of the Rousseauian assumption that a functioning democracy requires a strong sense of communal identity.

Stated in such general terms this argument is valid. If there really is a deep separation of interest between members of a political community, then the simple weight of numbers should be restricted in the making of decisions. There are several reasons why this might be so. Some of these reasons are consequentialist and prudential. Unless special interests are recognised, considerable problems of civil disobedience or civil disorder are likely to arise. Some of the reasons stem from a commitment to human rights: numerical majorities can deprive minorities of their rights, and to avoid this typically requires some non-majoritarian process of decision-making. Some of the reasons stem from the impossibility of a majority ever knowing what constitutes the interests of a minority that is distinct in outlook and circumstance. Certainly from beyond a veil of ignorance it would seem highly imprudent to consent to a system of single majority rule without any further constitutional protection if there was a prospect that you would end up a member of a culturally or politically distinct minority.

The difficulty is not with the general principle of respect for distinct political identity, however, but with knowing, for example, whether

Europe satisfied the conditions under which this principle can be unambiguously applied. How, in particular, might separate interests and peculiar customs be constituted? Part of the myth of nineteenth-century nationalism involved the assertion that a distinct social identity could be distinguished in terms of which peoples were constituted. One version of this myth was that nations were constituted from a common stock, so that at one time French schoolchildren had to memorise genealogies going back to Priam, because it was held that the French came from the Franks, who themselves came from Troy (Zeldin, 1977: 10). Other putative bases of national identity included: possession of a common language and literature, pride in common historic traditions, community of social customs or community of religion.

Ernst Renan and Henry Sidgwick, among others, effectively rebutted such arguments by pointing out that there were many nation-states in which none of these conditions held. One could find countries with a common language, like Ireland, which lack a common identity, and countries, like Switzerland, without a common language. Moreover, it is clear that social and economic developments since Sidgwick and Renan were writing (including the internationalisation of economic life, greater communication and travel, increased secularisation and the migration of peoples) have further undermined any such possible bases for nationality forming the basis of political identity in the modern nation-state.

There seem to me to be two possible consequences to draw from these observations in the present context. The first would be to search for a political unit other than existing nation-states, that might be a plausible candidate for political identity along the lines of some pre-existing social characteristic, like language or religion, and the most obvious candidate would be the 'region', meaning by that term an entity like Scotland, Pays Basque or Bavaria. The other alternative is to accept the nation-state as the focus of identity, but deny that this reflected any pre-existing social characteristic. Let me turn to consider the second line of argument.

The view to be considered here is that the nation-state may in practice be a focus of identity, even though there are no underlying social bases of unity like commonality of language or religion. Sidgwick puts the possibility with his customary clarity:

> I think, therefore, that what is really essential to the modern conception of the State which is also a Nation is merely that the persons composing it should have a consciousness of belonging to one another, of being members of one body, over and above what they

derive from the mere fact of being under one government; so that if their government were destroyed by war or revolution, they would still hold firmly together.

(Sidgwick, 1891: 214)

More recently, Brian Barry (1989: 168–70) has advanced a similar argument by distinguishing between ethnicity, statehood and nationality. Ethnicity is to be understood on the model of tribal relations, that is, in terms of the largest social group related as kin, and its most significant characteristic is that ethnic identity cannot be acquired by an act of will. Statehood is a juridical concept, in which membership is given by a set of legal rules. Nationality, by comparison with both of these concepts, is identified dispositionally as the willingness to make sacrifices in order to bring about or sustain a state in being. This disposition will typically transcend ethnic identification and it comprises more than the simple fact of common citizenship.

What I now wish to suggest is that this dispositional account of national identity can be generalized to other forms of political identity. As well as the consciousness of belonging to one another that goes with the concept of national identity, there can be a consciousness of belonging that goes with a number of different levels of social organisation: the neighbourhood, the town or city, the county, and the region, in addition to the nation. Each of these levels of social organisation can provide the opportunity for political cooperation, and in terms of the account of political identity that I am advancing, we are to think of political identity as based not upon a pre-existing social or cultural identity but instead as constituted by the existence of certain practices of political cooperation. As members of a political community we are to think of ourselves as persons linked to one another by the institutions in which we participate, but the existence of these cooperative practices itself is taken as the basis for our political identity.

In advancing this dispositional account of political identity, I do not mean to exclude the possibility that political units may on occasion reflect a deep structural or cultural affinity amongst individuals, such that those individuals see political self-government as the expression of an underlying ethnic or cultural unity. Separatist movements in Europe typically seek to revive or reassert traditional cultural forms of communal identification, in which languages or traditional sporting, literary and religious events provide key elements. Just as Irish nationalism in politics in the nineteenth century grew out of the revival of these cultural activities, so contemporary separatist movements in Europe draw upon the symbols of common identity to affirm a political identity. Yet, however widespread such movements are, it is clear that a general account of political identity in Europe cannot rest upon the positing of these cultural or linguistic identities, for many stable political units fail to exhibit the appropriate social or cultural characteristics. Few contemporary German *Länder* have long historical antecedents, for example. Nevertheless, within such political units there may well exist the conditions for a distinctive political identity, resting upon the practice of political cooperation.

If political identity exists in this form, then it is reasonable to suppose that it will issue in varieties of collective preference, depending upon the histories and practices of the regimes in question. Historically different political communities will have made different choices about matters of collective choice ranging from the number of swimming pools they have to their spending on science and education. On the present set of assumptions there is no need to assume that these choices express or reflect national character. They are simply the choices that have been made within the existing institutions of political cooperation, and they should be respected for that reason.

If this argument is taken seriously, then it leads to two implications. First, it undercuts any inference from the idea of political identity to the Europe of the Regions, leaving out of account the nation. The Europe of Regions requires that regional identities be rooted in social characteristics like language, culture or religion. Since there are no nation-states that exhibit the requisite degree of homogeneity, it would follow from a social identity thesis that the nation-state level would disappear between Community-wide institutions and the region. But this argument is undercut once we acknowledge that political identity does not require any pre-existing social identity, but merely the existence of a practice of political cooperation. The principle of reserving certain matters for decision at the level of the nation-state would follow, on this account, naturally from the fact that the nation-states of Europe have historically had large decision-making powers. Perhaps this is most clearly shown in the general acknowledgement that countries will not want to send soldiers to fight in a war that has been decided by a majority of *other* countries.

The second implication that might be drawn from this line of argument is a strong version of the subsidiarity principle. The principle of subsidiarity reserves decision-making competence to that level of government that can best decide on the matters at issue. Since nation-states have a large amount of decision-making competence, it would seem to follow, on the present argument, that they should retain as much as possible. Of course, this retention of decision-making competence will have to be restricted in certain ways once it is accepted that there are spill-over effects on other countries and once the task of completing economic integration has been accomplished. These concessions may, of course, open the way for many more powers at the European level over time, just as the interstate commerce clause of the US Constitution has opened the way for federal policies and programmes rather than state ones. However, given the existing powers and traditions of European countries, I assume that politically they are in a much stronger position to resist federal intrusion than the states of the union have been in the US.

I say that the second implication that might be drawn is that of a strong version of subsidiarity, but I think this is only one possible interpretation, and there is another. If identity is constituted by participation in a common set of political institutions, then there is no reason why identity cannot be fostered at the European level as much as at the level of the nation-state or the region. Indeed, instead of the view that individuals have one basic political identity from which all the others are derivative, we might suppose that individuals can have multiple identities ranging from the neighbourhood through the city and region to the nation-state and continental level, and perhaps even to the global level. Of course the concerns expressed and attended to at these levels will be different, but they may certainly be complementary and perhaps even inter-related (as when people are concerned about public transport in their city because they are worried about global climate change). So, to view political identity as constituted in the practice of political cooperation is to allow for a variety of bonds of union. In this sense a political system can encompass *both* de Tocqueville's 'one and the same nation' and 'the separate interests and peculiar customs' of the political institutions of which it is comprised.

Moreover, there is no general reason for believing that activities carried out at the level of the nation-state have more legitimacy than activities carried out at the level of continental Europe solely because of the differences of scale. Indeed, on some matters, for example, social security and social insurance, the arguments in favour of a large scale of organisation are considerable, because the pooling of risks is more extensive and hence the burdens of payment are more broadly spread. In these matters there is reason for thinking that the organisational advantages lie with the highest tier of effective government. In the US, a political system generally hostile to the federal organisation of social services, the old-age social security programme enjoys high levels of legitimacy compared to programmes like Aid to Families with Dependent Children, and in large measure this is to be attributed to the superior effectiveness and efficiency of the federal programme

(Marmor *et al.*, 1990, Chapters 4 and 5). Sub-federal political identities need be no bar to the efficient organization of public services at the federal level, especially when there are in-built economies of scale in respect of the service in question.

What conclusions can we draw from the argument so far? The first and most important inference, because it serves as a premiss of the remainder of the argument, is that political identity, as constituted by participation in a set of cooperative political practices, can take a complex and multiple form, within which individuals can possess a number of distinct, but related, identities. The contrast that de Tocqueville presupposes between a unified people and separate institutions and customs is overdrawn. The concerns attended to in respect of these political identities will vary, but if we consider the highest conceivable tier of government in Europe, namely, a set of federal European institutions, there is no reason in principle why this tier should not form a focal point for political identity. Moreover, in respect of those programmes for which it was responsible, there is reason to hold that the federal tier of government should be directly accountable to the citizens of Europe on the same terms as other systems of political authority are accountable. In practice, this would amount to transferring primary responsibility for government and legislation to a body securing the confidence of representatives of a majority of the population in a directly elected chamber. This is not to give the federal tier of government a broad range of programmes or unfettered power in the pursuit of those programmes. However, it is to imply that democratic accountability should not be mediated through existing national governments, but that legitimacy should be secured by means of majoritarian representation for those spheres of public policy for which the federal level is accountable.

THE STRUCTURE OF FEDERALISM

If I am right in supposing that the idea of political identity implies no barrier to the application of majoritarian principles of political accountability, then there are direct implications about the principles that ought to govern the locus of political authority within European institutions. In short, the principle ought to be that the authority to make decisions should rest with a team of elected politicians who enjoy the confidence of a majority of the elected representatives within a directly elected assembly. In practice, with regard to existing EU institutions, this would imply a decisive shift in the locus of authority away from the Commission and the Council of Ministers and towards the Parliament.

Given that the argument so far has operated within the premises of the theory of constitutional democracy, we can assume that the scope of the majority principle would exclude the power to change or alter the fundamental freedoms. This is a common restriction in constitutional democracies, and it draws upon the long-established principles of the separation of powers. What can we say, however, about the allocation of responsibility within the set of public policy questions properly decided by the simple majority principle? Although I have already argued that there are reasons of effectiveness and efficiency why some functions ought to be discharged at the highest level of authority within a federation, it seems impossible to supply a general formula that would enable impartial observers to allocate functions reasonably between different tiers of government. There are a number of reasons for this. Specific functions are rarely simple in themselves. Thus, we can distinguish between different levels of responsibility in respect of education, with some forms of education better regarded as the responsibility of higher tiers of government and other forms the responsibility of lower tiers. Responsibility for universities might appropriately be placed at a higher level of federal government than primary schools, for example. Moreover, technologies change. A function like pollution control that may have been suitably placed at a low level of government to deal with local pollution may be better placed at a higher level when production technologies give rise to trans-boundary pollution. Economies of scale can turn into diseconomies at a higher level of administration when local knowledge is essential to the successful discharge of a function, as is the case with decisions on land-use planning. In short, there are a variety of reasons why we should not expect a simple set of principles by reference to which we could allocate the functions of government within a federal European system.

In advancing the view that a rather traditional federal structure is not precluded by the complexity of political identity in Europe, I am also suggesting that a European federation could legitimately use the same decision-rule, namely, that of simple majority voting within a given sphere of competence, as other representative democracies. The scope of this rule would of course be bound by the protection of the fundamental freedoms and the allocation of political responsibility between different tiers of government. So, on the account of political identity that I wish to advance, the conditions for the legitimate exercise of political power resemble those of other federal political systems. Perhaps this is not surprising. After all, the problems faced by Europeans in constructing a workable and legitimate political constitution are not so very different from those faced by other peoples.

BIBLIOGRAPHY

Barry, B.M. (1989) *Democracy, Power and Justice*, Oxford: Clarendon Press.

Beetham, D. (1991) *The Legitimation of Power*, Basingstoke and London: Macmillan.

Berlin, I. (1969) *Four Essays on Liberty*, Oxford: Oxford University Press.

Calhoun, J.C. (1853) *A Disquisition on Government*, edited and introduced C. Gordon Post, Indianapolis: Bobbs-Merrill, 1953.

Lijphart, A. (1984) *Democracies*, New Haven, CT, and London: Yale University Press.

Marmor, T.R., Mashaw, J.L. and Harvey, P. (1990) *America's Misunderstood Welfare State*, New York: Basic Books.

May, K.O. (1952) 'A set of independent, necessary and sufficient conditions for simple majority decision', *Econometrica* 20: 680–4.

Mill, J.S. (1861) *On Representative Government*, in J. Gray (ed.) *On Liberty and Other Essays*, Oxford: Oxford University Press, 1991.

Rawls, J. (1972) *A Theory of Justice*, Oxford: Oxford University Press.

Riker, W.H. (1964) *Federalism: Origin, Operation, Significance*, Boston and Toronto: Little Brown and Co.

Rousseau, J.-J. (1762) *The Social Contract*, in G.D.H. Cole (ed.) *The Social Contract and Discourses*, London: J.M. Dent and Sons, 1973.

Sidgwick, H. (1891) *The Elements of Politics*, London: Macmillan.

Sidgwick, H. (1901) *The Methods of Ethics*, sixth edition, London: Macmillan.

Tocqueville, A. de (1835) *Democracy in America, volume 1*, ed. P. Bradley, New York: Vintage Books, 1945.

Zeldin, T. (1977) *France 1845–1945, volume 2, Intellect, Taste and Anxiety*, Oxford: Clarendon Press.

9 Emancipatory politics between universalism and difference
Gender perspectives on European citizenship

Ursula Vogel

CITIZENSHIP IN A EUROPE OF DIFFERENCE

What will the new Europe mean for women? Will the same processes that have exploded national and ideological boundaries and remapped the geographical terrain of politics also break down the patriarchal divisions bound up with the old European order in both West and East? Judged by the historic moment of women's involvement in the revolutions of '1989', the prospects already look bleak. 'Where have all the women gone'? (Einhorn, 1991: 16). This summary of failed hopes reflects upon developments which everywhere in East and Central Europe seem to have turned the clock back on the promise of women's full participation in the democratic process. Not only have the costs of economic transition fallen disproportionately on women, in terms both of higher unemployment rates and of the contraction of public child-care provisions (Corrin, 1992). What little public space was guaranteed to them under the old regimes, i.e. in the formal representations on decision-making bodies, has all but collapsed: 'Women are being "liberated" into the home' (*The Guardian*, 1 May 1992). At the frontiers of '1992', the most pessimistic projections conveyed similar apprehensions: in a Europe unified by the imperatives of a single, deregulated market the majority of working women would be relegated to a new economic underclass of poorly paid, ill-protected and under-skilled workers. Moreover, lack of organisational resources and lobbying power at the political level would but replicate the conditions which define their status as second-class citizens in most European nation-states (*Labour Research*, October 1989: 19–20; Local Government Information Unit, *Briefing*, September 1989: 2–3).

'How new, then, is the new for women?' (Crowley *et al.*, 1991: 1). If we widen the focus of this question to include other groups who are likely to lose out in the processes of disintegration and realignment, the social map of citizenship in the new Europe would bear a close resemblance to that of the old order. The internal coherence of this emerging multinational association would be guaranteed primarily by the common interests of those groups capable of taking advantage of the new opportunities of competitive expansion. As in the nation-state, the demands of political stability would have to be met by some common standards of minimal welfare provisions to compensate economically vulnerable 'minorities' – the unemployed, pensioners, ethnic groups, refugees, women. In this setting, group differences would crystallise into familiar hierarchical patterns. The challenge that the new Europe would pose to political theory would be of a quantitative rather than qualitative order. Arguments about citizenship would, no doubt, have to make allowance for size and complexity as well as for new institutional frameworks of community membership. But their normative core, embodied in universalist definitions of citizens' rights, could transfer easily from the plane of the nation-state to the next higher level of a dozen or more of such states.

We might, however, imagine another scenario of European integration – one in which the levelling of national boundaries will have the effect of deepening and transforming the impact of difference upon the assumed homogeneity of citizen status. The familiar divisions by class, gender and race would be multiplied by the plurality of legal and administrative systems and by the proliferation of languages, religions, ethnic and regional cultures. The multidimensional dynamic of diversity might well explode that capacity for assimilating conflicting group interests which common language attributes to 'pluralist democracy' and 'the nation-state'. On this reading, 'Europe' signals, at worst, a degree of fragmentation that would render the idea of citizenship meaningless; at best (which we will here assume), it expresses the idea of a polity constituted by difference. Its chances of cohesion would to no small degree depend upon whether those groups which in the first model are disposed of as 'minorities' can be integrated as citizens. If we understand the goals of integration in terms of a 'people's Europe', rather than in terms of imposed administrative uniformity, then difference of many different kinds must be the raw material of citizenship.

This Europe of difference confronts normative political theory with seemingly incompatible imperatives. In order to lend substance to the idea of a single European citizenship, it has to identify a core of universal entitlements and a common framework of institutional guarantees. Without some such unifying principles, however minimal, to define a common status of membership, there would be no base from which individuals (or groups) could invoke the mutual obligations that the members of a political community owe to each other. At the same time, political theory needs to treat group difference as an essential part of citizenship rather than aim at levelling it into uniformity. Difference, however, is itself an ambiguous term, with both negative and positive connotations. The conception of citizenship that we are looking for must allow us to distinguish between difference as an unjustifiable criterion of social and political inequalities, on the one hand, and difference in the form of legitimate claims to group autonomy, on the other.

What feminist political theory can bring to this task is an intellectual tradition firmly rooted in international solidarity and global orientations. As far as the history and politics of the women's movement are concerned, women have no fatherland. Nor does a theory that grew out of the European Enlightenment have any substantive links with the principle of nationality and its embodiment in the nation-state. While its philosophical origins as well as its political praxis thus commit feminism to universal values, its most distinctive and original contributions to political theory over the past two decades have, paradoxically, centred on a radical critique of the universalist foundations of modern citizenship. It has established the permanent contestability of the concept and of its presumed capacity to include all who are formally members of a given community. This critique has evolved from the experience that women's formally accredited status as equal citizens has had but limited purchase in 'engendering' the institutions of Western democracies (Phillips, 1991). It similarly reflects on the fact that feminist reinterpretations of political philosophy have largely failed to change the dominant orientations of that discipline (Pateman and Gross, 1986: 6; Shanley and Pateman, 1991: 1). In seeking to explain the persistence of women's exclusion and marginalisation, some writers have altogether abandoned the search for an as yet unrealised potential of genuinely universal principles in modern liberal and egalitarian doctrines. They have turned, instead, against the very universality of claims made on behalf of individuals as moral agents, right holders, citizens (Pateman, 1988; Young, 1989). The feminist critique of universalism bears upon the argument of this chapter in several important respects. It stresses the divisive and all-pervasive effects of gender difference, sometimes to a point of irremediable gender opposition at which the question of women's and men's common citizenship would become obsolete (Dietz, 1992: 76ff.). It points, on the other hand, to the positive attributes of 'difference' and to its potential for rebuilding the idea of citizenship from the basis of group identity and diversity. It should not be surprising that a political theory strung between these two poles will not offer neat or comprehensive conclusions. Its procedures will be experimental and its answers uncertain, imprecise and open-ended.

What does the feminist critique of universalist principles imply for the conceptualisation of European citizenship? I shall consider this question by looking at some of the policy statements in which the European Community has set out its commitment to gender equality. This narrow focus has obvious drawbacks. First of all, it does not encompass the whole of the 'new Europe' and settles for a confined space when the most urgent demand would be to think beyond the restrictive legacies of a divided Europe. Second, while the approach is not state-centred it is primarily concerned with questions of political, or 'constitutional', integration (Tassin, 1992: 170). It thus does not allow for the freedom of exploration of what we might derive from an imagined 'community' or from the diffusion of citizen activity into everyday practices of family life, friendships, neighbourhood, *ad hoc* groupings, social movements, etc., which have proved so effective in breaking the singular link between citizenship and the state (McClure, 1992: 123). Against both these wider settings, the perspective on the European Community has the advantage of linking the argument about universalism and difference to the concrete institutional features of an emerging polity. It will allow us, in particular, to assess the impact of an autonomous system of legal norms outside and above the nation-state; to identify the problems of social cohesion that gender divisions pose for a much enlarged community; and to point to new arenas of public debate across Europe where diversity itself can be seen to foster a sense of common membership.

Initiatives for 'improving the status of women in society' (Council Resolution on the Third Action Programme, 1991: 27) occupied a prominent place on the political agenda of European policy-makers in the 1970s and 1980s. If anywhere, it is in this field that the Community can be credited with innovative programmes and with the determination to wield the authority of an autonomous political association to extend the meanings of citizenship beyond the confines of the nation-state. Admittedly, the impact so far has been limited. Following the original intentions set out in the Treaty of Rome, Community laws have attached the rights of European citizens primarily to the status of individuals as workers (Meehan, 1991). My argument reflects this perspective and the constraints implied in it. It will deal less with women's political profile in representative institutions and decision-making processes than with their citizen entitlements to a just distribution of the rewards and opportunities of work. Since Community involvement in this domain has been dictated by the overall aim of promoting 'equality between women and men' (Community Charter, 1989), I shall examine the meanings of equality that could guarantee a common status of European citizenship to individuals of both sexes. In this, my intention is not to give a detailed and exhaustive account of legislative policies but, rather, to trace some decisive shifts in the normative orientations that have informed them.

On one reading of the equality principle – and it is the dominant one in our documents – women are to participate in the economic development of the Community on the same terms as men. Policies aim at the formal equalisation of rights, i.e. at the removal of all forms of legal discrimination against individuals on grounds of their sex. A second interpretation takes account of the fact that male and female workers are differently situated in relation to the rights and opportunities of citizenship. It endorses 'positive action' as a means of enabling women, as a group, to reach the starting-point of equality. Both these conceptions have problematic implications. They apply a 'universal' standard of citizen rights which, however, already incorporates certain assumptions about gender difference. They uphold the hegemonic or assimilationist thrust in the idea of citizen equality with its tendency to absorb and suppress the specificity of women's claims. A third formulation of equality aligns itself with the conditions of emancipatory politics. It tests the resourcefulness of universal ideas of citizenship by their capacity to respond to the significance of difference. As we shall see, this implies a redrawing of the boundaries between the public and the private spheres and, in consequence, a remapping of the constitutive terrains of 'political' theory.

To approach the possibilities of European citizenship from a gender perspective is not to claim a paradigmatic case capable of representing all the disparate forms of relevant group difference. There are, no doubt, certain affinities between gender, culture, ethnicity, class, or age as relations of difference. But each one of these is constituted within a particular context and by a specific history of exclusion. If we expect conceptions of citizenship to take account of difference, we cannot set out from yet another problematic assumption of homogeneity under the umbrella, for example, of 'oppressed groups'. We have to begin with the recognition of contextuality.

PATRIARCHAL EQUALITY: THE ASSIMILATION OF DIFFERENCE

The general principles which have informed the equality policies of the European Community can be found in the Treaty of Rome, in the

various Equality Directives, Recommendations and Action Programmes issued by the Council of Ministers and the Commission, and
in the decisions of the European Court of Justice. As stated in these
documents, European law consistently speaks the language of 'equal
treatment for men and women' (Byre, 1988). Thus the Social Charter
takes care to distinguish this domain of citizen equality from others
which refer to provisions of special assistance owed to adolescents, the
elderly, the disabled (Community Charter, 1989). The conspicuous
absence of the term 'working mothers' further illustrates the normative
symmetry in the status of women and men who, as workers, are entitled
to the same rights and have the same obligations. It is the comparison
between the sexes in relation to the same or similar categories of work
upon which claims to justice need to base themselves. As several judgements of the Court of Justice have shown, men too can avail themselves
of legal remedies against unequal treatment – on the same, strictly
gender-neutral grounds of comparative disadvantage (Kloss, 1992: 210;
The Guardian, 16 November 1991).

Many women in different member countries of the Community have,
no doubt, benefited from polices which have equalised classifications of
pay, access to employment, training and promotion and which have,
similarly, eliminated gender differentiation from the conditions of
retirement and of statutory and occupational social security (Carter,
1988, Chapter 6; Kloss, 1992). In asserting the authority of an
independent legal system Europe has helped to create 'a floor of basic
rights for the individual' (Byre, 1988: 20). Within the European context
the law has come to be seen as a 'more flexible, more principled and
more dynamic' force which can be used to fight women's battles in
countries with more rigid and inefficient legal systems (Hanna, 1992:
16). Most importantly in this respect, the European Court of Justice
has provided an autonomous tribunal, outside the nation-state, where
the normative force of the equality principle can be tested. These court
cases, whether brought by individuals against their employers or by the
Community itself against one of its member states, have, on the one
hand, lent higher public visibility to the systematic disadvantages which
still mark women's inferior status as citizens. They have, on the other
hand, exposed numerous traditional practices of differential treatment
as no longer capable of legitimation. That as individual citizens women
are entitled to the rewards and opportunities of work just like men, that
is, in their own right and not by virtue of their marital and familial
status, this simple postulate of unconditional equality has long been
absorbed into the proclaimed beliefs of democratic societies. But when
it is applied to concrete instances of discrimination in the workplace it

may still be perceived and resisted as a radical challenge. For it collides with habitual modes of thinking according to which differential treatment of women and men does not even appear as unjust discrimination but as the 'natural' ordering of social relations. European law thus provides an arena for normative debates which may not exist in domestic legal systems and in which customary expressions of gender difference take on the meaning of a violation of citizen rights. The recent decision of the Irish High Court to prevent a rape victim from having an abortion in Britain is a case in point. In the light of European law, this ruling constituted just such a violation. What was at issue here was not primarily the right to life of the unborn child but one of the basic, and least disputed, entitlements of European citizenship – the right of personal freedom of movement. To the extent, then, that the appeal to women's rights as European citizens might compel national governments to change their laws, 'the process of lawmaking would actually be important in raising consciousness. It would make rights more useful – and more used' (Hoskyns, 1988: 41).

However, will advantages of this kind outweigh the problematic assumptions that underlie the very principle of women's equality with men? How is this norm derived? Whose norm is it? The language of equal opportunities revolves around a single reference point – the rights of 'workers'. What this seemingly neutral category will not tell us is that many women would have nothing to claim if they were to appeal to the rights of European worker–citizens. They could not meet the normative prerequisites of entitlements which are tied to typical patterns of male employment. That is, the required symmetry in the situation of individuals as workers takes no account of the fact that the gendered, segregated structure of the labour market itself consigns the majority of women workers to positions from which they cannot compete with men on equal terms.

Indeed, there are good reasons to fear that, irrespective of those equality guarantees, the progressive deregulation of the European market will primarily and adversely affect women (Commission of the European Communities, 1991). Structural upheavals resulting from the drive towards increased competitiveness are expected to lead to job losses first of all in those sectors of industry where women are most heavily concentrated. Enhanced scope for flexibility in business strategies will, on the other hand, lead to an expansion of 'a-typical work' (i.e. part-time, freelance, on-call or home-based employment). While this latter tendency would actually increase the number of jobs available to women, it would, at the same time, enlarge and consolidate the female employment ghetto at the margins of the regular labour market.

For these would be jobs of low skill, low pay and minimal security to which, moreover, the rights of European workers do not yet apply. Driven by the dynamic of rationalisation the process towards European economic unity would thus exacerbate the structural inequalities between women and men 'which virtually every statistic so overwhelmingly confirms' (*Labour Research*, 1989: 22).

Women's continued isolation in a 'ghetto' outside the domain of formal equality illustrates the claim forcefully argued by Pateman and other feminist critics, namely, that the language of equal right itself masks a hierarchical division between male and female which is deeply embedded in the universalist legacies of normative political argument (Gatens, 1992; Pateman, 1988; Phillips, 1991; Young, 1989). The point is not that those premises have in the past not been consistently applied to women. The flaw cannot be traced to limiting historical circumstances alone. Rather, the moral and political significance of sexual difference is presumed in the abstract figure of 'the individual' as agent and right bearer. The hierarchical order of marriage and the separation of this private sphere of unequal right from the domain demarcated by political principles have traditionally guaranteed the equality of men as citizens, on the one hand, and the separate and subordinate status of women, on the other (Vogel, 1994). Although this divide is today no longer enforced by law, it lives on in the ideological codes and social practices that we have inherited from the past. It has become entrenched in conceptions of equality that take no account of women's position in the family and its constraining effects on the conditions of citizenship.

If, to return to our example, women's present disadvantages were but so many instances of their arbitrary, legal exclusion from the general rights of citizens in the past, then they could, indeed, be remedied by equalisation policies of the kind that we have discussed above. On the other hand, the remedy must, if the meaning of equality itself is still structured by patriarchal assumptions, fail to connect with the reality of women's lives. In that case, the promise of a European citizenship which bestows equal rights on women and men as 'workers' would remain an illusion. (Controversies in Britain about the equalisation of state pension rights have been a telling example of the burden that the paradigmatic figure of male employment and the inferior social value of domestic labour impose upon women). According to the European Court's 'Barber-judgement' of May 1990 the differential retirement age for women (at 60) and men (at 65) constitutes a case of sexual discrimination (in this instance, against men). The cheapest option, and the one favoured by the British government, of 'levelling upwards' (to 63 or 65) would meet the requirements of formal equality. The costs of that transition to equality, however, would fall on the great number of women workers who rely exclusively on the state pension scheme. Since they are prevented by long career breaks from building up adequate occupational pensions, their already inferior rights would be further diluted (Hughes, 1991: 18; Hunter, 1991: 16; 1992: 33).

THE IMPACT OF DIFFERENCE: ENABLEMENT FOR EQUAL CITIZENSHIP

Since the early 1980s the Community has initiated a number of special Action Programmes (covering the period from 1982 to 1995) to address the broader, non-legal causes of gender hierarchy in the labour market. Policy-makers acknowledge that despite undeniable achievements in the field of anti-discriminatory legislation 'inequalities continue to exist'; women's contribution to European economic development is still systematically undervalued (Council Resolution on the Third Action Programme, 1991: 26). These programmes are concerned less with the formal and uniform rights that pertain to women as individual citizens than with the collective disabilities of a 'distinct category of workers' (*Commission of the European Communities*, 1991: 147). Among the factors that have prompted a reorientation of equality policies the documents list in particular the persistent gap in pay levels, the tendency of worsening long-term unemployment among women, the barriers against their re-entry into the labour market (after a period given to family responsibilities), and the dismal outlook for young women without qualifications (Council Resolution on the Third Action Programme, 1991: 26ff.). What lends a specifically European emphasis to this familiar picture of entrenched disadvantages is the insistence that the permanent marginalisation of women would directly affect, and counteract, the Community's quest for political legitimation. Issues of gender equality are not 'minority' issues. When traced across the map of Europe the 'ghettos' of women's work will not appear as merely peripheral to an otherwise well-integrated economic system. They add up to a political problem that might jeopardise the very aim of integration. To neglect the development of human resources and skill potentials in half the Community's citizenry would leave the expected benefits of economic cooperation, i.e. a sound basis of economic growth, precariously exposed. More generally, without the full participation of women in the process of community-building, Europe would lack the essential safeguards of 'economic and social cohesion'.

Programmatic statements of this kind might, of course, be read as serving mainly rhetorical functions. The permanent exclusion of marginal groups from economic opportunities is, as we know, not incompatible with a nation's successful pursuit of growth and international competitiveness. Nor need it pose a threat to internal stability. The emphasis on the need for women's integration can, however, also suggest that for Europe the aim of social cohesion raises problems of a different magnitude and urgency. It is not accidental that such demands should have emerged together with more determined efforts to create 'a citizens' Europe' (Buckley and Anderson, 1988: 15). As a polity in its own right, Europe has no history. That is, unlike most nation-states, it cannot rely on long-established habitual modes of political identification amongst its citizenry. Bonds of common attachment cannot be derived from the legitimating power of tradition nor from the social and cultural homogeneity of the constituent population. To give women a stake in the community and a focus of civic allegiance could, from this perspective, be seen as an effective strategy to overcome Europe's deficit of political legitimacy.

In response to this challenge Community programmes have broadened the scope of equality to embrace policies of 'positive action' (*Commission of the European Communities*, 1991). They endorse a range of different measures that would assist women to move out of the female enclaves of low-skilled and badly paid work. Special resources of education and vocational training, as well as technical and financial assistance in setting up small businesses and cooperatives, are committed to the long-term goal of removing the causes of women's 'difference', i.e. of their characteristic vulnerability in the labour market. Added to this are proposals to encourage the public provision of child care in member states, to secure common standards of maternity benefits and of job protection during pregnancy, and to set up schemes of parental leave. Judged by their overall intention, these programmes can be said to shift the demand for equality beyond gender-neutral standards of citizen rights and towards gender-specific policies of enablement for citizenship. They aim to equip women with the means of reaching the common starting-point of competitive equality with men. If such policies were consistently and comprehensively pursued, they might, in theory at least, gradually erode all significant divisions between male and female work. So that perhaps towards the end of the next century a redrafted Social Charter would no longer have to target women's equality with men for special consideration. Gender difference would have withered away.

Would it, though? Who would bear the costs of women's enablement for citizenship? Let us consider three possible answers. Each of them marks the distance that separates the achievement of gender equality in the forms outlined so far from genuinely universal standards of entitlement. First, if we accept as a matter of realistic assessment that the organisation of work in an expanding capitalist market will increasingly rely on sectors of a-typical employment, some people will have to fill those jobs. They might, of course, be men. And while such a redistribution of disadvantages would go some way towards narrowing the particular gap between female and male work, it would generate new divisions elsewhere. (This raises a crucial question which, for want of space, cannot be developed here but which should not be excluded from a gender perspective on the constraints of universalist principles: how would women's successful bid for equality affect the rights of men – under conditions where the full entitlements of citizenship seem to be a scarce resource?) A second, and perhaps more likely, outcome is that policies designed to benefit the Community's women citizens will transfer their previous disabilities to non-citizens, i.e. to third-country nationals, immigrants, refugees – in most cases, women again (Dummet, 1991; Morokvasic, 1991; Yuval-Davis, 1991). Finally, if equality programmes give strategic priority to women's and men's full participation in paid employment and if this is to be the privileged public space to which the status of citizenship refers, will this not have the effect of further denigrating the social value of the kind of work that many women actually do? The rights and benefits that accrue to European citizens in their capacity as 'workers' would not be available to those women whose responsibilities lie primarily or exclusively in the private (domestic) sphere. Caring for the young, the old and disabled people at home does not provide a basis for citizen entitlements (Piachaud, 1991: 25).

The attempt to universalise citizen rights across the gender divide thus has problematic implications. Some of these are intrinsic to the idea of citizenship itself. Unless we adopt literally a 'universal' or global standpoint, the rights that pertain to individuals as citizens are always predicated upon membership of a particular legal community which, whatever its size, is demarcated by definite boundaries. Europe would be no exception. In relation to those outside its borders, citizenship in the European Community consolidates a condition of privilege. Its exclusiveness will act as a barrier against the claims of immediate neighbours in eastern Europe as well as against the pressing needs of people in the Third World. But, as our last example shows, the mechanisms of inclusion and exclusion operate also inside the Community, in the hierarchical ordering of spheres to which full citizen entitlements are attached. Women, and this is the salient point here, will be found on either side of such divides.

We have so far set the opportunities of European citizenship against a single dimension of difference between 'women' and 'men'. It turns out that the internal coherence of gender, as a category of critical analysis, is itself problematic. It is undercut and fragmented by multiple divisions between women that may crystallise around nationality and ethnicity as well as around social class and familial status. The remaining section of the chapter will focus on this last element in the multi-dimensional impact of difference. It will consider the division between the public and the private spheres which runs through the institutional structures of European democracies and which is, similarly, implied in the very understanding of what it means to be a citizen. The public–private dichotomy must be seen as the pivotal issue around which women's claim to political agency revolves (Okin, 1991). Moreover, in its more general formulation as a problem of political theory, it refers to definitions of gender difference which include all women. We shall see that recent policy statements of the Community confront this division in a number of concrete practices and areas of social life. The emphasis has shifted from simple equality towards the conditions of women's autonomy. What this shift would imply for the orientations of political theory will be outlined by reference to two contrasting models of emancipatory politics. When connected with these perspectives, Europe can suggest some distinct possibilities for rethinking the idea of citizenship. They centre less on the characteristic attributes of a 'state' or on institutional mechanisms of representation than on the features of a non-homogenous, non-exclusive public space in which difference can be voiced and where private concerns can become issues of political debate.

SHIFTING THE FOCUS TOWARDS AUTONOMY

If we trace the equality programmes of the European Community from the mid-1970s to the present we can discern a widening focus upon the gendered structure of all society's major institutions. The concern with specific instances of legal discrimination in the public space of work has broadened into a critical awareness that the root causes of patriarchal inequality lie elsewhere – outside the domains with which citizenship has traditionally been associated. In order 'to achieve lasting progress and a real change in attitudes, awareness-raising initiatives need to go beyond the sphere of employment' (Council Resolution on the Third Action Programme, 1991: 27). Patterns of family organisation have to be taken into account as well as the disparities in educational opportunities at school and, more generally, the strength of conventional beliefs about women's and men's roles in society which are deeply embedded in the political culture of European nations. The Third Action Programme, to cite but a few examples, includes measures against sexual harassment (the need 'to guarantee the dignity of women and men at work') amongst the conditions of equality (Council Resolution on the Third Action Programme, 1991: 31). Acknowledging the influence of the media upon customary perceptions of gender, it calls for innovatory programme developments 'to present a full, realistic picture of women in society' (Council Resolution on the Third Action Programme, 1991: 27). A report on sexual violence against women (Garcia, 1991; commissioned by the Council of Europe) may count as further evidence how far on the European level the commitment to gender equality has expanded beyond its original closely circumscribed brief. Perhaps the most far-reaching changes are entailed in proposals for parental leave 'designed to reconcile the family and occupational responsibilities of both women and men' (Council Resolution on the Third Action Programme, 1991: 27). The significant shift from 'workers' to 'working parents' as the reference point of equality envisages a fundamental redistribution of public and private responsibilities between the sexes and, on this basis, a redistribution in the resources of citizenship.

What do these perspectives on the ubiquitous and pervasive effects of gender difference imply for the orientations of political theory? How, in particular, do they reflect upon the universalist claims of modern liberal and egalitarian doctrines? If the dominant traditions of moral and political thought from Locke to Rawls have failed to account for the political significance of gender, there may be good reason to suspect that male domination is not contingent but endemic to modern theories of universal right (Young, 1987: 58). Some feminist critics have claimed that the philosophical resources of emancipatory politics cannot be found in those traditions (Benhabib and Cornell, 1987; Pateman, 1988; Young, 1987; 1989). They contain no open spaces or suppressed possibilities for endorsing women's autonomy. For universalism arose itself as the specifically modern form of legitimating patriarchal right (and, similarly, of racial domination, economic exploitation and the marginalization of ethnic groups). The unity of shared moral attributes and common values proclaimed in the universal idea of citizen equality is illusory. So are the assumed homogeneity of the public sphere and the impartiality of the public-spirited individual. The inclusion of women, as of other previously oppressed groups, into an undifferentiated concept of rights and the presumption of a uniform status of citizenship would but perpetuate their marginalisation. Rather than search for the conditions of integration, emancipatory political theory has to take the irreducible heterogeneity of group difference as its starting-point. It has to conceptualise citizenship not in terms of claims that pertain to the individual but in terms of group rights. In practice, that would imply the self-organisation of groups, separate political representation and procedural guarantees that special consideration be given to their viewpoints in matters which directly and uniquely affect them (Young, 1989). In Young's model, Social Movement politics and Rainbow Coalitions prefigure a community constituted by group-differentiated citizenship. It would preserve the separate identity and the plurality of values that express each group's specific experiences while providing a common space for public spiritedness. Insistence on group specificity can connect with the idea of citizen commitments because no claim that a group might bring to the public space would be excluded as merely private, or non-political. Young's approach has considerable merits in that it complements the meaning of difference, understood as disability, by the positive connotations of 'identity': by a sense of common social status, of shared attachments and experienced solidarity that derive from a common history. Moreover, it extends the perspectives gained from the analysis of gender to other forms of group difference. Finally, as a product of specific histories, group identity is not a natural or immutable given. Identities can and do change. And this historical openness links the idea of citizenship to an open-ended, experimental mode of politics, defined less by formal rights, institutional procedures and state provisions than by analogies with dialogue and conversation.

A second model of emancipatory politics suggests that we can draw on the universalist legacies of political philosophy if we develop their potential for genuine all-inclusiveness. To search for universal principles free from gender requires us to take 'gender massively into account' (Okin, 1989: 177) and to ascertain the many ways in which sexual difference has structured the classical formulations of citizenship. Okin's subversive reading of Rawls from premises that explicitly include women as equal participants in the original position – by placing a 'person's' gender among the particular circumstances hidden behind the veil of ignorance – testifies to the resourcefulness of universalist conceptions of political agency. It equally testifies to the magnitude of the task involved in such reconceptualisation. For whether or not those principles can gain a new lease of life depends on their capacity to spell out the requirements for the equal autonomy of women and men. The primary conditions of this equality would have to be established in spheres which have traditionally been of no concern to normative political theory – in the personal relations of marriage and the family. The model does not, as is sometimes feared, imply an 'unbounded concept of politics' with no clear distinctions 'between the polity and the every-day life of citizens' (Held, 1991: 6). It does, however, demand that such boundaries are not drawn along gender lines. That is, citizenship must at no point connect with even implicit assumptions about a natural division of labour between the sexes. The organisation of work would have to change in such a way as to allow men and women to equally share the responsibilities of paid and unpaid labour. Similarly, the attribution of definite social roles based on sex would have to disappear from legal and educational practices. What constitutes the 'political' in political theory could no longer be demarcated by its difference from, and opposition to, a private sphere of naturally female activities: 'A just future would be one without gender. In its social structures and practices, one's sex would have no more relevance than . . . the length of one's toes' (Okin, 1989: 171).

The implications of these two models of emancipatory politics can be summarised in three points. First, we have to reconsider the constitutive attributes of citizenship in ways that do not simply abstract from, and thus ignore, those differences between individuals which have historically served as grounds for exclusion or marginalisation. Second, the demands that group difference will make on the formulation of citizen rights can only be assessed if we also assume the presence and involvement of those groups with their specific claims in the terrains of citizenship. It follows, third, that the conditions of emancipatory equality are inseparable from the expression of diversity within institutional structures that allow for debate and exchange of experience.

CONCLUSION: EUROPE AS A FORUM OF EMANCIPATORY DEBATES

To ask whether Europe might be a more congenial terrain for developing these dimensions of citizenship is not to look for legal and institutional analogies with the nation-state. On the contrary, we need to refer the question to those features in which the emerging European polity differs most clearly from established political systems: to the as yet incomplete institutionalisation of political activity, the deficit of centralized power, to the uncertain direction of development and the multiplicity and diversity of political cultures. It is under such conditions that the concerns of 'minorities' may find the resonance which is usually denied to them in national politics. Hundreds of senior citizens descending on Luxembourg to set up a 'European pensioners' parliament' are a case in point (*The Guardian*, 10 March 1992). So are, in different ways, the expectations directed at a 'Europe of the regions' or the channels of Europe-wide cooperation between local government agencies. Similarly, the Third Action Programme reflects in many instances the impact that women themselves have had on the shaping of policy orientation. The clearer perceptions of what is implied in the demand for citizen equality are not owed to a God's-eye viewpoint of benevolent policy-makers. They have developed together with an increasing involvement of women in the formal and informal arenas of European politics.

Statements about Europe's capacity to develop the conditions of emancipatory politics will at this point necessarily be tentative and provisional. We can, however, identify some developments that lend credibility to such claims. They can be traced, for example, in numerous projects initiated by the Commission systematically to collect data and coordinate research about the condition of women in various parts of the Community in order 'to fuel policy debates' (Council Resolution on the Third Action Programme, 1991: 30). Comprehensive knowledge of this kind must itself count as a necessary prerequisite for rethinking women's role as citizens in ways that connect with their actual experiences and life-situations. The acknowledgement of the multi-disciplinary and global perspectives which the new specialism of 'women's studies' has brought to this task, and proposals to stimulate similar projects in universities and research centres across the Community, point in the same direction. This emphasis, too, reflects a significant shift towards a standpoint that does not consider women as objects of 'woman-friendly' policies but as agents who will themselves create the meanings of citizenship.

In considering the conditions from which Europe-wide citizen links might develop we should also stress the integrative dynamic inherent in diversity itself. The sheer number and rapid proliferation of women's networks and grass-root associations over the last decade could be taken as evidence of an emerging 'European fellow-citizenship' (Tassin, 1992: 189). It evolves less from the legal and administrative consolidation of citizen status than from the multiple sites and communicative processes of citizen activity. In encouraging an exchange of experience across a wide spectrum of different interests and practices, diversity acts as an effective mediator in the search for the 'best practice' which might establish the common grounds of European citizenship. This process draws on the characteristic qualities of the women's movement: on spontaneous, non-hierarchical modes of association, on the commitment to open debate and expression of difference, on the attention to local contextuality and, at the same time, to a praxis of international solidarity.

With these emphases the idea of citizenship could break free from preconceptions of a single political space or a unitary status defined by reference to the state. There is, however, the danger that arguments which postulate Europe as a 'public space of disparate communities' (Tassin, 1992: 189) will settle, somewhat complacently, at the opposite pole of heterogeneous particularities, local spontaneity, grass-root involvement without reflecting on the not unproblematic conditions of a *common* European citizenship. The merely polemical fixation on the 'dogma of nation-states' (Tassin, 1992: 189) and on any assumptions of community identity associated with that dogma, would carry us to the point of neglecting the constitutional elements in the construction of citizenship, of losing the focus on Europe as a polity. The analysis of this chapter has shown that the new Europe does, indeed, pose a challenge to that simple universalism which conflates equality with legal uniformity and homogeneity in the circumstances of citizenship. We have seen that a European polity has the potential to open up new spaces that are more hospitable to the expression of gender difference. We have also seen, however, that the constitutional affirmation of their equal rights as European citizens has provided women with valuable resources to free themselves from the traditional constraints of gender particularity. No theory of citizenship can build upon heterogeneity and group identity alone. Those new terrains of citizen activity are 'public' only in so far as constitutional principles and institutional procedures guarantee to all members of the community equal access and voice. This equality in turn requires a common floor of universal rights which pertain indiscriminately – and irrespective of any particular form of difference – to individuals as European citizens. 'European citizenship' is not a magic formula to simply substitute difference for equality, particularity for universalism. Nor does it hold out a definitive answer to the question how the tension between these principles could be resolved. If anything, it makes their precarious interdependence more transparent.

BIBLIOGRAPHY

Baldwin-Edwards, M. and Gough, I. (1991) 'European Community, social policy and the UK', in N.P. Manning (ed.) *Social Policy Review 1990–91*, London: Longman, pp. 147–68.

Benhabib, S. and Cornell, D. (1987) 'Beyond the politics of gender', in S. Benhabib and D. Cornell (eds) *Feminism as Critique*, Cambridge: Polity Press, pp. 1–15.

Buckley, M. and Anderson, M. (1988) 'Introduction: problems, policies and politics', in M. Buckley and M. Anderson (eds) *Women, Equality and Europe*, London: Macmillan, pp. 1–19.

Byre, A. (1988) 'Applying community standards on equality', in M. Buckley and M. Anderson (eds) *Women, Equality and Europe*, London: Macmillan, pp. 20–32.

Carter, A. (1988) *The Politics of Women's Rights*, London: Longman.

Commission of the European Communities (1991) *Employment in Europe*, Brussels: Commission of the European Communities.

Community Charter of the Fundamental Social Rights of Workers (1990) *Social Europe*, 1.

Corrin, C. (ed.) (1992) *Superwomen and the Double Burden: Women's Experience of Change in Central and Eastern Europe and the Former Soviet Union*, London: Scarlet Press.

Council Resolution on the Third Action Programme on Equal Opportunities for Women and Men, 21 May 1991, *European Industrial Relations Review*, 209, June 1991: 26–7.

Crowley, H., Einhorn, B., Hall, C., Molyneux, N. and Segal, L. (1991) 'Editorial. Shifting territories: feminism and Europe', *Feminist Review*, 39: 1–2.

Dietz, M. (1992) 'Context is all: feminism and theories of citizenship', in C. Mouffe (ed.) *Dimensions of Radical Democracy*, London: Verso, pp. 63–85.

Dummet, A. (1991) 'Racial equality and "1992"', *Feminist Review*, 39: 85–90.

Einhorn, B. (1991) 'Where have all the women gone? Women and the women's movement in East Central Europe', *Feminist Review*, 39: 16–36.

Garcia, A. (1991) *Sexual Violence against Women: Contribution to a Strategy for Countering the Various Forms of Such Violence in the Council of Europe Member States*, Strasbourg: Council of Europe, European Committee for Equality between Women and Men, EG (91)1.

Gatens, M. (1991) *Feminism and Philosophy: Perspectives on Difference and Equality*, Cambridge: Polity Press.

Hanna, L. (1992) 'Will women voters forgive John Major for loading the dice against them at Maastricht? Lynn Hanna consults EOC chair, Joanna Foster', *The Guardian*, 21 January.

Held, D. (1991) 'Editor's Introduction', in D. Held (ed.) *Political Theory Today*, Cambridge: Polity Press, pp. 2–21.

Hoskyns, C. (1988) '"Give us equal pay and we'll open our own doors": a study of the impact in the Federal Republic of Germany and the Republic of Ireland of the European Community's policy on women's rights', in M. Buckley and M. Anderson (eds) *Women, Equality and Europe*, London: Macmillan, pp. 33–55.

Hughes, M. (1991) 'Men's struggle for equality gathers pace as women fight move to raise retirement age', *The Guardian*, 16 November: 18.

Hunter, T. (1991) 'Women to pay the price of retirement age changes', *The Guardian*, 21 December: 16.

Hunter, T. (1992) 'Major employers call for flexible retirement age', *The Guardian*, 27 June: 33.

Kloss, D. (1992) 'Equal treatment of men and women', in S. Bulmer, S. George and A. Scott (eds) *The United Kingdom and European Community Membership Evaluated*, London: Pinter Publishers, pp. 205–11.

Local Government Information Unit, *Briefing*, September 1989, 'What future does 1992 hold for women in Europe?', London: Local Government Information Unit, pp. 2–3.

McClure, K. (1992) 'On the subject of rights: pluralism, plurality and political identity', in C. Mouffe (ed.) *Dimensions of Radical Democracy*, London: Verso, pp. 108–27.

Meehan, E. (1991) 'European citizenship and social policies', in U. Vogel and M. Moran (eds) *The Frontiers of Citizenship*, London: Macmillan, pp. 125–54.

Morokvasic, M. (1991) 'Fortress Europe and migrant women', *Feminist Review*, 39: 69–84.

Okin, S. (1989) *Justice, Gender, and the Family*, New York: Basic Books.

Okin, S. (1991) 'Gender, the public and the private', in D. Held (ed.) *Political Theory Today*, Cambridge: Polity Press, pp. 67–90.

Pateman, C. (1988) *The Sexual Contract*, Cambridge: Polity Press.

Pateman, C. and Gross, E. (eds) (1986) *Feminist Challenges*, London, Sydney and Boston: Allen & Unwin.

Phillips, A. (1991) *Engendering Democracy*, Cambridge: Polity Press.

Piachaud, D. (1991) 'A Euro-charter for confusion', *The Guardian*, 13 November: 25.

Shanley, M.L. and Pateman, C. (eds) (1991) *Feminist Interpretations and Political Theory*, Cambridge: Polity Press.

Tassin, E. (1992) 'Europe: a political community?', in C. Mouffe (ed.) *Dimensions of Radical Democracy*, London: Verso, pp. 169–92.

Third Action Programme on Equal Opportunities for Women and Men (1990) *European Industrial Relations Review*, 209, June 1991: 27–31.

Vogel, U. (1994) 'Marriage and the boundaries of citizenship', in B. van Steenbergen (ed) *The Condition of Citizenship*, London: Sage Publications, pp. 76–89.

Young, I.M. (1987) 'Impartiality and the civic public: some implications of feminist critiques of moral and political theory', in S. Benhabib and D. Cornell (eds) *Feminism as Critique*, Cambridge: Polity Press, pp. 56–76.

Young, I.M. (1989) 'Polity and group difference: a critique of the ideal of universal citizenship', *Ethics* 99: 250–74.

Young, I.M. (1990) *Justice and the Politics of Difference*, Princeton, NJ: Princeton University Press.

Yuval-Davis, N. (1991) 'The citizenship debate: women, ethnic processes and the state', *Feminist Review*, 39: 58–68.

10 Basic income and the political economy of the new Europe[1]

Philippe Van Parijs

> The interest of the [European] Community in a guaranteed minimum income goes back at least to the beginning of the 1980s, and the advent of the Single Market has intensified this concern. . . . The growing links of the East European countries could well reinforce these concerns with a minimum guaranteed income, in view of the increasing insecurity which citizens of the eastern countries are likely to face as they move towards a market society.
>
> (Room, 1991: 6)

If the new Europe is the one that arises as the European Union's economic integration deepens and as its links with eastern Europe strengthen, then the issue of a guaranteed minimum income is of central importance to it. But what sort of guaranteed minimum income should one go for? Along with a number of academics and organisations across Europe, I have been arguing for a number of years that, whatever the short-term strategy, the ultimate objective must be the introduction of an unconditional basic income, i.e. an income granted to every citizen or permanent resident on an individual basis, without means test or willingness-to-work conditions.[2]

Here is obviously not the place to present a comprehensive defence of this controversial proposal.[3] I shall restrict myself to highlighting the intuition behind it by sketching the argument for basic income stemming from a concern with poverty and emancipation, respectively. Next I shall present at more length the argument that emphasises basic income as a strategy against unemployment, by comparing it to two alternative strategies often put forward in today's European debate: statutory working-time reduction and employment subsidies. This aspect of the case for basic income is particularly relevant in the context of this book, as persistent mass unemployment constitutes the most conspicuous threat to the European Union's claim to keep offering an appealing socio-economic model to the world. Against this background, I shall next sketch the proposal of a (partial) European basic income. By way of conclusion, I shall spell out the main links between the subject of this chapter and the central issues of the volume.

POVERTY AND EMANCIPATION

It would be ludicrous to maintain that poverty is simply a question of monetary income. Yet it is even more ludicrous to claim that poverty can be overcome without some form of guaranteed minimum income. If I am firmly in favour of the totally unconditional form of guaranteed minimum income represented by a basic income, it is because any form of conditional guaranteed income presents in a high degree one at least of the following three drawbacks (and often all three at once):

1 Owing to the intrusions into an individual's private life which it legitimises and the social stigma that attaches to it, conditional assistance is humiliating for those receiving it.
2 Since conditional assistance is restricted to those in need of it, it is withdrawn as soon as anyone starts to manage on her/his own and therefore has the effect of catching recipients in the unemployment trap.
3 Conditional assistance allows many of the most deprived to slip through the safety net which it claims to provide, because ignorance or intimidation prevents them from claiming their entitlement.

A basic income, by contrast, would give rise to no humiliation, it would eliminate the unemployment trap and tighten as far as possible the mesh of the net. Moreover, at any given level of minimum income it would be more expensive than conditional forms of benefit only if the 'cost' were naïvely measured by the volume of financial flows to be handled by the State. If instead the cost were measured by the real resources (in working time, in paperwork, etc.) which a community needs to devote to managing its transfer system, the opposite would be the case.

Emancipation is not just a matter of income either. But it is not possible without a minimum of financial autonomy. The problem is how we can ensure that every person – and particularly those millions of women in Europe who have no income of their own and live in total economic dependence on their spouse – will enjoy that autonomy, while avoiding both of the following pitfalls: either driving women back into the home, which traps them in the family cell; or obliging all women to take up work outside the home, which is tantamount to forced labour. In order to achieve financial autonomy for every individual, male and female, and avoid the first pitfall, one might consider implementing what in eastern Europe used to be known as the 'anti-parasite' law: making gainful employment both a legal obligation and a legal right of every citizen, to be supplied by the public authorities if the private sector fails to provide it. This avoids the first pitfall, but clearly not the second. To ensure financial autonomy without recourse to forced labour, one solution would be what is sometimes called a 'housewife's wage'. This avoids the second pitfall, but evidently not the first; such a payment would be analogous to the repatriation allowance which some wish to see paid to migrant workers, nappies, pots and pans here playing the role of the country of origin. To achieve financial autonomy for everyone and steer a course between both pitfalls is not, however, impossible. That is precisely what is achieved by a basic income.

THE END OF FULL EMPLOYMENT?

Those who advocate a basic income as a way of fighting poverty or promoting emancipation were as justified in their views two decades ago as they are now. However, a further reason has been apparent for some years now; and it is the strength of this reason which explains why the idea of a basic income has been arousing interest in ever wider circles.

For nearly two decades, most west European countries have been experiencing a situation of massive unemployment. Millions of Europeans are vainly seeking work. There are not enough jobs to go round which are both economically viable (their cost does not exceed what demand is willing to pay) and socially adequate (the earnings from them are not less than the minimum necessary to meet the needs of a household). In order to put an end to this massive unemployment, it initially seemed obvious that we should try to boost the rate of growth. But in view of the speed with which technical progress was eliminating jobs, it rapidly became apparent that a fantastic rate of growth would be necessary even to stabilise employment, let alone to reduce the number of the unemployed – a rate of growth, indeed, which even if it were possible, would hardly be desirable. Alternatively, one might then want to consider a substantial reduction in workers' earnings, the idea being that by reducing the relative cost of labour, technical change could be redirected in such a way that fewer jobs were sacrificed. Even a relatively modest growth rate would then be able to stabilise and, gradually, reduce present levels of unemployment. However, such a policy would not only hamper productivity growth and run the risk of upsetting the stability of demand. Above all, it would impose an unacceptable standard of living on a large part of the population – all the more so in that a reduction in wages would need to be coupled to a parallel reduction in unemployment benefits and other replacement incomes, so as to preserve work incentives.

If we cannot or will not rely on either accelerated growth or reduced earnings, do we then have no option but to regard full employment as an impossible target? We are, indeed, condemned to this view if by full employment we mean a situation in which virtually everyone who wants a full-time job can obtain one which is both economically viable (without any subsidy) and socially adequate (without any additional allowance). But we are not if we are willing to redefine full employment by leaving out one, at least, of the three conditions implicit in the foregoing sentence. Corresponding to each of those conditions, there is a potential strategy for reducing unemployment which involves neither an increase in the rate of growth nor a reduction in the level of income.

THE THREE DILEMMAS OF WORKING-TIME REDUCTION

The first is the social redefinition of 'full time', i.e. a reduction in maximum working time, whether through a reduction in the maximum number of years worked (extension of compulsory school attendance, lowering of the retirement age, sabbatical years, etc.) or through a reduction in the maximum number of hours worked per year (longer holidays, the 30-hour week, etc.). Since there are not enough jobs for everyone who would like one, let us not allow a small number of people to appropriate them: they must be rationed. If this strategy is to be taken seriously as a way of solving the unemployment problem, the reduction must be both dramatic in its extent (unemployment in Europe is still exceeding 10 per cent) and neutral in its effects on wages (otherwise the negative indirect impact is likely to cancel out the positive direct impact of the sharing of jobs). Working time must therefore be reduced by some 10 per cent on average with a corresponding (average) reduction in gross earnings levels.

However, such a strategy comes up at once against three unavoidable dilemmas. First, either the across-the-board percentage reduction in gross earnings is not differentiated according to pay levels (hourly wage levels are simply retained unchanged), in which case the lowest wages will fall below the social minimum; or a greater reduction in the highest gross earnings is introduced, thus protecting those with the lowest incomes and maintaining the overall wage bill at the present level, in which case the relative cost of the least skilled jobs increases considerably, stepping up the pressure for their elimination through mechanisation. In other words, a dramatic and financially neutral reduction in working time is necessarily detrimental to the least qualified jobs – either because it kills the supply (they pay less than replacement incomes) or because it kills the demand (they cost firms a lot more per hour than they used to).

That is not all. Unemployment is very unevenly distributed, both in terms of regions and in terms of skills. This generates a second dilemma. Either the reduction in working time is undifferentiated across the board – which would lead to massive inefficiencies (bottlenecks for certain skilled jobs and in certain regions, high cost of retraining in new skills, and of moving either the work force or the means of production). Or it is so devised as to affect the various categories of workers only in so far as there are job seekers with the required skills – which ensures that the system is not plagued with the inefficiencies just mentioned but imposes unacceptable inequalities (surgeons and executives, for example, being allowed to continue to work sixty hours a week, whereas primary school teachers and hairdressers might not be allowed to work more than ten).

Finally, when we think of reductions in working time, we are mainly thinking of wage-earners. But what of the self-employed? Here again, a hard choice has to be made: either they are to be treated in the same way as waged workers and their work must be shared, which would entail intractable enforcement problems (an inspector would have to be able to check exactly how many hours a butcher works in her/his own back-yard) without much of a guarantee that these efforts would lead to any increase in people working, except in the labour inspectorate; or no reduction is imposed on the working hours of the self-employed, in which case the enforced reduction in the waged workers' hours would mostly serve to increase the number of the 'fake self-employed', i.e. wage-earners artificially detached from the salaried staff of a firm so as to allow them to work 'for themselves' for as many hours as they want. It would, furthermore, constitute a flagrant injustice, victimising those who have no option but to be and remain waged workers.

SUBSIDISE THE EMPLOYER OR LIBERATE THE EMPLOYEE?

Awareness of these dilemmas helps us to understand why the campaign to reduce working time, even in those countries in which the trade union movement has been sympathetic, is moving at a pace which is insufficient even to make up for the new rationalisations. This forces us to take another possibility into account. Whereas it is not possible to provide everyone seeking employment with a job which is sufficiently productive – without external intervention – to be both economically viable and socially adequate, it may be possible to use those activities which are sufficiently productive to 'subsidise' others, rather than (unsuccessfully) trying to share out 'productive' jobs amongst all.

Two options, profoundly different in their consequences, are on offer. One consists, in its pure form, of flat-rate employment subsidies: a lump sum of money is paid to the employer for each person (s)he employs. The other option, in its purest form, is the introduction of a basic income: the same sum is paid directly to every citizen (or permanent resident), and hence to every actual or potential worker, no strings attached.[4] In many ways, a general flat-rate subsidy and a universal basic income are similar. In particular, they both address head-on the first dilemma mentioned in connection with working-time reduction: the least skilled can be employed at a lower cost to their employer, without this needing to take them below the 'social minimum', because of the wedge between direct labour cost and standard of living generated by the subsidy or the benefit.

There is, however, one fundamental difference between the two approaches. In the first, the pressure to take up employment is kept intact. In the second it is reduced. As a result, poorly productive jobs made viable by the first approach are likely to be just as unattractive as those which existed previously, whereas those made viable by the second approach can only exist if workers with the right skills find them sufficiently attractive. If the motive in combating unemployment is not some sort of work fetishism or the fear of leaving part of the population without a job to keep it busy, but, rather, a concern to give every person the possibility of taking up gainful employment in which (s)he can find some accomplishment, then there is no doubt that the basic income approach is to be preferred. If, moreover, for the reasons outlined earlier, we cannot hope to eliminate unemployment by accelerating growth, lowering wage levels or imposing a reduction in working time, then basic income provides the only viable strategy for effectively fighting unemployment in the sense in which it is essential that the latter should be fought.

A STRATEGY FOR THE NEW EUROPE

Basic income provides, moreover, a strategy that has been made particularly relevant by the changes that are now occurring, east and west, and giving Europe a new shape. Why?

'1989', the 'democratic revolutions' in eastern Europe have most probably sealed the fate of the socialist dream – the idea that state control over the means of production could provide the core of a desirable society. But it does not follow that there is no major breakthrough ahead, that we are stuck – at best – with roughly the sort of capitalism we have got, and that the battles left are essentially of a defensive nature: to protect civil liberties, the welfare state and our ecosystem against the powerful pressures deriving, directly or indirectly, from capitalist competition. The potential breakthrough that is worth fighting for is precisely the introduction of a basic income. It builds on the conquests of the welfare state in order to achieve for people's real freedom what the abolition of serfdom and slavery did for their formal freedom. This breakthrough is fully consistent with a market society. It provides a 'capitalist road to communism', a way of remaining true to the valuable emancipatory ideal incorporated in the communist 'realm of freedom', while dismissing the institutional framework of so-called 'communist' regimes as an inappropriate way of pursuing it.[5] The collapse of these regimes makes basic income capitalism more relevant than ever as an attractive horizon for European societies.[6]

After '1992' and the establishment of the Single European Market, the introduction of at least a partial basic income is becoming far more than a sheer horizon. Increased mobility of both people and capital, increased competition in all areas make it imperative and urgent to set up at least an elementary social protection on a European scale. How could this be done? Social insurance systems are structured in such complex ways, and in ways that differ so much from country to country, that trying to harmonise them to any significant extent looks like a hopeless task. One might then think of trying, more modestly, to introduce a European guaranteed minimum income scheme – on the pattern of British 'supplementary benefits', the Dutch '*bijstand*', the Belgian '*minimex*', the German '*Sozialhilfe*', the French '*revenu minimum d'insertion*', etc. But if this scheme is to be uniform across the European Community, it will either (if low) badly damage the situation of the worst off in the more affluent countries of the Community, whose current minimum income level is higher than the European one would be; or (if high) create a disastrous unemployment trap in the less affluent countries, whose current median wage is close to what the European minimum income would be. And if it is not uniform across countries, it can be safely expected to generate all sorts of unfortunate consequences, whether of a pragmatic or a symbolic nature (selective migration to high-benefit countries, feeling that there is a hierarchy of 'castes' of European citizens, whose membership is determined by nationality, etc.).

The roads thus sketched can and will be tried – at least as thought experiments. But my forecast is that, as a result of this process, more and more people will start thinking about a comparatively very simple alternative option.[7] Why not introduce, say at the same time as the European currency, what could be called a Eurogrant? A Eurogrant is a basic income at a comparatively low level (say, 200 ECU per month) paid unconditionally to every adult permanent resident of the EEC, and financed directly by a European tax, for example (in part at least) a uniform taxation of private and corporate energy consumption. This Eurogrant would of course not replace all welfare state provisions (old-age pensions, unemployment benefits, student grants, disability allowances, means-tested minimum income guarantees, etc.), these would only be reduced by an amount equal to the grant, and abolished only if they did not exceed this amount.[8]

In low-wage countries without a guaranteed minimum income, this would amount to introducing a form of income guarantee that does not create an unemployment trap. It would also provide those countries (and particularly their poorer regions), which tend to consume far less energy per capita than others, with a large, stable and non-stigmatising net transfer of resources that reaches their citizens directly, instead of having to pass – with a heavy 'leaky bucket' toll – through a maze of programmes and organisations.[9] In high-wage countries with a guaranteed minimum income, on the other hand, the introduction of a non-means-tested Eurogrant is more like the introduction of a right to work than like the introduction of a right to an income. For contrary to what happens under means-tested income maintenance systems, no-one would have to give up her/his Eurogrant when finding a job. Hence, though the proposed package would not remove the unemployment trap, because of residual income supplements provided nationally, it would significantly reduce its depth. Such a scheme, moreover, could serve as a partial substitute for European agricultural policies. It would help to guarantee small farmers a regular income, and would constitute overall a large net transfer from the cities to the countryside.

For many, including myself, this partial basic income would only count as a first step. But it is now high time to focus on it and look closely at the legal, economic, political and sociological problems its implementation will raise. This is the way forward for this – radical but realistic – strategy for today's Europe.

BASIC INCOME AND POLITICAL THEORY

Having thus delineated how and why I view basic income as a central component of the institutional structure of a desirable new Europe, let me now try to spell out what this approach presupposes with respect to the questions which form the focus of this book.

Structure of political authority

Subsidiarity – understood as the demand that the state, or some larger-scale public authority, should not attempt to provide what civil society, or some smaller-scale public authority, can provide better – has a lot to commend itself. For it tends to locate decision-making at the points where information about the needs to be met is most accurate and where control over the use made of the resources is likely to be closest. Moreover, it makes maximal room for spontaneous variety and responsible experiments. There is nothing wrong, in my view, with subsidiarity so conceived. But is it not blatantly at odds with the notion of a basic income introduced, funded, administered by a European state? Not at all, if appropriate attention is paid to the limits explicitly stated in the principle itself, and if the latter is not turned into something else with which, in the field of social policy, it is all too often confused.

First, then, the principle itself justifies the state taking over from civil society, or a larger-scale public authority from a smaller-scale one, when the services considered are better provided at those levels. This is the case, in particular, in those areas in which environmental externalities and/or distributive issues are essentially and significantly involved. Why? One reason is common to both these categories of cases. In an open economic environment, whichever area 'does the right thing' – by appropriately taxing polluters or by achieving a high level of redistribution – at the expense of lower profits, will pay a high, possibly prohibitive price, due to capital migration towards other, less 'virtuous' areas. Hence, locating decisions at a level that covers a significant portion of the relevant economic environment may well be a precondition for anything substantial being durably done. There is one further reason for attributing to a larger-scale authority the task of dealing with one category of externalities – those which are largely borne by people who are not just distinct from the economic agents responsible for them but who live in a different political area. In this case, a higher-level political authority is not only necessary to enable each area to adopt environmental policies which are in its own interest. It is also required, or at least most useful, to effectively prevent the export of nuisances or risks. And there is of course also one additional reason for entrusting the task of dealing with distributive issues to a larger-scale authority as soon as distributive justice is viewed as a matter which transcends the boundaries of particular areas. Hence, there is little ground for doubting that organizing on a European level the eco-funded basic income suggested above is fully consistent with the subsidiarity principle, as stated.

There is, however, an alternative interpretation of the subsidiarity principle in the field of social policy which is plainly inconsistent with any basic income proposal. It consists in construing subsidiarity as the demand that a public authority should only play a role in the attempt to solve a person's 'social problem' if all lower levels prove inadequate: the local authority should only intervene if the family or neighbourhood cannot handle the problem; the province or region if the local authority is not up to it; the national state if sub-national entities cannot cope; and the EU if all else has failed. If such a principle is meant to govern transfer policies, it is clear that the latter can only be conceived in the form of remedial, targeted, means-tested actions focusing on the needy, and not at all in the universal, unconditional form characteristic of basic income. I do not need to restate at this point the fundamental reasons why I believe the latter kind of transfer policy should be preferred to the former. What matters here is that the two construals of subsidiarity are logically independent, and hence that one can consistently be committed to one while rejecting the other.

Pattern of social and economic rights

This distinction between two meanings of subsidiarity is also useful for the sake of understanding the pattern of rights into which a European basic income would fit. For while the latter would no doubt replace some of the transfer schemes that currently exist on a national scale and affect the levels, funding structure and significance of many others, beyond this common base (which might also include child benefits, for example), transfer systems would vary a great deal across European nations and regions. This variation, it is fair to say, would partly be the sheer reflection of a regrettable but unavoidable mess. But it would also be the expression of differences between median preferences in different areas and of a concern that plenty of room should be left for experiments.

Cultural diversity

Diversity in the level, funding and structure of these supplementary schemes is one of the ways in which cultural diversity could keep expressing itself in the area of social and economic rights. One country may go for more generous maternity leave arrangements, another for more heavily subsidised child-care facilities. One country may want to facilitate early retirement, while another wants to encourage pensioners to keep working on a part-time basis. One country may refuse to subsidise homeopathic medicines, another life-prolonging operations on people over 75. The more generous the European basic income, the more numerous, perhaps, the number of national transfer schemes that are thereby made redundant, but also the more leeway for the expression of cultural differences. For a high unconditional income financed on a European level reduces the competitive pressure on the various countries involved and makes it easier for each of them to experiment with social policies that significantly diverge, whether temporarily or permanently, from those that would maximise its competitiveness.

Europe and the world

The massive inequalities that exist between Europe and the Third World are morally unjustifiable. A European basic income, as such, will do nothing to alleviate them. Indeed, it is only sustainable if tough immigration policies keep preventing the massive inflow of Third World citizens eager to improve their living standards. But the massive migration of people is not a sensible strategy for reducing the world's inequalities. The migration of profit-seeking capital and technology makes a lot more sense, preferably channelled selectively so as to encourage reasonable military, monetary, demographic and environmental policies, and also the introduction and protection of civil, political and social rights.[10] But this is not enough. If inequality on a world scale is to be kept under check, permanent transfers are needed from richer to poorer areas. If the arguments developed above are correct, a basic income on a world scale would be the ideal and largely the sheer recognition that those who are in no position to make use of their equal right to consume the resources of the earth (and in particular to pollute) should get due compensation from those who can only consume as much as they do because not everyone does. If only for technological reasons, this ideal is currently out of reach. But it can none the less be helpful as a guiding principle, as actual transnational transfers can gradually be reshaped so as to resemble it more – reliable, paid directly to the people, in cash, *ex ante*, without clawback.

Universalism versus contextualism

Both the intuitive plausibility and the political potential of the universalist, justice-based arguments I have presented in favour of a European basic income are by no means context-insensitive. They are heavily dependent on the constitution of a European audience and discussion space. Only the latter can induce a shift from bargaining between self-interested European countries to arguing on the basis of a sense of justice as equal concern for all Europeans. The significant discrepancy that appears on many issues between the positions of the Council of Ministers and that of the European Parliament is an indication of the difference the jump from bargaining to arguing can make.[11] But giving more power to the European Parliament is not enough for the emergence of a relevant European public forum. Bridging the ethnic, linguistic, cultural, political gaps through countless international encounters, dialogues, debates of all kinds and sizes, is no less important. The initiative which led to this book is one example of what is needed.

NOTES

1 Part of this paper was the author's contribution to the hearing on 'The guaranteed basic income and the future of social security', for the Social Affairs Commission of the European Parliament (Brussels, November 1986), revised versions of which have appeared in *L'Europe en Formation* (Nice) 275, été–automne 1989; *Mensuel M* (Paris) octobre–novembre 1991, pp. 27–30; *Garantir le revenu*, Gilles Gantelet et Jean-Paul Maréchal (eds) Paris: Transversales, 1972, pp. 74–82; and *Green Light on Europe*, Sara Parkin and David Fernbach (eds) London: Heretic Books, 1991, pp. 166–76.

2 The European literature on basic income has grown very quickly in the last few years. In English, Walter (1989) provides a good, though now outdated, general introduction. Van Parijs (ed.) (1992) and Van Parijs (1995) concentrate on the ethical issues. Atkinson (1995) presents and discusses the most relevant aspects of the economic literature. Further information on the present state of the European debate is provided by the Citizen's Income Bulletin (Citizens Income Study Centre, St Philips Building, Sheffield Street, London WC2A 2EX) and by the Newsletter of the Basic Income European Network (BIEN, c/o Chaire Hoover, Place Montesquieu 3, 1348 Louvain-la-Neuve, Belgium, BIEN@econ.ucl.ac.be). BIEN also has a web site which provides, among other things, an integrated and annotated bibliography on basic income (since 1986) in several European languages (http://www.econ.ucl.ac.be/ETES/BIEN/bien.html).

3 I have tried to do so in Van Parijs (1995).

4 An intermediate option would consist in paying the allowance directly to each (actual or potential) worker, but only on condition that (s)he actually works or makes her/himself available for suitable full-time work.

5 On this 'capitalist road to communism', see Chapters 8 to 10 of Van Parijs (1993).

6 The specific relevance of a basic income to the future of eastern Europe is discussed by Roland (1989) and Standing (1991).

7 I argue for the same conclusion from a somewhat different angle in Van Parijs (1996a).

8 A scheme of this sort was proposed on a national scale by the Dutch Scientific Council for Government policy in an important report (WRR,

1985). Although these proposals only mention the taxation of energy as one possible source of funding, it would be neat if a significant (though still very partial) European basic income could be fully financed by a uniform European tax on energy (which an increasing number of people are now advocating). On the basis of rough calculations, however, a partial basic income of 200 ECU (or about £130) per month would require a tax of about 650 ECU per TEP, compared to a current European average of about 100 ECU and a current average tax-inclusive price of 270 ECU. (See Genet and Van Parijs, 1992, for further figures and calculations.) It follows that either a basic income of 100 ECU a month could only be phased in very gradually, or that different sources of funding must be tapped.

9 The redistributive impact of even a modest basic income financed by a uniform energy tax would be incomparably greater than the one currently effected by the European Social Fund and the Fund for Regional Development. The same countries are net beneficiaries and net contributors under both schemes, with the sole exception of Britain, currently a net beneficiary, who would become a net contributor. But the extent of inter-country redistribution (as measured by the average absolute level of the twelve countries-net contributions or benefits) involved in a basic income of 200 ECU a month funded by a European tax on energy would be 26 times greater than the redistribution currently achieved by Europe's so-called structural funds. In other words, a basic income of 8 ECU a month (financed in this way) would be sufficient to redistribute as much from the rich areas to the poor areas as is currently done. See again Genet and Van Parijs (1992).

10 For a comprehensive overview of the arguments for and against the free movement of capital versus people, see the useful collection edited by Barry and Goodin (1992).

11 The distinction between bargaining and arguing is illuminatingly elaborated by Elster (1991). I use it to justify increasing the power of the European Parliament as part of an exercise in justice-oriented democratic engineering in Van Parijs (1996b) and Van Parijs, P. (1997). 'Should the European Union become more democratic?' A. Follesdal and P. Koslowski (eds), *Democracy and the European Union*, Berlin and New York, Springer, pp. 287–301.

BIBLIOGRAPHY

Atkinson, A.B. (1995) *Public Economics in Action: The Basic Income/Flat Tax Proposal*, Oxford: Oxford University Press.

Barry, B. and Goodin, R.E. (eds) (1992) *Free Movement: Ethical Issues in the Transnational Migration of People and of Money*, Hemel Hempstead: Harvester-Wheatsheaf and University Park, PA: Pennsylvania State University Press.

Elster, J. (1991) 'Arguing and bargaining in two constitutional assemblies', the Storrs Lectures, Yale Law School.

Genet, M. and Van Parijs, P. (1992) 'Eurogrant', *BIRG Bulletin* 15: 4–7.

Parijs, Van, P. (ed.) (1992) *Arguing for Basic Income: Ethical Foundations for a Radical Reform*, London and New York: Verso.

Parijs, Van, P. (1993) *Marxism Recycled*, Cambridge: Cambridge University Press.

Parijs, Van, P. (1995) *Real Freedom for All: What (if Anything) can Justify Capitalism?*, Oxford: Oxford University Press.

Parijs, Van, P. (1996a) 'Basic income and the two dilemmas of the welfare state', *The Political Quarterly* 67(1): 63–6.

Parijs, Van, P. (1996b) 'Justice and democracy: are they incompatible?', *Journal of Political Philosophy* 4(2): 101–17.

Parijs, Van, P. (1997) 'Should the European Union become more democratic?' in A. Follesdal & P. Koslowski (eds), *Democracy and the European Union*, Berlin & New York: Springer, pp. 287–301.

Roland, G. (1989) *Economie politique du système soviétique*, Paris: L'Harmattan.

Room, G. (1991) 'Towards a European welfare state?', in G. Room (ed.) *Towards a European Welfare State?* Bristol: SAUS, pp. 1–14.

Standing, G. (1991) 'Towards economic democracy and labour flexibility', in G. Standing (ed.) *In Search of Flexibility: The New Soviet Labour Market*, Geneva: I.L.O., pp. 363–97.

Walter, T. (1989) *Basic Income: Freedom from Poverty, Freedom to Work*, London: Marion Boyars.

WRR (1985) *Safeguarding Social Security*, Report 26, abridged English version, The Hague: Wetenschappelijke Raad voor het Regeringsbeleid.

11 European citizenship: A mirage?

Percy B. Lehning

INTRODUCTION

All the chapters in this volume have been concerned with the basis and implication of European identity and citizenship. Some have argued for a culturally weak conception of citizenship and some for a stronger conception, but all agree that we need some account of identity. Moreover, from the range of papers, it is also clear that citizenship is a multi-dimensional phenomenon, covering social and cultural aspects as well as political participation.

The purpose of this chapter is not to recapitulate the previous arguments but to evaluate existing practices and institutions in the European Union in the light of the complex concept of citizenship. A prime example of such a concept is 'liberal democratic citizenship'. When justifying one set of political arrangements relative to others, 'liberal democratic citizenship' – with its two constitutive elements, rights and identity – ultimately makes reference to the interests of individuals, and does not stop at the interests of collective entities like cultures, churches, communities or languages. The two elements of citizenship must be experienced in a geographical context, regardless of the fact how this geographical context is defined. The function of citizen can be discharged at a multitude of levels, from local government and functional interest groups through to the cosmopolis.

This individualist assumption is in line with the fact that we have to take into account the social and cultural pluralism of modern societies, and that from a liberal perspective citizens should have the equal ability to choose their own conception of the good. It is, in fact, a minimal democratic criterion: the interests of each person are entitled to equal consideration. Liberal democratic citizenship is, then, dissociated from identity based on '*ethnos*', because there is no necessary connection between 'descent' and interests. When discussing (European) citizenship, '*demos*' and '*ethnos*' are separated. A European *demos* cannot be based on ethno-cultural terms, on an idea of ethnic homogeneity. To be sure: cultural and ethnic pluralism is not denied, but what is denied is that this kind of pluralism should play a role when developing a 'sense of community' on a national as well as on a European scale.

To be able to generate a public identity, 'shared citizenship identity', certain institutions and practices of political cooperation have to be in existence, not only at the level of a nation-state, but also at the level of the European Union. It requires a democratic process with accountability, rooted in the political culture of the European Union, based on shared principles of democracy and social justice, which serve as the common denominator. This forms the base for 'constitutional patriotism' on a pan-national scale. The principles of social justice that should apply to the Union as a whole are the same that are basic to any welfare state, confronting the risks of sickness, old age, invalidity, unemployment, and poverty in all parts of the Union.[1]

In the following, it is this concept of 'liberal democratic citizenship' that will be taken as the yardstick to evaluate the actual situation in the European Union with regard to citizenship. In answering the question if there is a fit between the normative conception of 'European citizenship' and the reality of the European Union, an eclectic use of research into 'the state of the European Union' is made.

I, eventually, come to a rather gloomy conclusion. Not only is there no fit between 'liberal democratic citizenship' and the actual situation, but the requirements that allow one to speak of 'European citizenship' seem difficult to be realised. Therefore, it seems that one has to come to the conclusion that it is a mirage to speak of 'European citizenship'.

EUROPEAN CITIZENSHIP AND A 'PAN-EUROPEAN WELFARE STATE'

When looking for a match between the political theoretical conception of 'European citizenship' and the empirical reality of the European Union, it seems we find support for the arguments for the two elements of citizenship, identity and rights, in a remark made by Streeck. In his 'Reflections on the political economy of European social policy' he argues that the coming about of European-level social policy suggests that European unity must be grounded in some form of popular European identity and he adds that this identity requires in turn 'a policy of redistributive justice based on an advanced version of common European citizenship' (Streeck, 1995a: 408).

He follows this remark, referring to the ideas of Marshall on citizenship and on the evolutionary sequence of citizenship rights and the acquired legitimacy and unity in modern polities, that European national states have to accept the development of the Union 'into a "Europe for the citizen" – social policy and all – or else the integration project will die from lack of popular support' (Streeck, 1995a: 408–9).[2]

To be able to answer if the West European nations are indeed about to merge into a 'United States of Europe' (USE), into a 'Europe for the citizen', or at least into a steadily increasing 'pool' of 'shared sovereignty' – an economic, political as well as cultural entity of its own – we have to be more specific. With regard to a match between the liberal democratic conception of European citizenship and the actual situation in Europe, the question is: is there a European welfare state, a 'transnational synthesis' of national welfare states, with 'European social citizenship' being one backbone of the 'United States of Europe'? 'Does the EU play a significant role, or do national welfare states remain largely untouched?', when we focus on traditional components of the welfare state?[3] Can we speak, in other words, of a 'pan-European welfare state'?

Pierson and Leibfried argue that the Union has used political power to supersede, supplement and modify operations of the economic system to achieve results which the economic system would not achieve on its own. They conclude that, in that sense, 'Social Europe' already exists. They add that the Union is also 'becoming a formidable actor in the field of social policy by introducing "market compatibility requirements", which restrict certain social policy options of member states that conflict with the construction of the single market' (Pierson and Leibfried, 1995a: 3). In fact, a system of shared political authority over social policy is emerging in Europe, 'though one that is far more decentralized than the arrangements of traditional federal states' (Pierson and Leibfried, 1995a: 4).

But is this the same as a 'pan-European welfare state'? The conclusion Pierson and Leibfried themselves draw is that, although actual and potential European social policy is of considerable significance, '[s]ocial policy has in fact taken a backseat to the single-market project; hopes (or fears) of some pan-European welfare state can be put to rest' (Pierson and Leibfried, 1995a: 4).

We have, however, still to ask if this 'considerable significance' of social policy is in fact enough of an indicator to say that there is, indeed, a match between one of the constitutive elements of the political theoretical conception of liberal democratic citizenship and the actual world of the European Union. To conclude so would be much too hasty. A more concrete indicator has to be used, before we can give a convincing answer.

As an indicator of the first aspect of liberal democratic citizenship, we will use 'social rights' that define a general floor of income and living conditions below which no member of the political community should fall. After all, the regimes of poverty policy are the most exposed parts of social citizenship.[4] Does, then, empirical research show us that we can speak of a 'European welfare state built on a European poverty policy'?

Discussions on a 'Social Europe', on the 'social dimension' of Europe, on the 'Social Charter', test the limits of European unification. Here the poverty issue is of special relevance, since it is morally clear-cut and marks the 'North–South' divide in the Community itself. Addressing this issue would mean designing programmes aimed at all European families. Leibfried has noted that the EU social policy mandate is, however, mostly focused on employees and their families and not on the European citizen *per se*. And this goes for the EU Social Charter as well. His conclusion is that 'the evolution of "pre-federal" European institutions, of Europe's "incomplete federalism", has been strongly moulded by "negative integration"' (Leibfried, 1993: 134).

An empirical requirement for 'European citizenship' or a 'Social Europe' to come about should be then, or so it seems, a 'positive mode of integration': an integration that is much more ambitious and complete than a pure and simple common market goal, one that only removes obstacles. It aims at constructive action, at a 'positive state', a movement from 'freedom' to 'social rights' in a unifying Europe (Leibfried, 1993: 134).

But is a 'positive integration' conceivable as a by-product of on-going European economic integration? Could a 'Social Europe' eventually emerge from the different existing welfare systems in Europe? Here, once again, Leibfried's conclusion is a negative one.

> [The] divergence of [welfare state] regimes does not lend support to the notion that a European welfare state might grow via automatic harmonisation, building from the national towards the EU level. A 'bottom up' strategy for EU 'social integration' policy seems stillborn.
>
> (Leibfried, 1993: 143)

There are two scenarios left:

1 Policy disharmony in welfare policy is here to stay, or may be transformed into a process of automatic disharmonisation at the bottom, the problem being that needs-centred social policies are

rather difficult to standardise and 'are least likely to be protected by European development' (Leibfried, 1993: 145).[5]

2 Policy disharmony may also, on the other hand, provoke pressure for European 'social cohesion', which might bring about a European policy frame for poverty policy – or for all social benefits – primarily tied to social citizenship.[6] This second scenario seems, however, unlikely.

Based on his research, Leibfried is of the opinion that European development will most likely leave all poverty and welfare policy at the local or state level, at the sub-European level, one of the main reasons being that it is hard to start from a common European denominator. In fact, the 'easy common ground is missing on which a European welfare regime could be built' (Leibfried, 1993: 143).[7]

It seems fair to say that the founding of a United Europe depended mainly, if not totally, on the 'four freedoms' that are important for economic integration: the free movement of persons, goods, capital and services. At the fore is thus 'economic citizenship'. The fact that political as well as social citizenship have, until now, only been marginal in the process of European unification leads Leibfried to conclude his research, noting that:

> Unity in such a restrictive frame would turn into a unity of 'possessive individualism', a unity of markets only. It will not be the unity of an enlightened 'Social Europe' synthesising its traditions of democracy and solidarity, of civil and social rights, and building on its traditions of merging the citizen and the social state.
>
> (Leibfried, 1993: 150)

In relation to the test for a match between the liberal democratic conception of European citizenship and the actual situation in Europe, we have to conclude – focusing on the traditional components of the welfare state – that national welfare states remain largely untouched and that the EU does not seem to play a significant role. Integration definitely does not mean harmonisation, when talking about a European policy frame for poverty policy.

But has this conclusion not been reached too early? Should we not investigate if steps taken towards European citizenship at Maastricht in 1991 have allowed for 'the metamorphosis of the "market citizen" (1957–91) into the "full-fledged" EU citizen – a new synthesis which includes a European welfare state trajectory, building on universal rights?' (Leibfried, 1993: 150–1). To be more specific: has 'Maastricht' not brought the actual situation in the European Union more in line with the conception of liberal democratic European citizenship?

Streeck has a straightforward answer: three years after Maastricht there was little doubt that the battle for an EU social policy had been lost once more. The Social Charter, for instance, was adopted only as a non-binding 'social declaration' of the European Council, and 'references to *citizens* were replaced with references to *workers* to avoid the appearance of an expanded social policy mandate for the Community' (Streeck, 1995a: 402–3). Integration is once again identified with deregulation and political disengagement from the economy, and the inter-governmental character of the community was confirmed by the Single European Act. 'A free European market, if this is all that is to be, does not "require" a "Europe of the citizen"; in fact, citizenship makes the market less "free"' (Streeck, 1995a: 413). Thus, 'Maastricht' has not meant a metamorphosis of the 'market citizen' into the 'full-fledged' EU citizen.[8]

Although Pierson and Leibfried think Streeck's analysis exaggerates the power and cohesiveness of member states and organized business, while oversimplifying their attitudes towards EU social policy, they add that the European Union is not, and undoubtedly will not become, a federal welfare state like those of traditional nation-states (Pierson and Leibfried, 1995b: 433).[9] In fact, they conclude that 'national welfare states remain the primary institutions of European social policy, but they do so in the context of an increasingly constraining multitiered polity' (Leibfried and Pierson, 1995: 44). And they stipulate that the (national) welfare state is at the moment not only one of the few key realms of policy competence where national governments still reign, but given the popularity of most social programmes, national administrators are in fact reluctant to lose authority over social policy (Pierson and Leibfried, 1995a: 34).[10]

Our conclusion from the research of 'European Social Policy' is that the first requirement to be able to speak of liberal democratic European citizenship is not met. When we focus on the traditional components of the welfare state, national welfare states remain, indeed, largely untouched, and there is to date no 'pan-European welfare state'. Soysal's remark that 'the welfare state is universal only within national boundaries' nicely sums up this conclusion (Soysal, 1994: 139).

EUROPEAN CITIZENSHIP AND THE MAASTRICHT TREATY

In our second test we have a close look at what the Maastricht Treaty has to say on 'Union citizenship'.[11] Is this a domain where we can speak of a metamorphosis of the 'market citizen' into the 'full-fledged' EU citizen?

With regard to 'Union citizenship', the Maastricht Treaty gave, first of all, birth to the concept of a common citizenship for the European Union. This can be seen as an act of symbolic importance, 'as it postulates the existence of a common popular sovereignty to complement – or rival – the common sovereignty of states' (Duff, 1994: 29). In that sense it may be seen as a radical change because that idea had, until the signing of the Treaty, only substance in the context of the nation–state.

However, it should be noted that, at the same time, citizenship of the Union is limited to citizens of the member states and confined to an extension of electoral rights, to vote and to stand, in local and European elections for citizens residing in an EU country other than their own, a confirmation of the existing right to petition the European Parliament, the establishment of an ombudsman to investigate charges of maladministration by EU institutions, and a sharing of consular services outside the EU.

Also the concept of Union citizenship is based on the existing principle that nationals of member states have certain rights in some circumstances to move freely across national borders in the common market. But although this right of freedom of movement of EU citizens throughout the territory of the Union is reaffirmed, there is no stipulation about the rights that they may carry with them.

The Treaty also confirms the obligation to adopt a uniform electoral procedure. The existence of trans-European political parties is recognised for the first time. They are expected to contribute to 'forming a European awareness and to expressing the political will of the citizens of the Union'.

As for the European Parliament, which lays claim to be the repository of the pooled popular sovereignty of the European citizen, it looked as if it was to gain most. Although it was not granted the right of direct legislative initiative, it was given the right it has exercised for some years to request the Commission to propose legislation. Duff claims that this has significance (Duff, 1994: 30).

When we analyse the discussion in the aftermath of Maastricht, judgements of the conception of 'European citizenship' as formulated in the Treaty are, however, in general, not very positive. Duff's conclusion is that, although the extension of civil rights adds up to a modest step in the history of European integration – and a significant step forward from the previously wholly superficial harmonisation of passports – it nevertheless 'does not attempt to define more modern civil rights and duties. *An EC citizen is defined as a national of a member state*' (Duff, 1994: 29–30; my italics).

Jessurun d'Oliveira's evaluation is even more negative. The way citizenship is conceived in the Treaty is 'nearly exclusively a symbolic plaything without substantive content'. He stresses that the notion of Union citizenship is crystallising around the freedom of movement. And this right does not form part of a political right linked to democratic systems of government, but forms part of the fundamental economic freedoms of the European market. It means that the mobility of economically active persons has now been elevated to the core of European citizenship and expanded into mobility for persons generally (Jessurun d'Oliveira, 1995: 65–6; 82–3). This underwrites the conclusion of Leibfried we mentioned earlier in our discussion of social policy and 'social rights', namely, that in unifying Europe 'economic citizenship' was at the fore. We see that the Maastricht Treaty has not changed this. The 'market citizen' still has priority.

One of the core aspects of citizenship is the distinction it should be able to make between those who 'belong' and those who do not, the function to *exclude* others. Does the bundle of rights connected with the notion of Union citizenship indeed fulfil this function of exclusion? In fact, the rights and obligations of the European citizen as granted by the Maastricht Treaty do differentiate only very partially between citizens and non-citizens.[12] For instance, persons who do not possess the nationality of one of the member states are not excluded from the rights which are presently being bestowed upon Union citizens, when we consider the example of local elections. In The Netherlands, for example, the distinction between nationals and resident foreigners has been seen as a democratic problem. *All* foreigners who otherwise comply with residence conditions, will have eventually these – local – voting rights (Jessurun d'Oliveira, 1995: 78).

Second, the freedom of movement is granted to large categories of non-nationals, such as nationals of the EFTA countries, or even to 'everyone', or normally to those legally resident in the territory of one of the member states, regardless of the Maastricht Treaty. The problem we encounter here is that Union citizenship not only lacks a cohesive notion, but also that the political dimension is clearly underdeveloped: no instruments for participation in the public life; in fact no public life itself, as distinguished from public life in the member states; a weak parliament; and next to no access to the European Courts (Jessurun d'Oliveira, 1995: 83).

Our conclusion is that the potential contribution of the Maastricht Treaty provisions for citizenship to the further development of European Union should not be overestimated. In general, it changed very little. National control in the area remains strong. This form of citizenship represents hardly an extension of EU powers and an erosion of national sovereignty. It affects directly only a certain number of citizens and applies mainly to their relationship with the member state in which they reside.[13]

Has 'Union citizenship' as formulated in the Treaty, these comments notwithstanding, some importance in the context of the conception of liberal democratic European citizenship? After all, the idea in the Maastricht Treaty of 'Union citizenship' which is related to a community of states seems to mark a significant departure from the traditional link between nationality and citizenship in the nation–state. Does this aspect of the Treaty not show that the Union concept of citizenship represents a loosening of the 'metaphysical' ties between persons and a state, in fact could it not be seen as a symptom of cosmopolisation of citizenship, and as a clear indication that the member states have to a large extent become multicultural and multi-ethnic societies? Could the Union concept of citizenship not, in fact, be 'the nucleus of modern active citizenship', and may it not be useful as 'a laboratory for this procedural concept of proto-cosmopolitan citizenship'? (Jessurun d'Oliveira, 1995: 83–4).

Aspects of the conception of citizenship, as formulated in the Treaty, are certainly in line with political theoretical arguments for the liberal democratic conception of European citizenship developed. After all, a central aspect of that conception of (European) citizenship is to surpass differences based on ethnic or cultural traits, and to cope with pluralism in the form of multi-ethnic societies. At the same time, however, we should recognise that the way 'citizenship' is worked out in the Treaty precludes the realisation of the liberal democratic conception of citizenship. In fact, Jessurun d'Oliveira himself seems to agree with this conclusion. As it stands, he remarks,

> Union citizenship is misleading in that it suggests that the Union is a state-like entity. This connotation is less adequate than ever as the Union moves more and more away from federal and supranational aspirations. . . . *To indicate the position of people under the Maastricht Treaty as citizenship is nearly as gross a misnomer.*
>
> (Jessurun d'Oliveira, 1995: 84; my italics)

Our conclusion from this analysis of the idea of Union citizenship formulated in the Maastricht Treaty has to be that the requirements to be able to speak of liberal democratic citizenship on the level of the European Union are – once again – not met. There are, however, still some other ways of exploring a potential match between our political theoretical ideas and the 'real world' of the European Union.

EUROPEAN CITIZENSHIP AND IMMIGRATION

Our conclusion so far is that the concept of citizenship used as a practical matter of fact within the European Union has not left the confinements of the nation–states. What, however, can we say if we include in our analysis the problem of 'third-country people', that is to say people who are not members of the nation–states that form the European Union? Does the way the Union *as a Union* deals with the problem of these third-country people, with 'immigrants', give us reason to speak of a situation in which the conception of citizenship is realized? Could immigration policy be said to be creating a 'pan-European state'? Does this show us the road to 'European citizenship'?

We mentioned earlier that the way 'Union citizenship' was defined in the Maastricht Treaty, the rights and obligations of the European citizen as granted by it, do differentiate only very partially between citizens and non-citizens, and in that sense was not adequate to make the distinction between those who belong and those who do not.

However, when we talk about the function to *exclude* others, the Union as a Union tries to keep a clear boundary between the members of the Union and 'the rest' of the world. There is a strong agreement that the external boundaries of the Union as a whole should be upheld at all costs. That is of course the function of the Schengen agreement which aims at drawing the borders of a supra-nationality through common visa and immigration procedures. At the same time the Maastricht Treaty and other EU conventions declare that immigration policies will comply with 'international commitments' to human rights and the 'humanitarian traditions' of EU states. And thus, constrained by its own discourse, conventions, and laws, 'the Community establishes, and compels its member states to provide an expanding range of rights and privileges to migrants from both EC and non-EC countries' (Soysal, 1994: 159).

The question we have to pose is on what criteria this migrant policy is based. Is it based on a pan-national conception of citizenship and thus a conception that transcends the boundaries of the nation–state? An answer can be given by using Soysal's research on the typology of membership models. She has analysed the variations in incorporation regimes, the cross-national differences revealing how host states (including European states) and their foreigners encounter each other.

Her conclusion is that it is, first of all, not guestworker cultures and situations that predict how they participate in and interact with host societies. Her research shows that it is the 'institutional repertoire of host political systems, which determines the rationale for both state and migrant action' (Soysal, 1994: 5). Distinct models of membership provide the schemes within which new entrants to the polity are incorporated. Soysal

> highlight[s] the emergence of membership that is multiple in the sense of spanning local, regional, and global identities, and which accommodates intersecting complexes of rights, duties, and loyalties. Turkish migrants in Berlin represent an example of this emerging form of membership. . . . As foreign residents of Berlin, Turkish migrants share a social space with foreigners from other countries and with German citizens. They pay taxes, own businesses and homes, work in factories and in the service sector, receive welfare, rent government-subsidized apartments, and attend schools. . . . Either selectively or concurrently, they invoke, negotiate, and map collective identities as immigrant, Turk, Muslim, foreigner, and European.
>
> (Soysal, 1994: 166)

One could well agree with this statement, especially if it is seen as a normative statement of how things in fact ought to be. It is in line with the requirements of a liberal democratic conception of European citizenship. It is much too soon, however, to conclude that we have eventually stumbled on a match between those requirements and the reality of the European Union. There remains an empirical problem with Soysal's statement. Let us quote her once more, and see what the conclusion of her research into the different membership models is.

> While the basis and legitimation of membership rights have shifted to a transnational level, membership itself is not really organized in a new scheme. . . . [T]he responsibility of providing and implementing individual rights lies with national states. . . . Actually, the very transnational normative system that legitimizes universal personhood as the basis for membership also designates the nation–state as the primary unity for dispensing rights and privileges. . . . Hence *the nation–state remains the central structure regulating access to social distribution*. The material realization of individual rights and privileges is primarily organized by the nation–state, although the legitimacy for these rights now lies in a transnational order.
>
> (Soysal, 1994: 143; my italics)

This conclusion shows that priority is still given to national sovereignty which ordains that every 'nation' has a right to its own territorially delimited state, its own membership rules, and that only those who belong to the nation have the right to participate as citizens of the state.

And territorial belonging (and identity) are presumed to be determined by the parameters of national contiguity and homogeneity (Soysal, 1994: 7).

We thus have to conclude that this investigation into another possibility of a fit between the liberal democratic conception of European citizenship and the situation in the European Union has to be negative. The way the Union *as a Union* deals with the problem of membership gives us no reason to speak of a situation in which liberal democratic European citizenship is realized. Membership policy does not create a 'pan-European state' and is not the road to European citizenship.

EUROPEAN CITIZENSHIP, THE 'DEMOCRATIC DEFICIT', AND IDENTITY

Looking for another possibility of a match, especially with the second element of liberal democratic European citizenship, leads us to investigate if certain practices of political cooperation are in existence in the European Union. How do we fare with the requirements of a democratic process with accountability, based on shared principles of democracy?

If we look at the frequency with which the 'democratic deficit' is mentioned in the context of the European Union, it seems a foregone conclusion that with regard to the second element of liberal democratic European citizenship, we will find no fit. But before we can draw that conclusion we have to analyse, first of all, what exactly is meant when speaking about the 'democratic deficit'.[14]

Sbragia notes that the deficit, in the eyes of many, is due to the lack of power exercised by the European Parliament: the institution representing the individual citizens of the member-state countries does not have enough of a say in the workings of the Community (Sbragia, 1992: 277). For Shirley Williams the 'democratic deficit' should be understood as the gap between the powers transferred to the Community level and the control of the elected Parliament over them. Her problem is that this gap is filled by national civil servants operating as European experts or as members of regulation and management committees, and to some extent by organised lobbies, mainly representing business (Williams, 1991: 162). Clearly here 'deficit' is the lack of control the European Parliament has.[15] She 'concludes that the loss of accountability to national parliaments has not been compensated by increased accountability to the European Parliament' (Williams, 1991: 155).

In both cases we have an example of Neunreither's reminder (1994: 299–300) that the European Parliament has argued over the years that the democratic deficit is basically *institutionally* and more specifically a parliamentary deficit. This raises the question of how exactly we are to describe the democratic deficit. Three main elements of a democratic deficit should be distinguished:

1 The institutional or parliamentary deficit.
2 A deficit concerning the intermediate structures characterised by the absence of genuine European political parties and European media.
3 The deficit in relation to the European citizen which a union of states with far-reaching powers of decision-making like the EU should have.

These distinctions can be elaborated by formulating that there is, in fact, a system of dual legitimacy. The first legitimacy is based on the democratic institutions of member states and the fact that national parliaments have agreed by ratification of the EU Treaty to the partial transfer of powers to the European Union and the exercise of power by the Community institutions according to these treaties. Institutions like the European Council, Council of Ministers, the Commission, the Court of Justice and the Parliament rely on this first basis of legitimacy. Neunreither concludes that a democratic transfer of power from the member states to the Community has taken place; otherwise the institutions could not do what they are doing democratically.

A second source of legitimacy has been building up, mainly based on the direct elections to the European Parliament. These elections gave rise to a new and direct and rather independent source of the democratic exercise of power. The European Parliament represents the second source of legitimacy of the European Union, the *direct* one. The legitimacy of the Council of Ministers is clearly based on a *derived* legitimacy stemming from national systems. Both the Commission and the Court of Justice find themselves between these extremes: their institutional legitimacy derives from the treaties and the competence assigned to them, while personal legitimacy of the members, both of the Commission and the Court of Justice, is based on appointment by the member governments with increasing but still limited involvement of the European Parliament (Neunreither, 1994: 312).

Taking these different sources of legitimacy into account, one could conclude that the institutional system of the Community is based on democratic principles. A more important point, however, especially in the context of our own analysis, is raised by Neunreither. If there is this system of dual legitimacy, it is clear that there only can be full legitimation if both dimensions, the institutional and the direct one, are fully built up. The institutional deficit, especially the parliamentary one, could be eventually reduced. More problematic is the lack of direct legitimacy. The democratic deficit lies beyond institutional competence: '*Legitimacy also depends on the consent of the citizen*, not necessarily on individual political decisions taken, but on the system itself. There must exist some kind of identification between citizen and the political system' (Neunreither, 1994: 312). This of course fits in with the argument for the democratic premiss, namely, that accountability is normally essential to the exercise of political authority, which is based on the belief in the legitimacy of that authority by citizens. Citizens are to think of themselves as persons linked to one another by the democratic institutions in which they participate, and the existence of this cooperative practice itself is the basis of their political identity.

The problem of the Union is, however, that democratic institutions have, in one way or another, to rely on the ultimate source of public power: the people. And, as Neunreither has noted,

> as far as the EU institutions are concerned, a first difficulty lies in the fact that there is no EU citizen, as such, and there is no European Union people. ... When speaking about 'the people', this term is not yet used in its singular form as far as the European Union is concerned. It is still the twelve 'peoples' of the member states which constitute the popular basis for a democratic exercise of government.
>
> (Neunreither, 1994: 311)

This analysis of the problem of direct, non-institutional legitimacy shows us that there is, in other words, no praxis of citizens who actively exercise their political rights, based on an idea of European constitutional patriotism; certain practices of political cooperation are not in existence in the European Union.[16] We have to conclude that we cannot speak of a democratic process with accountability, based on shared principles of democracy.

Needless to say, the democratic deficit is of direct influence on the question of shared citizenship identity, if this identity is indeed constituted by participation in a common set of political institutions on the pan-European level.

The description of the actual situation in the Union gives little reason to suggest that there is such a cooperative practice, and the reality, of course, one has to admit, is that citizens do not feel part of the political entity in which decisions are taken. In general, it is safe to say that citizens in Europe identify themselves much more closely with their member states and, to some extent, their regions than with the European Union.[17] The specific case of, for instance, the Danish referendum is an example of this. It showed that, far 'from Community social policy advancing citizen identification with supranational union, national identification remains so strong that it stands in the way of Community social policy' (Streeck, 1995a: 413).[18]

The idea of a liberal democratic conception of European citizenship which is related to a community of states, and which would mark a significant departure from the traditional link between nationality and citizenship in the nation–state, is clearly not (yet?) shared by citizens of the nation–states of the Union. A sense of solidarity and tolerance among the citizens of the Union to encourage the emergence of a new pan-national, shared citizenship identity, a 'sense of community', has not developed. According to Sbragia's analysis, for example, it is still national territory that is the most important shaper of most aspects of life.

> It is nearly impossible to overestimate the importance of national boundaries as key organizers of political power and economic wealth within the Community. National identity, political party organizations, party systems, partisan identity, interest groups, . . . are all defined by national territory. The ties across territory are relatively weak in critical areas. . . . Feelings of solidarity are also constrained by national boundaries in the central area of taxation.
>
> (Sbragia, 1992: 274)

In the context of our discussion, we have to conclude that 'European citizenship' is not based on a European '*demos*', but still consists of '*demoï*'. As long as a European '*demos*' is non-existent, the idea of 'belonging' to a European Union as one of a citizen's identities, the hope of realising European citizenship is very dim indeed.

It should be added that if, on the other hand, citizenship is based on a communitarian or *Gemeinschaft* outlook, based on *ethnos*, or *ius sanguinis*, it would be difficult to envisage a new form of citizenship at the European level. And the fact that the normative content of the concept of liberal democratic citizenship is dissociated from national identity based on '*ethnos*' means of course that a European *demos* cannot normatively be based on ethno-cultural terms, and should also never become one (leaving aside the improbable situation that this would ever empirically come about).[19]

Is there a solution to this problem that citizens in the European Union identify themselves much more closely with their own member state and, to some extent, their regions than with the European Union, such that they do not feel part of the political entity in which decisions are taken? The question is not only if the ambitious goal for deepening the European Union can be reached without a transformation of major elements of the European political culture, but also which institutions should play a role in this transformation.[20]

THE DEMOCRATIC DEFICIT: A TERRITORIAL SOLUTION?

We have seen that in Sbragia's analysis it is national territory that is a major element in defining identity. It has also been remarked that the debate over an appropriate role for national governments in decision-making is linked to the issue of making the Community somehow accountable to the electorate, so that it is rendered more democratic. And it is added that a federal structure, based on a 'citizens' Europe', stands as an alternative to a Europe of nation-states (Sbragia, 1992: 259).

This fits in with our own political theoretical analysis. This is also true with regard to the statement that the Parliament 'is too weak to provide the kind of democratic accountability conventionally implied by the term *democracy*' (Sbragia, 1992: 277). And in line with the distinction between institutional legitimacy and 'direct' legitimacy, Sbragia remarks that although it could be argued that the Community is indeed democratic since the member governments are democratically elected, it is in fact the indirect link between the individual citizen and the directives approved by the Council of Ministers that troubles those who believe that the link between voter and policy-maker should be more direct, more robust.[21] She notes that, from the perspective of committed federalist, the representation of governments in the Council of Ministers and the European Council is less legitimate than the representation of individual voters. She adds that 'representation' as used in political discourse refers to voters rather than to governments. This is, according to Sbragia, due to the fact that 'the representation of the individual voter has come to dominate notions about democracy and therefore has a much greater legitimacy than does the representation of territorial government as an institution' (Sbragia, 1992: 278).

This remark hints at the direction of Sbragia's solution to the problem of the democratic deficit, and it takes as a point of reference the distinction she makes between 'dominant notions' about democracy, based on the representation of the individual voter, and – evidentially – non-dominant notions of democracy, based on territorial representation. She claims that the representation of governments rather than individuals

> is so unusual that it does not fit conventional notions of democracy. Even though these governments are responsible to directly elected legislatures, indirect representation is viewed with deep suspicion by

current theories of democracy. In a similar vein, the participation of constituent units in the exercise of the general or federal power is so atypical that scholars of federalism have felt impelled to categorize it as a deviation from normal federalism.

(Sbragia, 1992: 288)

The 'unusualness' of the representation of governments, the 'deep suspicion of current theories of democracy' about this, the 'dominant notion' of representation of the individual voter instead of governments, has evidently in Sbragia's view prevented theorists from looking at (other) methods that would facilitate integration. According to her, the representation of territorially based governments does in fact provide a method of facilitating integration, of achieving federalism, without submerging the interests of the constituent units. She claims that it does offer the possibility of federalisation through indirect rather than direct representation or, as she elaborates, of combining direct and indirect representation in a way that gives the collectivity of national governments (but not individual governments) the right of absolute veto. Her conclusion is that it 'thus presents an alternative to models that assume that federalization must necessarily be characterized by either supranational executive or by parliamentary sovereignty' (Sbragia, 1992: 289).

Why have we overlooked this type of solution to integration? The answer is not that representation of territorially based governments could not provide a method of facilitating integration, or that it should be discarded because it deviates from 'normal federalism'. The basic question is if there are not good reasons for the 'deep suspicion by current theories of democracy' about the idea of representation of governments rather than individuals, and that there may be more to this suspicion than that it is 'so unusual that it does not fit conventional notions of democracy'.

It was argued that the conception of liberal democratic citizenship is based on a minimal democratic criterion: the interests of each person are entitled to equal consideration. Therefore justifying one set of political arrangements relative to others ought ultimately to make reference to the interests of individuals, and cannot stop at the interests of collective entities like cultures, churches, communities, languages *or territorial governments with 'institutional self-interest'.*[22]

In addition, the democratic premise means that political institutions should be accountable to the population in the form of a representative assembly responsible for matters of government. This premise is essential when describing the requirements for a 'federal model of democratic authority'. This may be labelled by Sbragia 'the conventional notion of democracy', but this labelling gives us no reason to abandon the democratic premiss.

There is another point to be noted. If Sbragia's analysis is correct that national territory is the most important shaper of most aspects of life, and thus the major element in defining identity, the proposed territorial solution to the democratic deficit will also preclude any hope of reaching a political identity that would liberate itself from the confinements of political identity based on the nation–state. If participation in a common set of political institutions at the European level is not seen as necessary, then there is no reason to think shared citizenship identity would ever be fostered at the level of the European Union.

Sbragia's solution to the democratic deficit at the level of the European Union, by arguing for representation of governments instead of that of voters, has on closer analysis nothing to do with coping with the democratic deficit, but with the question of how a loss of autonomy of national governments, or loss of power of territorial entities, should be prevented.

If we want to look for a solution to the 'democratic deficit' that is in line with the liberal democratic conception of European citizenship, we will have to look – once again – to the democratic premiss and the principles that ought to govern a federal model of democratic authority based on it.

EUROPEAN CITIZENSHIP AND ENLARGEMENT: NEW PROBLEMS

One of the problems about the basis of the legitimacy for cross-national political institutions is related to debates in political theory about size and democracy. If, as argued, one of the constitutive elements of the idea of European citizenship is shared identity, indeed, a shared citizenship identity that will supersede rival identities based on national identities in the first place, we should point out the importance of taking measures to encourage development of a moral commitment to the Union, a commitment that should consist of developing a sense of solidarity among the citizens of the European Union.

There is, however, a problem of size that we have not mentioned before. The problem of size also raises the issue of the place of opportunities for participation in maintaining democratic legitimacy. Is the problem of size, then, an insurmountable threshold for the conception of liberal democratic citizenship with its democratic premiss of accountability of political authority, when this premiss requires that political authority within European institutions should rest with a directly elected representative European assembly, responsible for matters of government? And if we would argue that in the present situation of the Union, size is not a barrier to the liberal democratic conception of citizenship, how about potential enlargement of the Union?

Enlargement raises, in fact, additional problems for any conception of European citizenship. In his analysis of 'The Europe to come' Perry Anderson explains that the rationale for Britain's pressure for not only rapid integration of the Visegrad countries into the EU, but for the most extensive embrace beyond it, is based on the idea that the wider the Union becomes the shallower it must be, for the more national states it contains, the less viable becomes any real supra-national authority over them (Anderson, 1996: 6).

The calculation is that the more member states there are, the less sovereignty can practically be pooled, and the greater is the chance that federal dreams will fold: expansion must mean *de-federalisation.*[23] From the perspective of the conception of liberal democratic citizenship, this should be considered to be a negative development. But enlargement would raise another problem with regard to the liberal democratic conception of citizenship. Anderson raises a fundamental difficulty of enlargement of the Union, one of a purely political nature. Doubling the membership of the Union would cripple the institutions of the Union.

> Proliferation of partners, regardless of adjusting voting weights and regardless how the inequalities between them were finessed, threatens institutional gridlock. *Rebus sic stantibus*, the size of the European Parliament would swell toward eight hundred deputies; the number of Commissioners rise to 40.
>
> (Anderson, 1996: 8)

Any discussion of liberal democratic citizenship, also one in a European context, should start from the premiss that this context should be a democratic one. The consequences of enlargement show the implications of holding on to the democratic premiss of accountability and a representative assembly. A discussion of 'size and democracy' may in that perspective have consequences for how we judge the desirability of enlargement of the unit we are speaking of.[24]

EUROPEAN CITIZENSHIP: A CONCLUSION

Is the European Union to be conceived of as an association of states, or at least entities with some political independence, or is it to be conceived of as a representative of a single people? Are we talking of a Union of collectivities or of a society of individuals? Is the Union to be considered an example of inter-governmental cooperation? Is it a quasi-federal system? Is it a multi-tiered system? As we have seen, there is among experts on 'Europe' disagreement on these questions.[25]

Whichever way one may look at the present process of political integration in the Union, either as an inter-governmental bargaining process, or as a multi-levelled, highly fragmented system in which policy 'develops', in all instances the representation of populations has been indirect, with implications both for democratic accountability and for democratic legitimacy.

Earlier we referred to Streeck's (negative) conclusion about progress towards a European social policy. In our concluding remarks it is relevant to pick up once again his analysis. In fact, it shows in a nutshell all the discrepancies between each of the constitutive aspects of liberal democratic European citizenship and the actual situation in the Union.

> The European Community was created without citizen identification and supranational legitimacy, on the weak and indirect legitimation conferred on it by its member states. . . . It is true that a federalist European state-building project would be jeopardized by lack of citizen identification with 'Europe', and would therefore require that the 'democratic deficit' be closed and redistributive social policy be developed. *But the reigning integration project is not a federalist one.* The present European accommodation between the sovereignty of nation–states and of self-regulating markets precludes supranational political development or requires it be kept at a minimum. There are neither institutional nor economic nor political reasons for national governments promoting economic union to help European civil society build supranational political resources capable of remodelling the Community into an interventionist federal welfare state.
>
> (Streeck, 1995a: 414; my italics)

Although, then, one may disagree what the Union exactly is, one thing is certain. The requirements to be able to speak of liberal democratic European citizenship are not met. With regard to the democratic premiss and the accountability of political authority, the conclusion with which Pierson and Leibfried end their own research is even more telling. They write: 'What is emerging in Europe is a multi-levelled, highly fragmented system in which policy "develops" *but is beyond the firm control of any single authority*' (Pierson and Leibfried, 1995b: 433; my italics). If it is indeed the case that the European Union is developing 'beyond the firm control of any single authority', one could conclude that it does not make sense at all to speak about 'accountability', or about 'the democratic content' of this Union. We have to surmise that we do not even know where 'the locus of authority' is.

On top, as if this is not enough, it seems to be the case that we do not need shared citizenship identity at all, to be able to have an *economic* union. According to Streeck,

> the uniqueness and, indeed, the genius of Monnet's design, . . . lay exactly in its uncoupling of progress on supranational organization from progress in *the formation of supranational patriotism*. The European Community was conceived as a political regime that would have to, and could, survive and grow without the popular legitimacy that previous modes of state building had required. In Monnet's pragmatic approach, European unity was to be based for the foreseeable future not on collective acceptance of a common identity but on the functional interdependence of political–administrative decisions and organized interests in an internationalized 'mixed' economy.
>
> (Streeck, 1995a: 412; my italics)

We can add that the founding of a United Europe depended mainly, if not totally, on the 'four freedoms': the free movement of persons, goods, capital and services, on, in other words, 'economic citizenship'. The concept of 'Union citizenship', formulated in the Maastricht Treaty, did not change this direction the Union has been taking.

If the perception of citizens of any sub-unit is that it is unfairly disadvantaged or that it is under-represented in key federal institutions, if there is a lack of mutual understanding and mutual distrust, these may be factors that have the potential to destabilise a union. It is reasonable to suppose that a federation based merely on a *modus vivendi* – one in which pan-federal identification, tolerance and solidarity do not develop – will remain inherently unstable.

The conclusion to be drawn is that consensus on a liberal democratic conception of citizenship seems to be the only viable basis for a stable social union in *and between* modern democratic societies that are characterised by the fact of cultural and ethnic pluralism.

If one is in favour of a democratic European Union, from whatever size, 'the gradual encroachment of these ideas' should be stimulated. It seems the only way to go forward to a united Europe, that is not only the Europe of Auschwitz, but also of Srebrenica.

NOTES

1 See for an extensive argument for this conception of 'liberal democratic citizenship', 'Pluralism, contractarianism and European union', Chapter 7 in this volume.
2 See for these ideas on citizenship, Marshall (1964).
3 This is the central question Leibfried and Pierson ask in their research of 'European social policy' (Leibfried and Pierson, 1995: 43).
4 See Leibfried (1993: 133–4).
5 There is, however, a possibility for harmonisation in some work-centred social policies such as 'health' and 'work safety' issues. These policies are structured in a fairly comparable way and the European institutions have stronger mandate here (Leibfried, 1993: 145).
6 Leibfried's argument is based on his idea that 'in the context of currency union some such non-incremental development is likely'. And the road to a European welfare state 'with a monetary union on the books may have to be travelled speedily' (Leibfried, 1993: 143; 150).
7 The fact that this common ground is missing and that trying to harmonise, for instance, social insurance systems to any significant extent looks like a hopeless task is, of course, one of the reasons van Parijs argues for a 'Eurogrant', a basic income at a comparatively low level. See Van Parijs, 'Basic income and the political economy of the New Europe', Chapter 10 in this volume.
8 In fact, Streeck notes that, '[b]y defending national democracy against supranational welfare state building, European citizens in effect defend the freedom of the integrated market from redistributive political intervention, although this may not be the outcome they have in mind' (Streeck, 1995a: 413).
9 They discuss four limitations on member-state power: 1 the autonomous activity of EU organizations; 2 the impact of previous policy commitments at the EU level; 3 the growth of issue density; 4 the activity of non-state actors (Pierson and Leibfried, 1995: 434).
10 See for a similar argument, Streeck (1995a: 417).
11 The elements of the Maastricht Treaty, as given in this paragraph, are based on Duff (1994) and M. Anderson (*et al.*) (1994).
12 See also Soysal: '[I]t is no longer a simple task to differentiate permanent non-citizen residents of Western nation–states in terms of the rights and privileges they hold' (Soysal, 1994: 130). The line between citizen and non-citizen is more and more blurred.
13 See also Streeck's conclusion in this regard (Streeck, 1995a: 413). And see Anderson on what more comprehensive citizenship could have contained, which would have meant 'a truly radical innovation pointing clearly in the direction of a federal future for Europe' (Anderson *et al.*, 1994: 122).
14 See for the 'standard' version of the critique of democracy in Europe also Weiler *et al.* (1995).
15 It should be pointed out that 'lack of control' is not the same as stating that the European Parliament is a weak parliament. Tsebelis elaborates the role of the Parliament as a *conditional agenda setter* (Tsebelis, 1994: 128). See also Guy Peters (1992) for examples of the power of the EP.
16 See on 'constitutional patriotism' and European citizenship, Habermas (1992; 1996).

17 See Neunreither (1994: 313). See on the strongness of regional identification also Judt (1996: 116–18). With regard to this territorial identification Judt remarks on Habermas's ideas on 'constitutional patriotism', and notwithstanding Habermas's disassociation of identity with the historical national unit: 'It does not work' (Judt, 1996: 119).

18 At another place Streeck has noted that the negative Danish vote can be seen as both a legitimate exercise of democratic self-determination, a decision to secede, from a European Community that is advancing towards 'political union' and a refusal to join (the expanded Community) (Streeck, 1995b: 186–7).

19 In this regard the so-called Maastricht decision of the German Federal Constitutional Court should be considered carefully. It has a 'No-*Demos*' thesis, and argues in fact that the emergence of a pre-existing European *Demos defined in ethno-cultural terms* is a precondition for constitutional unification or, more minimally, for a redrawing of political boundaries. See for several objections to this *Demos*-as-*Volk* thesis: Weiler *et al.* (1995: 9–24). See also Habermas on the 'tragic irony' of the argument of the Court that extension of the Union requires certain cultural homogeneity among its people (Habermas, 1996: 137).

20 See Neunreither (1994: 313–14).

21 It should be noted in passing that in the European Union not all *governments* are elected. *Parliaments* are indeed elected, and voters are sometimes in for a surprise which (coalition-) government eventually will take power. The Netherlands is of course a classic example of this situation.

22 In the context of the German system of federation, the 'second chamber' represents what Fritz Scharpf has labelled the 'institutional self-interests' of the executive branch of the *Länder* governments, the *Länder*'s dominant political authority (Scharpf, 1988: 254).

23 Anderson adds that the problem of scale may cut both ways. It 'might force just the cutting of the institutional knot the proponents of a loose free-trade area seek to avoid. Widening could check or reverse deepening. It might also precipitate it' (Anderson, 1996: 8).

24 See also Dahl (1983: 103–4; 107) for an argument that one cannot decide from within democratic theory what constitutes a proper unit for the democratic process: that process presupposes a unit.

25 See also the ruling of the German Constitutional Court, that ruled in 1993 that the Community was not a *Bundesstaat*, a federated state, nor even a *Staatenbund*, a federation of states. It was, said the Court, a *Staatenverbund* – something more like a confederation. Middlemas renders it as 'close association dependent on national entities' (Middlemas, 1995).

BIBLIOGRAPHY

Anderson, M. *et al.* (1994) 'European citizenship and cooperation in justice and home affairs', in A. Duff, J. Pinder and R. Pryce (eds) *Maastricht and Beyond*, London and New York: Routledge, pp. 104–22.

Anderson, P. (1996) 'The Europe to come', *London Review of Books*, 25 January 1996, 18(2): 3–8.

Dahl, R.A. (1983) 'Federalism and the democratic process', in J.R. Pennock and J.W. Chapman (eds) *Liberal Democracy*, New York and London: New York University Press, pp. 95–108.

Duff, A. (1994) 'The main reforms', in A. Duff, J. Pinder and R. Pryce (eds) *Maastricht and Beyond*, London and New York: Routledge, pp. 19–35.

Habermas, J. (1992) 'Citizenship and national identity: some reflections on the future of Europe', *Praxis International*, 12(1): 1–19.

Habermas, J. (1996) 'The European nation-state: its achievement and its limitations. On the past and future of sovereignty and citizenship', *Ratio Juris*, 9(2): 125–37.

Jessurun d'Oliveira, H.U. (1995) 'Union citizenship: pie in the sky?', in A. Rosas and E. Antola (eds) *A Citizens' Europe; In Search of a New Order*, London: Sage, pp. 58–84.

Judt, T. (1996) *A Grand Illusion?: An Essay on Europe*, New York: Hill and Wang.

Leibfried, S. (1993) 'Towards a European welfare state? On integrating poverty regimes into the European Community', in C. Jones (ed.) *New Perspectives on the Welfare State in Europe*, London and New York: Routledge, pp. 133–56.

Leibfried, S. and Pierson, P. (1995) 'Semisovereign welfare states: social policy in a multitiered Europe', in S. Leibfried and P. Pierson (eds) *European Social Policy: Between Fragmentation and Integration*, Washington, DC: The Brookings Institution, pp. 43–77.

Marshall, T.H. (1964) 'Citizenship and social class', in *Class, Citizenship and Social Development*, New York: Doubleday. (The essay was first published in 1949.)

Middlemas, K. (1995) *Orchestrating Europe*, London: HarperCollins.

Neunreither, K. (1994) 'The democratic deficit of the European Union: towards closer cooperation between the European Parliament and the national parliaments', *Government and Opposition*, 29(3): 299–313.

Peters, B. Guy (1992) 'Bureaucratic politics and the institutions of the European Community', in A.M. Sbragia (ed.) *Europolitics: Institutions and Policymaking in the 'New' European Community*, Washington, DC: The Brookings Institution, pp. 75–122.

Pierson, P. and Leibfried, S. (1995a) 'Multitiered institution and the making of social policy', in S. Leibfried and P. Pierson (eds) *European Social Policy: Between Fragmentation and Integration*, Washington, DC: The Brookings Institution, pp. 1–40.

Pierson, P. and Leibfried, S. (1995b) 'The dynamics of social policy integration', in S. Leibfried and P. Pierson (eds) *European Social Policy: Between Fragmentation and Integration*, Washington, DC: The Brookings Institution, pp. 432–65.

Sbragia, A.M. (1992) 'Thinking about the European future: the uses of comparison', in A.M. Sbragia (ed.) *Europolitics: Institutions and Policymaking in the 'New' European Community*, Washington, DC: The Brookings Institution, pp. 257–91.

Scharpf, F. (1988) 'The joint-decision trap: lessons from German federalism and European integration', *Public Administration*, 66: 239–78.

Soysal, Y.N. (1994) *Limits of Citizenship: Migrants and the Postnational Membership in Europe*, Chicago and London: University of Chicago Press.

Streeck, W. (1995a) 'From market making to state building? Reflections on the political economy of European social policy', in S. Leibfried and P. Pierson (eds) *European Social Policy: Between Fragmentation and Integration*, Washington, DC: The Brookings Institution, pp. 389–431.

Streeck, W. (1995b) 'Inclusion and secession: questions on the boundaries of associative democracy', in E.O. Wright (ed.) *Associations and Democracy*, London and New York: Verso, pp. 184–92.

Tsebelis, G. (1994) 'The power of the European Parliament as a conditional agenda setter', *American Political Science Review*, 88(1): 128–42.

Weiler, J.H.H. *et al.* (1995) 'European democracy and its critique', *West European Politics*, 18: 4–39.

Williams, S. (1991) 'Sovereignty and accountability in the European Community', in R.O. Keohane and S. Hoffmann (eds) *The New European Community: Decision-making and Institutional Change*, Boulder, San Francisco and Oxford: Westview Press, pp. 155–76.

Index